The Butchers, the Baker

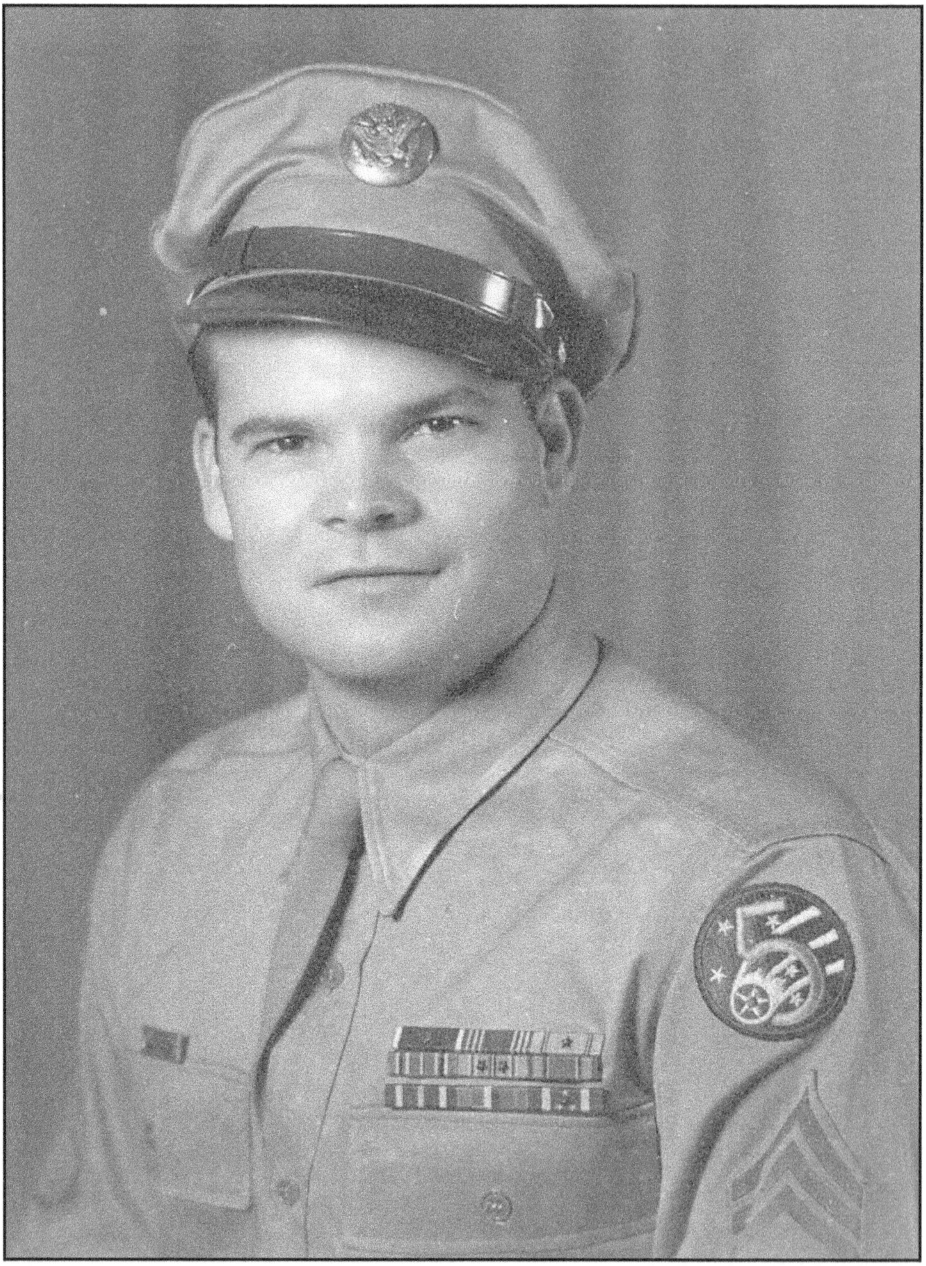

THE BUTCHERS, THE BAKER

The World War II Memoir of a United States Army Air Corps Soldier Captured by the Japanese in the Philippines

by

VICTOR L. MAPES *with*
SCOTT A. MILLS

McFarland & Company, Inc., Publishers
Jefferson, North Carolina, and London

To Americans and Filipinos
who fought bravely and successfully
to delay Japanese conquest of the Philippines.

Those who survived military operations
were surrendered and often faced brutality and death
in marches, camps, and prison ships.

The present work is a reprint of the library bound edition of The Butchers, the Baker: The World War II Memoir of a United States Army Air Corps Soldier Captured by the Japanese in the Philippines, *first published in 2000 by McFarland.*

Frontispiece: *Staff Sergeant Victor L. Mapes, 1947*

LIBRARY OF CONGRESS CATALOGUING-IN-PUBLICATION DATA

Mapes, Victor L., 1917–
    The butchers, the baker : the World War II memoir of a United States Army Air Corps soldier captured by the Japanese in the Philippines / by Victor L. Mapes with Scott A. Mills.
       p.   cm.
    Includes bibliographical references and index.

    ISBN 978-0-7864-3879-2
    softcover : 50# alkaline paper ∞

    1. Mapes, Victor L., 1917– . 2. World War, 1939–1945 — Prisoners and prisons, Japanese. 3. World War, 1939–1945 — Personal narratives, American. 4. Prisoners of war — Phillippines — Biography. I. Mills, Scott A., 1924– . II. Title
D805.P6M36   2008
940.54'72522'092 — dc21   [B]   99-37721

British Library cataloguing data are available

Cover photograph: Staff Sergeant Victor L. Mapes, 1947; USS *Narwhal* that carried Mapes to safety in 1944 (U.S. Naval Historical Center)

Manufactured in the United States of America

McFarland & Company, Inc., Publishers
  Box 611, Jefferson, North Carolina 28640
   www.mcfarlandpub.com

Contents

Preface

Victor Mapes and Scott Mills met several years ago at a reunion of the Americans who had been evacuated from the Japanese-occupied Philippines by the submarine *Narwhal* during World War II. The *Narwhal* combined patrols against enemy shipping with deliveries of arms to Philippine resistance forces. After unloading its cargo, the *Narwhal* picked up Americans who wanted to leave.

Mr. Mapes was at the reunion because he had been evacuated from Mindanao by the *Narwhal* in 1944 — Sgt. Mapes had escaped from a Japanese prison ship that had been torpedoed offshore. Mr. Mills was at the reunion because he was writing a book about a missionary family who also had been evacuated by the *Narwhal* in 1944, but on another patrol and from a different island. In 1945 Ensign Mills was aboard a landing ship in the invasion of Okinawa, and later that year his ship joined the fleet that was assembling to invade Japan when the war ended.

Conversation between Mapes and Mills revealed that Mapes had written down a great deal of his war experiences while a patient at Walter Reed Hospital, which he had entered in late December 1944 for a stay of over two years. But he had never completed his story of three years in the Philippines as an Air Corps soldier and then as a POW. We decided to complete the account because of Mapes's amazing odyssey and survival.

During the next few years, lengthy talks resulted in this memoir of Victor Mapes's time in the Philippines. The great bulk of the memoir consists of what Mapes saw and did. In addition, we reported the comments of other servicemen who were at the same place at the same time as incidents described by Mapes. For a broader context, we provided brief historical remarks on the Japanese attack on Clark Field, General Wainwright's surrender on Corregidor, and General MacArthur's drive to retake the Philippines.

Apprentice Seaman Scott A. Mills, 1943.

1

Threats of War

November 1, 1939,
to December 8, 1941

I kept my hands in my pockets to keep them warm as I walked along a downtown street in Fort Wayne, Indiana. It was a blustery November 1, 1939, and I was taking a look around town before returning home to St. Cloud, Florida — I had been visiting friends near Fort Wayne. I was about ready to go to a movie and get warm when a huge poster of Uncle Sam stopped me short — he pointed at me and demanded, "I want you."

I read the rest of Uncle Sam's message carefully. He declared that the Army Air Corps had a program for young, red-blooded Americans who wanted to get ahead. The Air Corps offered men who were physically and mentally sound an extensive field of training with pay, good food, medical care, and a chance to see the world. This all sounded too good to be true. At 21 I longed to get out from under my father's watchful eye while I did the heavy work on our family's dairy farm. I headed for the Army Recruiting Office, persuaded by Uncle Sam but also feeling patriotic because of the world situation.

World War II had started just two months before when Hitler ordered his German troops into Poland. England and France had declared war against Germany but had not been able to save Poland. Now the war in Europe had come to a nervous pause, but on the other side of the world Japanese force continued to fight in China, as they had been doing since the early 1930s.

Upon entering the recruiting office, I faced a neatly dressed old sergeant with a lot of stripes on his sleeves, showing his long years of military service. He got up, shook my hand, and gave me a friendly smile. He had me sit down and then painted a rosy picture of service in the Army Air Corps. I was convinced but wanted a few days to think it over. But the sergeant insisted that the two openings he had for service in Panama or in Hawaii might not last. The idea of Hawaii began to fill my head — the hula girls, blue surf, the paradise of flowers and palm trees. My silence made the sergeant think I was backing out, but he didn't have to worry — intrigued by beautiful Hawaii, I enlisted that very day. On December 10, 1939, I sailed from New York on the troop ship *Chateau Thierry* and arrived in Hawaii on December 29, 1939.

Our contingent of Army Air Corps recruits immediately went into basic training at a tent site at Hickam Field. There we stayed even through the New Year holidays until we finished and got our first pay. Then a group of us put on civilian clothes for a night in Honolulu. Our first stop was a barbershop, where pretty Japanese girls talked us into getting the works — a shampoo, shave, and massage in addition to a haircut. The total cost was $3.50, a big chunk out of a monthly paycheck of $21. Then we hired a taxi and visited bars and a few Japanese restaurants. Finally, we strolled along the streets of Waikiki, smoking big cigars and thinking we were big shots. But I noticed GIs were not liked in most places — I sensed we were tolerated because we were suckers with our money. Hawaii seemed to be like the States in its low opinion of servicemen at that time. That first night in Honolulu made me start looking forward to the end of my enlistment and getting back home.

Basic training over, I was assigned to the reactivated 14th Bomb Squadron in the spring of 1941. In the new squadron we all soon made a rating, and Air Corps life took on a brighter hue. But the Air Corps expansion at Hickam Field was so great that it outran facilities to train airmen. While we waited to be trained, we were assigned such duties as cutting lawns. Hoping to avoid such boredom, I signed up for the Cooks and Bakers School and was temporarily assigned to Schofield Barracks to attend classes. In the middle of June 1940, I graduated with a 95 average as a first cook and returned to the 14th Squadron at Hickam Field.

Meantime World War II had expanded. After the conquest of Poland in the fall of 1939, Hitler's forces had paused until the spring of 1940. Then the German war machine struck westward and won astounding victories over the Netherlands, Belgium, Norway, and France. France capitulated on June 22, 1940, just 17 days after it was invaded. Only the English Channel and British determination stopped an immediate invasion of England. Before crossing the channel, the Germans had to destroy the British Air Force. But British pilots prevailed over massive German air attacks in August and September of 1940. The invasion of England was called off.

At Hickam Field in June 1940 there was still a shortage of training slots for airmen, so I was glad to share a pastry job with another cook. Being free of duty every other day, I wandered around off base, but, not knowing anyone, I grew very lonely. I longed to go home.

One evening I was moping along a narrow street in Honolulu near the Nuanna Canal when a beautiful hymn sounded through the darkness and interrupted my gloomy thoughts. It was one of my favorites, and it thrilled my soul. Moving closer, I forgot my loneliness and instead thought of home and my church there. I looked in the church door, not wanting to be noticed, but an elderly white man saw me and invited me inside. I said I was not properly dressed and preferred to just stand outside and listen. Finally, however, I took his urging as the beckoning hand of God. I decided I should not turn my back on Him now, as I had often done since joining the Air Corps.

It was a wonderful experience to worship in this church, where Hawaiians, Puerto Ricans, whites, blacks, Chinese, Japanese, and others sat together. Some were well-dressed, others were not, but everyone was happy. I sensed their friendliness as I sat down by a Hawaiian to sing and listen to the sermon. For the first time since being in the Air Corps I felt at home. After the service, I shook hands with members of the congregation, who invited me to come next Sunday. On the way back to the base, I felt like I had taken a refreshing bath. I went to the church many times, made friends, and was invited to their homes. The more I became acquainted with them, the more I wanted to stay in Hawaii when my service time was up.

One day a Navy tug pushed a British cruiser into Pearl Harbor for repairs — the cruiser had a large hole in its side, inflicted by German action. On July 23, 1941, German aggression in Europe affected the Pacific in a more drastic way. The Vichy government of unoccupied France, a German puppet, gave permission to the Japanese to land troops in Indochina, which was a French colony. On July 25, 30,000 Japs landed in Saigon. The same day President Roosevelt froze all Japanese assets in the U.S., thus halting U.S.-Japanese trade. The effect was to stop American exports of scrap iron and oil to Japan — crucial to the Japanese war effort in China. The next day President Roosevelt placed all armed forces of the Philippines under the command of General Douglas MacArthur, who was named commander-in-chief of U.S. forces in the Far East.

The worsening situation came home to us in the 14th Squadron. When I enlisted, it had been possible to purchase a discharge after one year of service. But now three years of service became mandatory. Each airman at Hickam Field was trained to use a machine gun and .45 pistol. The latter was to be carried at all times. We camouflaged our planes and loaded them with live bombs and ammunition for their daily and nightly flights. We stood guard duty day and night and had orders to shoot any suspicious characters. Yet we thought we were in a safe spot in case of war. Our ships freely came and went, and patrol planes roared overhead at all times. Most people in Hawaii thought an attack was impossible.

Meantime, my friends at the church and plenty of work as a baker — now for 5,000 men — had changed my outlook. I had so many things to think about that time was passing quickly. More planes and men were arriving in Hawaii, but more intensive training and less free time meant fewer customers for the merchants downtown in Honolulu. The merchants squawked in the papers, radios, and in letters to the top command. Now, they treated servicemen with a lot more respect than before.

Early in the afternoon of September 16, 1941, the 14th Squadron mustered in the dayroom. As 1st Sgt. George Scott called out our names, he directed each of us to one side of the room or the other. I was put in the group that was to stand by for immediate departure for an unknown destination. I protested to Captain Marshall Gray that I shouldn't go because of my heavy responsibilities in baking for a large mess, and good prospects of being promoted as a cook. But the captain insisted that I had been greatly honored by being selected to be in the elite 14th Bomb Squadron. But I did not feel honored. In fact, it was a good thing I didn't know what was in store for me.

We were to stand by with only what we could carry and be ready to leave at a moment's notice. Everyone had to quickly dispose of civilian clothes, sports equipment, books, and radios. Several men even owned second-hand cars that were left behind or given away. I had no car, but I had to break a date that night with my steady girl, an attractive Chinese mestizo. We were going to see a movie, *Nice Girl*, starring Deanna Durbin. I couldn't reach my girl by phone and never saw her again.

We embarked that evening on the troop ship *President Pierce* while hula dancers and a band performed for us on the dock. We found the 200th Anti-Aircraft Regiment from New Mexico already aboard — they had sailed from San Francisco on August 28. As we steamed out of the harbor, I stood at the rail, watching the waving palms along the beach, the city lights beyond, and the distant dark mountains. I hated to leave, and a voice inside whispered for me to slip overboard and swim ashore in the darkness. That was out of the question. But I knew I might be sailing into hardships, heartbreaks, and misery.

Sgt. Scott told us to sleep on deck with life belts handy. I used mine as a pillow and stretched out. From the darkness of the blacked-out ship, I gazed at the thousands of stars, which made brilliant dots in the black sky. Venus was so bright it cast a shimmering path on the ocean's surface. But sleep soon claimed me. When I awoke the next morning, I noticed the cruiser *Phoenix* sailing off our bow as escort, changing course from time to time. I soon realized that the *President Pierce* was also sailing a zigzag course to foil torpedo attacks.

I was given the job of inspecting lifeboats and keeping them drained. In my spare time I studied maps of the South Pacific, trying to figure out where we were going. Several days out, we sighted bits of wreckage and then a violent storm struck. The ship pitched and rolled constantly, making many seasick, but I was not affected. Our escort looked like a submarine as it dived under and through the monstrous waves. When the storm subsided, the *Phoenix* was no longer to be seen. It must have been ordered elsewhere.

In calmer water we passed the 180th meridian, marking the International Dateline. It was the shortest Sunday I had ever known — one-hour long. A chaplain from the 200th AA Regiment used the interlude to preach a sermon. We sailed on across the endless Pacific, passing south of Guam. Then we continued westward past the Japanese-mandated island of Yap, which appeared at a distance off our port bow and then was gone. It looked like we were headed for the Philippines, but was that our final destination?

On September 30, 1941, a few vague spots showed on the horizon ahead of us. As we steamed onward, green, misty islands took shape, some rising steeply out of the water. We were approaching the Philippine Islands, consisting of eleven large islands and hundreds of smaller ones, with a total area about that of Arizona. We had traveled six time zones westward from Hawaii — considerably greater than the distance across the U.S., which includes four time zones.

The next day the *President Pierce* weaved its way slowly through the San Bernardino Strait, passing close to many small islands. I tried to imagine what inhabited them — probably snakes and crocodiles as well as creatures unknown to me. My boyhood in rural Florida had aroused an interest in all wild things. As we steamed onward, signs of civilization appeared, and later we could see the imposing Manila Hotel and several other large buildings.

Manila Bay was full of craft, from dugouts to merchant ships, as well as old-type U-boats and other naval vessels — some anchored and some moving about. After anchoring, an officer opened our sealed orders, and we finally learned we were to be stationed at Clark Field, one of the two major bomber bases in the Philippines. The 200th Anti-Aircraft Regiment also on board was likewise going to Clark Field, 50 miles northwest of Manila.

As I leaned over the rail, I wondered what the first woman I saw would

N

LUZON

PHILIPPINES

Clark
Field

Manila

Mariveles

Pacific Ocean

Romblon

Maricalom

See
Enlargement

Cagayan

Siari

Malaybalay

Iligan

MINDANAO

Davao

Zamboanga

19°

15°

11°

7°

121°

125°

PHILIPPINE ODYSSEY
From Clark Field 12/24/41 to Departure on NARWHAL 9/29/44

•••◀•••◀••••• Retreat from Clark Field to Cagayan
— — — — — Various Sea Transports as POW
∘∘∘∘∘∘∘∘∘∘∘∘ Foot/Truck Transports in Retreat and as POW
◀◀◀◀◀◀◀◀ Evacuation from Siari on U.S. Subarine NARWHAL

SCALE: 3/4 INCH = 141 MILES

Map by Henry Harer

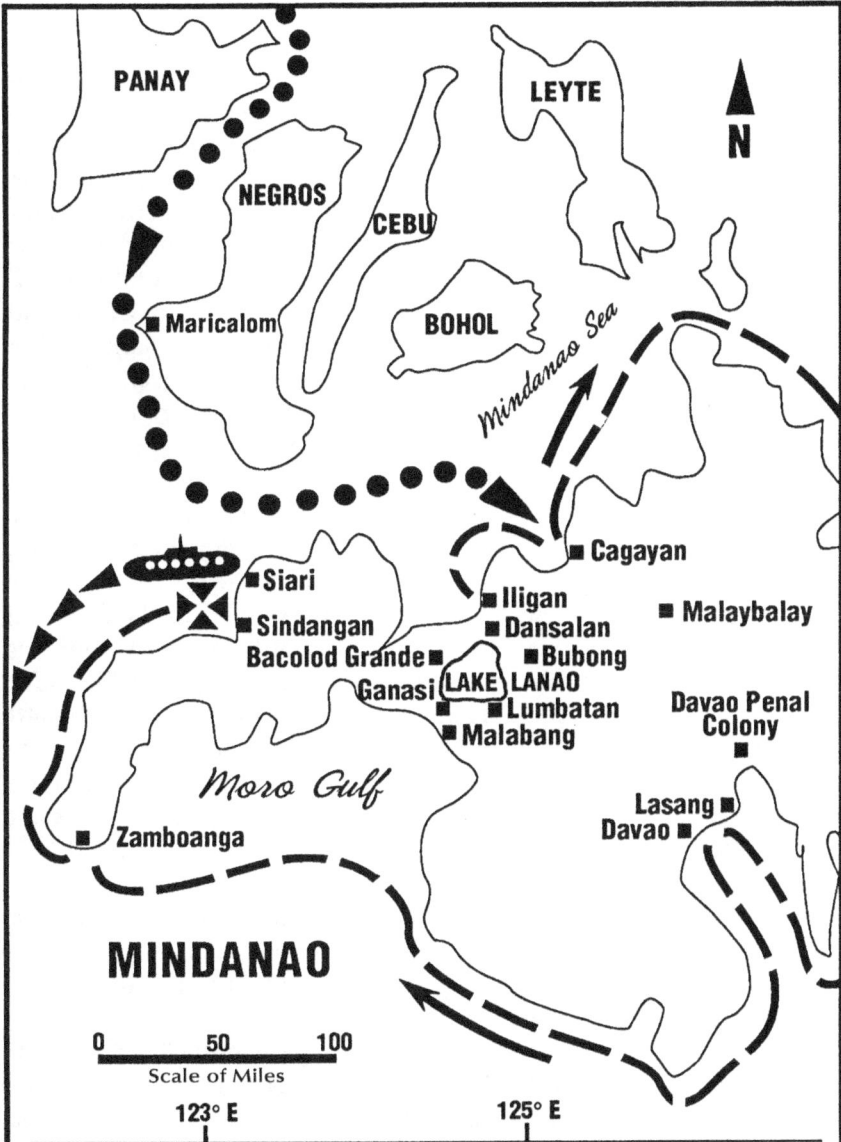

PANAY

LEYTE

NEGROS

CEBU

Mindanao Sea

BOHOL

■ Maricalom

■ Siari

■ Cagayan

■ Iligan
■ Dansalan

■ Malaybalay

■ Sindangan

Bacolod Grande ■

■ Bubong

Ganasi ■

LAKE LANAO

Davao Penal
Colony

■ Lumbatan

■ Malabang

Moro Gulf

Lasang ■

Davao ■

■ Zamboanga

MINDANAO

```
0        50      100
Scale of Miles
```

123° E   125° E

SEA ROUTES AND LAND LOCATIONS
Legend of Sea Travel

●●●◄●●●◄●●● SS MAYON ● Bataan to Cagayan (12/29/41 to 1/1/42)

———— Various Transports as POW (7/7/42 to 9/8/44)

✕ Sinking of SHINYO MARU
(9/8/44)

Survivors' Rendezvous with U.S. Submarine NARWHAL
(9/29/44)

◄◄◄◄◄◄◄◄ NARWHAL Departure Route (9/29/44) Map by Henry Harer look like. I soon saw her. She was in a small boat and wore a large straw hat and a shapeless dress that matched her figure. While marching down the gangplank, a local band played for us. On shore Filipinos wanted to carry our baggage for a few centavos, which we didn't have. But when we showed them American money, they went wild. Some Americans threw coins to see them scramble — causing the Filipinos to bump their heads. Conscious that the Filipinos were very poor, I watched uncomfortably as the men threw coins until we were ordered to board buses for Clark Field.

A very large pilot, Lt. Kelso, had ridden down from Clark Field on his motorcycle to escort us. Now, the buses formed a column and followed him through the city. It bustled with bicycles, horse-drawn carts, automobiles, buses, and people — a welcome sight after the long voyage from Hawaii. Outside Manila, a typhoon had left water everywhere. People in the villages were wading in the filthy water up to their armpits, but regardless of their plight they called out in cheery voices "Hello, Joe!" and waved as we passed.

We arrived at Clark Field after dark, hungry and tired. While eating a cold supper, we were greeted by some of our 14th Squadron comrades, whom we had left in Hawaii. They had already settled in at Clark Field after flying out the nine B-17s — or Flying Fortresses — that made up the 14th Squadron. They had made stops at Midway, Wake, Rabaul, Port Moresby on New Guinea, and Darwin, Australia — the pioneer flights by that route. We now had at Clark Field a typical bomb squadron of 220 officers and men, of whom 60 were pilots and air crew and the remainder ground crew. The 14th was the first squadron of the 19th Bomb Group to arrive in the Philippines. The 19th would reach a total strength of 35 B-17s, based at Clark and Del Monte Airfield, 600 miles to the south.

After talking some with the air crew about our assignment at Clark, we went to our quarters, which were made of palm leaves thatched on split bamboo. Each bunk had mosquito netting, but one of the boys awoke to find himself entangled. He thought an animal was attacking him, and his yells woke us all up. We were jumpy anyway, thinking we were near real jungle.

The next morning after breakfast, dozens of small black men, naked except for loin cloths, began to scavenge through the garbage cans where we had dumped our leftovers. They were 4½ feet tall and called Negritos. General Arthur MacArthur, father of Douglas MacArthur, had recognized the Negritos' ownership of the region where Clark Field was later located, and the Negritos had agreed to share use of the region with the Americans. That was in 1898, and the agreement still held. Besides helping themselves to leftovers, the Negritos traded with servicemen, exchanging bows and

B-17 Flying Fortress. These great bombers were in short supply following the early Japanese attacks on U.S. airfields. (National Air and Space Museum, Smithsonian Institution [SI Neg. No. 95-9156].)

arrows for combs, knives, nail clippers, and mirrors. They searched the base endlessly for old bottles, clothing, and any discarded item of interest.

Life was easier at Clark Field than it had been at Hickam. We were paid two pesos for every dollar we had received before. It was to our advantage because one peso bought more in the Philippines than one dollar did in Hawaii. Many of the men would buy whiskey by the case. At Clark every man had a Filipino bunk boy, who would make your bunk, shine shoes, wash and iron, and do your KP duties, all for a few pesos a month. Another bonus — we worked only half a day because of the heat. Another change was permission to grow beards.

I thought the first beard I saw at Clark belonged to a man of 35, but he said he was 22. Not having to shave daily, he bought a beer or two with what he had been spending on razor blades. I joined the crowd of beards and competed for the prize given for the best-looking one. *Life* magazine carried pictures of the various styles, and the Air Corps at Clark Field was called the "Hair Corps."

Adjacent to Clark Field was Fort Stotsenburg, home of the Philippine Scouts, who made up the bulk of General Wainwright's 26th Cavalry Division. The Scouts asked us to watch their precision drilling. In spotless uniforms they marched on the parade ground to the beat of a lively band. The Scouts treated us like brothers and invited us into their homes in Margot and Sloppy Bottom Villages, where we met their families.

Beyond the vicinity of Clark Field, we visited nearby villages and towns. The town of Angeles had two popular bars, the Moonlight and the Star, where the men found wine, women, and song. The same town had a taxi-dance hall. There, for a few centavos, beautiful girls danced with you to dreamy Spanish music. But I spent most of my free time riding around the countryside with a member of the 28th Bomb Squadron who owned an old car. We drove over the mountains to swim in Subic Bay and parked at different places to ride horses and bicycles or be pulled in carriages by small, underfed ponies.

After we were eligible for three-day passes, ten of us from the Air Corps decided to hike to the top of the tallest mountain near Clark Field, Mount Pinatubo. Because our Philippine guide didn't tell us how rough the trail was, we brought too much gear and had a hard time keeping on our feet. One of us slid into a swift stream while thundershowers soaked all of us.

In the mountains we encountered wilder Negritos than those around Clark Field. They set snares and traps for animals and cleared small patches of jungle to plant beans and potatoes. Usually when we sighted one of the little men, he would dash away into the jungle with a weird yell that warned others that our party was approaching. Occasionally we would run into one of their hunting parties carrying ugly arrows, but they did not harm us for we were well armed, and their fierce little faces with their teeth filed to points would disappear. Our guide told us that they had been known to attack intruders. When we crossed a river on a fallen log, he told us this was the boundary line between the Negritos and a tribe called the Zambal, who were not pygmies but who were more dangerous.

Just as it was growing dark, we came to a clearing and found a deserted cabin that had been the scene of the murder of a few Philippine Scouts by the Zambalenos. We were tired enough to stop there for the night, anyway. Yet our hopes for a good night's sleep did not work out. The wind began to rattle the tin roof and whistle between the old boards, making eerie noises that kept us awake most of the night.

Everyone was glad when dawn came. Only three of my buddies, Bill

Knortz, Ben Ferrens, and Verge Haifley, joined me in the final climb to the top of Pinatubo while the rest stayed behind. On the way I slipped into a moss-covered fissure that was deep enough to frighten me, but I scrambled out. Knortz crawled to the top first. Finally all four of us lay at the top, breathless after the steep climb in the thin air. As we looked out, the sun occasionally broke through the surrounding clouds and fog to give us views of Clark Field, Iba Air Field, and the China Sea. Closer, we could see fires of the savage Zambalenos beyond the cabin.

On our easy downhill return, we soon were breathing normally. Our comrades were waiting at the cabin, having spent the day sleeping and target shooting. It was too late to go on so we spent another night at the cabin. This time the cabin noises didn't bother us, and we had a good rest. Next day we came upon 30 of the wilder Negritos. They seemed peaceful enough when their chief gave a handful of arrows to the driver of the truck that was taking us on to Clark Field. But then all of them tried to climb on the truck — a dangerous overloading. They apparently thought the arrows were some kind of payment for a ride. We were barely able to restrain them without using force. Back at Clark we had missed Thanksgiving dinner, but someone had saved cold turkey for us.

Our easygoing life at Clark did not last. The 28th Bomb Squadron arrived with its B-17s to join our 14th Squadron as part of the 19th Bombardment Group, and two tank outfits arrived. Now there were long lines at the PX and movies, and a shortage of water caused some of us to bathe in the Bambam River. The bars in Angeles were too crowded to be enjoyable. Clark Field had grown up overnight and was a threat to Japan's back door.

One day a strange plane flew over. At first we assumed it was one of the Dutch aircraft working with us, but we soon realized it was a Japanese observation flight. Yet nothing was done about it. Believing war was close at hand, I wrote a long letter home and the following Saturday boarded a train for a final fling in Manila with my buddy, Sgt. Merrill B. Forsythe of Hillsboro, Florida. We boarded a third-class car that was already nearly filled with Filipinos, mestizos, and Negritos. Some passengers carried chickens and bundles of wood while a few had pigs underfoot.

In Manila we took a room at the YMCA. After cleaning up, we went to the dining room and ordered a big meal with all the trimmings. But just as we began to eat, a fire alarm went off and a loudspeaker told everyone to go to the ground floor and stay there until further notice. I thought war had begun, but it was only practice for an air raid. We were soon back at our dinner but hurried because we wanted to see as much of the city as we could before a real attack.

We stopped first at the Panama Café, which was crowded with drinking parties of civilian women and men but few servicemen. My buddy and I looked like members of the Merchant Marine because of our beards and civilian clothes. The Filipino girl who brought our drinks wore becoming clothes and expensive, high-heeled shoes. When we invited her to join us, she sat down but declined to drink. She said she was a devout Christian, had lost her parents, and now was supporting her sister, who was a student. We invited her to see Manila with us, but she politely declined.

Then we hailed a taxi and visited many places, always taking our Filipino driver with us and treating him as a comrade. Driving between bars, one of us would distract him while the other set back his meter. He never seemed to catch on. When he delivered us back to the YMCA, we all were a little drunk and he was happy with a few pesos. Next afternoon at Clark everyone took it easy, telling of the good times he had had in Manila, Angeles, or San Fernando—small talk when we knew war might start at any moment.

The following morning, Monday, December 8, 1941, I was awakened by the excited tones of men gathered around the cook on duty. Up early to prepare breakfast, he had heard the first radio reports of the Japanese attack on Pearl Harbor and heavy American losses there. Later we found that the battleships, the kings of the fleet, had been lined up in Pearl Harbor; all had been hit. Hickam Field, where I had been stationed before coming to the Philippines, had also been bombed. Later I learned that the three places where I most likely would have been had been hit the hardest.

The attack on Pearl Harbor put us in hot water that was close to the boiling point. We were practically at the Japs' back door and could be attacked in minutes and cut off from the rest of the islands. Although later reports only confirmed the bad news, some men found the attack hard to believe and suggested the reports were only propaganda to warn the United States of the growing menace in the Far East. When stationed at Hickam Field, the same men had seen the heavy Navy bombers going out on patrol in Hawaiian waters every hour on the hour. They also remembered the many alerts and maneuvers we had undergone there. Thus, the reported sneak attack did not seem likely. But continuing reports of the damage to our old home made the boys talk in a grave manner, especially when we were ordered to dig foxholes and draw our allowances of weapons, ammunition, steel helmets, and gas masks. After equipping ourselves, we came back to the barracks and sat beside a radio with grim faces, digesting every particle of news. Someone brought in word that the 26th Cavalry Division next door at Fort Stotsenburg was preparing to resist landings of Japanese paratroopers.

We learned later that the news of Pearl Harbor had reached General MacArthur's Command in Manila at 3 A.M. that day. At 5 A.M. MacArthur's air chief, General Lewis Brereton, sought but was refused permission to bomb Japanese installations on the island of Formosa, 220 miles north of Luzon and the nearest Japanese base for attacking the Philippines. After Brereton was rebuffed again at 7:15 A.M., he ordered our 17 B-17 bombers at Clark Field to take off and cruise aimlessly to save them from being caught on the ground — 16 bombers did so but the 17th had generator trouble.

Our bombers had been in the air some time when we learned that Japanese aircraft had attacked Baguio about 40 miles due north of us — a rich mining center and the summer capital of the Philippines. The only victims were a few soldiers on leave at nearby Camp John Hayes and a few civilians. Since Baguio did not seem very important, we conjectured that the Japs' intelligence was not good or that they planned to establish a military base there. Finally, Baguio might have been attacked to throw us off guard before bombing elsewhere — perhaps Clark Field.

About 11:30 A.M. the 16 B-17s came back and landed. The hungry pilots and crews rushed off the field to eat while the ground crew refueled and checked the engines. We learned later that at 11 A.M. General Brereton had finally been given permission to bomb Formosa, and so the B-17s had been recalled to refuel and prepare for the mission.

2

Clark Field
Under Attack

December 8–12, 1941

The attacks on Pearl Harbor and Baguio made for a morning of anxiety at Clark Field. After noon chow, no one felt like his normal siesta. I talked to my fellow cooks while waiting to hear Don Bell, a radio commentator who had served in China as a Marine. He always grabbed our attention with his lively presentation, and his message always boiled down to, "The Japs are preparing for war right under our noses." Now our popular newscaster came on, but instead of talking about Pearl Harbor he startled us by reporting that "Clark Field is being bombed by the Japs at this very minute. Yes, it is being smashed by our enemies. They have already hit Tarlac, a city nearby." We laughed and wondered what was going on — no bombs were falling around us. We suspected the news was propaganda, but for what purpose?

We knew that General Wainwright had ordered the 26th Cavalry Division at neighboring Ft. Stotsenburg to prepare for action. East of Clark at Sloppy Bottom, the 200th Anti-Aircraft batteries were camouflaging their guns. At Clark the Air Corps was digging foxholes and setting up machine guns while the 803rd Engineers dug zigzag trenches. Our planes, which had been ordered aloft during the morning as a protective measure, were now lined up in the open while being refueled and serviced.

We were still joking about the "attack on Clark" when I noticed some men back of the 28th Materiel barracks who were scanning the sky in the direction of the Bambam River and Zambales Mountains. Curious, I joined them. I looked up into the clear, blue sky and saw two perfect formations of aircraft — 27 in each at about 20,000 feet. Someone remarked about the beautiful formations the Navy flew and wondered where they were going.

But something inside me said these planes meant danger! Suddenly, I was convinced the planes were Japanese. I told the other bystanders to run for the nearby dugout. I ran inside the 28th Materiel kitchen, through the dining room and into the dayroom, yelling we were about to be attacked. The men were listening to the radio, waiting for more from Don Bell. At my warning, they hurtled through the screened windows instead of running for the doors.

I ran back through the kitchen where I picked up a gas mask and steel helmet. I headed for the closest dugout, but it was already full. I called to others to follow me. Others ran across the open field in the direction of nearby Ft. Stotsenburg. Just as I got into a dugout, the Japs released their first bombs, which seemed to fall across the Bambam River. A captain stood stupefied at the edge of the hole. I tried to pull him down, but he protested, "Get your hands off me, soldier," and cussed the hell out of me.

I looked up at the fearful sight of enemy planes attacking us in perfect formation and without challenge. At first the bombs looked like they were falling short, but the first one hit nearby. Then the captain crawled in next to me. The bombs began a march of destruction, "walking" step by step, shaking the ground more with each step. Exploding bombs and the constant roar of enemy aircraft filled our ears as hell broke loose. The fires that were ignited spread smoke everywhere while wounded and dying men shrieked in pain.

Our planes, caught on the ground, were useless. It seemed the Japs knew that this was our lunch hour and our planes would be down — clay pigeons for them to destroy at their leisure. We always thought afterward that a fifth columnist* had tipped off the Japs or they had detected the landing of our planes by listening to our radio traffic.

Only the 200th Anti-Aircraft batteries fired steadily at the enemy aircraft, adding to the din of Japanese aircraft and bombs. The first wave of planes was so high that the anti-aircraft shells burst far below their targets. Another hindrance for the defenders was the smoke from burning hangars, planes, and gas trucks that blotted out the attacking aircraft from the ground.

One of the bombs walked right up to our hole, almost stepping on us. It landed so close that it shook everything, even our teeth. Worse, it

---

*Subversives within a country who assist invaders. First used in 1936 to describe rebel sympathizers inside Madrid when four columns of rebel troops were attacking that city.

caved in the framework of our foxhole. We had to dig through the dirt to get air. We broke free and pulled our comrades out after us.

Just then enemy fighter planes swooped in low and began strafing. Bullets hit all around us and killed and injured many. Yet, the smoke prevented the Japs from seeing us well. Our men were firing machine guns, rifles, and pistols at the strafing aircraft. I saw one American hit in the chest with shrapnel. As he placed both hands around the ugly wound, he cried out, "Look at me! Look at what those yellow bastards did to me!" He asked us to tell his folks what had happened and to get even with the Japs for him. Then he died.

After our hole collapsed, we ran for an old building where we took cover under the edge of its concrete floor. In case the building were hit, the lucky ones near the edge might have a chance to crawl out. We were wretched-looking, covered with sweat and dirt, our clothes torn and some of us bleeding. Now planes roared over the building to strafe the roof above us. Some men ventured out to fire at the Zero fighter aircraft as the planes skimmed over the building. Then they took cover again to reload and muttered to each other, "Maybe we'll have better luck next time." They came to realize that to hit a moving plane, one had to fire well ahead of it, and then it was mostly pure luck to score a hit with a rifle. I lay there gathering my senses, wishing I had a gun. I recalled that earlier in the raid, some of the Zeros had flown low east of Clark to Sloppy Bottom, where ground fire brought down two of them. As the raid continued, I wondered if the Japs would drop paratroopers to capture Clark Field.

The thought came to me, "How do I stand with God?" To which my inner voice kept repeating, "Blessed is he who endureth to the end." I began to pray, like others around me. I asked forgiveness and entreated His guidance.

After what seemed like a decade, the raid ended with the hum of Jap planes dying in the distance. Those motors seemed to be rejoicing over the smoke, fire, and explosions they had left behind. Then the angry voices of trucks and tanks came as a defiant response as the vehicles rushed from the field to ward off a possible land invasion. Ambulances darted about, picking up the dead and wounded. The field was filled with the shrill yells of men fighting fire and taking care of the wounded. The forgotten radio was still playing a gay tune, as if the field was not lying in ruins. We had been baptized into the horrors of war. The behavior of different individuals during the raid was sometimes predictable but not always.

A fellow climber to the top of Mount Pinatubo, Bill Knortz, who was Superman and Gary Cooper combined, had studied judo (Japanese wrestling) in Hawaii and earned the black belt, a prized achievement. During the raid, he was draped with belts of machine gun ammunition, exposing himself to enough danger to fire twice as many rounds as other machine gunners.

Equally brave was Christopher, a small fellow who wore glasses and seemed frail and timid. Some men called him a sissy — he did look out of place among us. No one thought he would be of any use in action, but during the frightening and prolonged attack, Christopher stayed with the teletype, sending and receiving messages while everything around us blew up.

Then there was a camera bug who became so absorbed in taking pictures that he forgot the danger. A fellow airman pushed him away from a gas truck just before a bomb exploded. But the near victim walked back and took a close-up picture of the exact spot where he had been standing. The bravest ambulance driver was Andre — he did not wait for the raid to end before driving out to care for the wounded.

The Chinese manager of the PX was not as lucky. After diving into the nearest foxhole, he remembered he had left money in the cash register and ran back to retrieve it. As he neared the PX, a bomb hit him dead center and he disappeared. Only his wooden shoes were found, as if he had simply stepped out of them.

Almost before the sound of the departing aircraft died out, we were startled to hear music. It was the 200th AA Band marching around through the wreckage playing "God Bless America," "My Old Kentucky Home," and similar tunes. Col. Emeral Cane had ordered the band to perform. Then he called everyone together for a short speech. He didn't say much. His main message was that we had to clean up the field so we could have a chance to fight back next time.

Our first job was work we had never done before. We gathered truckloads of our comrades' bodies, many with mangled arms and legs and some without heads. We also found many still alive who were crying out in pain and agony from shrapnel and bullet holes, or just staring into space. Blood was everywhere, and there was the odor of burnt human flesh as well as burning wood and fabric. We had only three or four ambulances so we used trucks to get the wounded to Ft. Stotsenburg. There, much suffering continued because the hospital did not have enough equipment, doctors, or medicine to handle us as well as the wounded Filipinos of General Wainwright's 26th Cavalry Division. Survivors not working with casualties were fighting fires. Even many who were bleeding worked to fight the blazes, which billowed smoke high into the sky.

The heavy-bombing part of the attack had lasted about 18 minutes. The strafing and dive-bombing lasted about 35 minutes. Casualties at

Clark were 143 wounded and 93 killed. The raid had blown into thousands of pieces most of the 16 shiny, new B-17 bombers, which had been aloft during the morning.

The destroyed bombers had constituted half of the 35 B-17s in the Philippines. The other half had been moved to Del Monte Airfield on the large island of Mindanao — hundreds of miles out of the range of the nearest Japanese airfields on Formosa.* But the supporting ground crews had stayed behind — the bulk of squadron manpower. They and the 17 B-17 bombers still at Clark were within easy range of Formosa, 300 miles to the north.

The enemy force attacking Clark Field that day consisted of 54 bombers and 36 new Zero fighters. We knew of only two Japanese aircraft that were shot down, one at the Bambam River and the other at Margo Barrio, where the families of the Filipino officers of the 26th Cavalry Division lived. The Negritos got to the body of one enemy pilot first. They carried it over to Clark, asking us the whereabouts of General Wainwright. We gave directions — rather perplexed that the gift corpse for the general lacked a head.

I believe the 200th Anti-Aircraft batteries should be credited for shooting down the two enemy planes, although others at Clark scored some hits. While almost everyone else was under cover or taking sporadic shots, the 200th was out there with their anti-aircraft guns, plugging away. Most of this gallant outfit were Mexican-American boys from a National Guard outfit in New Mexico. I had several good friends among them.

The end of the day found me and two other volunteer cooks preparing food for the battered men of other outfits. The cooks at the 28th Materiel mess did not show up, nor did their Filipino helpers. Many of our hungry eaters had torn and greasy clothes that smelled of smoke because they had been fighting fires. I opened everything I could get my hands on in the mess hall stores and brewed plenty of hot coffee. The men ate everything that we put before them.

As it grew dark my helpers, Ishmael Gudgeon, Jerry Coty, and I, looked for our outfit but could find none of our men. The firefighters and rescue workers were exhausted and moving off the field — the wrecked barracks were no place for rest. Furthermore, the Japs might come over again at any time to bomb or drop paratroopers. Everyone straggled away into the jungle toward Margot Barrio. It was so dark when we stumbled into the brush that we didn't go very far, fearing that the men already hidden would be jumpy enough to think we were Japs and shoot.

---

*In the following days, a few Del Monte B-17s flew back to Clark at dusk and were serviced during the night for raids against the enemy invasion of Luzon.

After deciding to stay where we were for the night, we threw together a rough, V-shaped barricade, using a dead log, a huge tree, and many limbs. We lay down uncomfortably inside, fighting mosquitoes and ants. Occasionally we heard a rustle in the brush that died away quickly, leaving us to wonder whether it was a sneaking Jap, a Yank, or a cobra wandering about. Lying down for the night seemed to be a bad idea so we sat up and peered in different directions into the jungle with our backs to each other. Shots during the night made us wonder if Yanks were firing at their own men. Explosions were still going off around Clark Field. There were also distant booms that we thought were Jap attacks elsewhere. To stay awake, we talked about the war, home, and the uncertain future. We promised each other that if one of us were killed, the others would look up his family. Yet, as dawn broke, our only physical complaint was lack of sound sleep.

Others stirred from their hiding places in the jungle close by. I got up, stretched, and looked over the ruins of Clark Field. An aircraft engine roared — it was a P-40 pursuit plane trying to take off. Suddenly, it hit a bomb crater, lurched out of control, and smashed into a B-17. Both exploded, destroying planes and pilot. Thus began the second day of the war.

I didn't have to look far for my outfit. A lieutenant, whom we shall call John Doe, and Sergeants George Scott and John Chandler had located the 14th Squadron command post close to where I had slept. At first we had difficulty rounding up our men, but the 28th Materiel Mess Hall proved to be a good place to look. In the absence of regular mess, everyone was raiding the food stores. The sergeants and I told our men to gather up all the chow they could carry and report to our command post. There, in a thicket among coral rocks, we pitched the tents and set up a kitchen with gas field ranges. Other units located near us.

Soon all the Air Corps men were cleaning up the field, repairing the few planes that could be put in service again, dismantling others, and moving useful equipment into the jungle. The likelihood of another attack made the men jumpy, but they kept busy and Clark Field again took on an orderly appearance.

You could see signs that many were still shocked from the raid. Some of the fellows slept in their helmets and shoes while others would not even remove their helmets when bathing. An extreme case was my likable friend, Punchy. He was a real talker, especially after drinking. He would brag about what a good fight he would put up, but the first bombing took all the fight out of him. He dug himself an air raid shelter, not a common foxhole, under the biggest tree he could find. He stayed there for two days, not even coming out for chow. We urged him to climb out, but he finally asked us to bring him a sandwich. We found that his shelter was so deep that he could not hear planes landing or taking off. Another kid went nuts, even forgetting his name. One fellow who studied religion and was thought to be an authority on it burned all his religious books and pamphlets, and denounced God because He had allowed the Japs to attack us.

The second day after the attack, December 10, and again on December 12, enemy aircraft attacked the 26th Cavalry Division at neighboring Ft. Stotsenburg. Their strafing killed many of the Philippine Scouts who were preparing to leave for northern Luzon to defend against Japanese landings.

The next day, December 13, we had plenty to worry about ourselves when the Japs mounted their second attack on Clark Field. This time, however, our few remaining planes had already taken off to attack Japanese forces to the north. After we sighted the enemy aircraft, I beat my helper into our foxhole, but not by much. He was Willard Rosselle, a chubby airman from Wisconsin. I thought I had been hit by a flying timber until I saw Rosselle's grinning face beside me. Looking out, we saw an airman dash into the open and just stare at the approaching bombers — he was shell-shocked from the first raid. Comrades pulled him into a foxhole before the bombs began to fall.

Our foxhole could not protect us from the debris and shrapnel flying all over the place so we climbed out and built a barricade around us of sacks of sugar, flour, rice, and potatoes. We had just settled inside when a bomb came screaming down and exploded about 50 feet from us and tore a hole in our barricade. Rosselle and I grabbed a cleaver and hatchet and dug deeper into the foxhole — so energetically it looked like we were trying to reach the States. We did as much in a few minutes as Rosselle had reluctantly done for me the past three days. Even after the bombers had disappeared, we were still digging inside our chow barricade. As we dug, I was singing "What a Friend I Have in Jesus." A squadron clerk staggered up and interrupted us.

During the raid he had been caught in the open so he had fallen forward and hugged Mother Earth. He had remained safe despite the bombs falling all around him. But now his face showed he was scared out of his wits. He was shaking and his vocal chords refused to work. However, his voice came back shortly, and then the three of us joked about the whole matter while eating some of our barricade. We felt secure because of the dirt and rocks we had piled around us with our furious digging. Rosselle and I decided that from then on, we would dig foxholes that were deep enough.

A few bombs were still exploding here and there when we were ordered to move our kitchen to the other side of the fields, into a banana patch near the Bambam River. Now, demolition crews were setting off unexploded bombs but some were going off of their own accord at unexpected moments. When these sporadic explosions finally ended, the silence brought a momentary sense of calm.

We were still moving kitchen equipment when our planes came straggling back from combat operations. As we watched, two Zero fighters dived out of the sun and attacked an incoming B-17 that had survived the first enemy raid. The big bomber burst into flames almost immediately. In moments, little dots appeared in the sky suspended from white chutes. While the men floated helplessly earthward, the Japs dived after them. All drifted to the ground, some of them certainly wounded or dead. But a half hour later, all of the parachutists walked into camp none the worse for the jump except for scratches and bruises.

One of the parachutists was Bob Altman, who stopped to help us relocate the kitchen. He was sad and subdued, telling us that the crew's respected pilot, Captain Colin Kelly, and Sgt. William J. Delahanty had not gotten out of the plane. Altman went on to say that his chute and shrouds had been hit several times on the way down. While tracers flew all around him, Bob closed his eyes and prayed. But his only injury was a slight scratch near his eye. Their B-17 had dropped all of its bombs in an attack on the battleship *Haruna* and badly damaged it.* Their safe return seemed almost certain when the two Zeros attacked only three miles from Clark. When the B-17 was hit, Captain Kelly ordered his crew to bail out — his prompt orders had saved everyone except himself and Sgt. Delahanty.

The press reported in the U.S. that Captain Colin Kelly had steered his burning plane into a Japanese battleship. Bob Altman's account was correct except that the damaged ship was the heavy cruiser Ashigara. *It survived the attack, was repaired, and operated until the war ended.*

3

Last Trip to Manila
December 12–22, 1941

As it grew dark on the day of the second raid on Clark, the men gathered in the banana patch to wait for chow. Then the boys were unsettled by the sound of someone trying to open a toolbox with a hammer. Inside the box was a wrench that was needed to set up the field range to cook dinner. But that didn't matter to the toolbox owner — he jumped about and yelled in almost insane efforts to stop the pounding. Other men were close to cracking while they waited hungrily for their supper. Finally, it was ready, and after eating everyone felt better. Now the squadron was exhausted, and each man hunted for a place to sleep. We posted guards, sweating out the possibility of Japanese paratroopers. We didn't sleep well because the slightest sound could wake up and unsettle one man or another, who in turn awakened others. I felt more calm than many, and thought of myself as a seasoned veteran.

My experience as a kid in the Florida everglades and my Eagle Scout training were coming in handy. I had always dreamed of jungle adventures, but they did not include hiding in a banana patch at the edge of a battered airstrip, only to exist and wait for the worst.

The next day we cut off all the lower leaves of the banana trees so we could move around freely but stay hidden by the top foliage. We set up our field ranges for the kitchen and prepared separate places for trucks, jeeps, water, and food. Our command post was well hidden a short way off. Nearby, other outfits were doing the same things. The banana patch was a beehive of activity. The bees had one thought — to stay concealed from the birds.

At this time I was promoted to sergeant and took the top position in the kitchen in place of Sgt. Palmer, who had advanced to the slot left vacant when Sgt. Delahanty was killed in Captain Colin Kelly's plane. However, Palmer still helped me run the kitchen. Things were also different because our Filipinos, hired to do routine work in the kitchen—kitchen police (KP) jobs—never showed up after the first raid on Clark Field. Now our own men rotated for the detested duty. In their spare time everyone looked for food and brought in cans and sacks scrounged from the warehouses, post exchanges, and ice plants at Clark and Stotsenburg.

Whenever the air raid siren sounded its dreaded song from the control tower, the boys on the airstrip ran for their lives. They were quickly joined by the tower watchman, who had to scramble to the ground after giving the alarm. The pilots did what they could in the repair efforts but were angry and disgusted when they had to take to foxholes instead of climbing into their fighter planes to engage the enemy. The bombs whistled just over our heads but hit the airfield in front of us since the Japs did not realize where we were. Still, we feared they might release their bombs too soon or find our hiding places. They never found us, though—not thinking we would stay so close to the airstrip in a place as unlikely as a banana patch. We had a visitor every day who would come over and circle slowly overhead just as we were sitting down to eat. We dubbed him "Oscar" or "Photo Joe" and felt he knew when we ate—actually he was probably choosing the best time of day to take pictures. Worried, however, we ate just twice daily, changed our mealtimes from day to day, and dispersed while eating so a number of us would survive an air attack.

In the early days of the banana patch, Bill Knortz and others began to acquire discarded machine guns and take knives, rifles, and pistols from the wrecked planes. With these assorted weapons, our beards, and tattered clothes, we were a spectacle. Many of the boys reveled in our looser kind of life. But there were drawbacks, like the lack of running water.

We had not had a bath in several days—the last time an air raid had caught us we were in the Bambam River and had to run for cover, nude. My swarthy, good-looking friend from Philadelphia, Sgt. John G. Murdoch, felt as dirty as I did. He joined me in searching for the showers in the wrecked barracks at Ft. Stotsenburg—its Filipino occupants, the 26th Division, had gone north to fight the Japs. The first shower room we found still worked. Delighted, we peeled off our filthy, sweat-stained clothes and showered for the first time since the Japs' first raid. We washed each other's backs and whooped with glee—our yells brought more men and noise to the showers. We forgot the war—I closed my eyes and remembered showering at home when my kid brother complained about my taking so long and mother hurried me to get ready for supper. But these dreams were shattered when two men shouted that the air raid had sounded and Japanese planes were expected at any moment. Having no place to go, we just sweated it out in the shower space. The raid was short, and we were unharmed. Yet I vowed never again to forget we were at war.

We put on some discarded clothes that were cleaner than ours and headed back to the banana patch. Murdoch and I, however, turned aside to look into another barracks, hoping to find something useful for the squadron. I crawled through a hole torn by a bomb fragment and gazed at the body of a Filipino Scout — his hand clutching the crucifix he had worn around his neck. In the wreckage I spotted a bloodstained M-1 rifle — a weapon we knew of but had not seen. I brought it out to show Murdoch and asked him if he thought I would be allowed to keep it. I had always wanted an M-1 because my obsolete Enfield frightened me — it had been known to blow up in men's faces. Back at the banana patch, my commanding officer, Major Emmet O'Donnell, told me I could keep my prize. I couldn't get the bloodstains off, but a lieutenant showed me how to use it and an old sergeant gave me some infantry training involving both the M-1 and Colt .45 automatic.

Shortly thereafter, Major O'Donnell moved up from CO of our 14th Squadron to Commanding Officer of the 19th Bombardment Group, of which the 14th was a part. We were glad to still be in his larger command because he was a great leader. At one time he was so determined to fight the enemy that against the wishes of his superior officer, Col. Eubanks, O'Donnell took to the air in a B-17 that had no tail gun. But he found and destroyed parked planes in northern Luzon and hit other targets before returning safely.

Now however, Japanese advances and dwindling delivery of supplies made us downhearted — we were too far from the U.S. Furthermore, we felt the general public wasn't too concerned over a war in a place they knew of only from geography class. As Christmas neared, Knortz and others composed a slogan, "Get your foxhole dug early and avoid the rush — only a few more days for Christmas shopping."

On December 22, 1941, Lt. John Doe, Bill Knortz, Sgt. James Palmer, Cpl. Richard Hough, and I got on a truck and headed for Manila for supplies and parts. We drove on empty streets through Angeles past the town's once overflowing bars and dance halls. The Filipinos we passed on the road threw up two fingers to make a "V" and shouted over and over, "Victory Joe." It warmed our hearts that they stuck with us even though we were losing. Several villages had been bombed and strafed, but elsewhere Filipinos were working in muddy rice paddies, threshing rice by hand, and fishing. Several times Japanese aircraft forced us to pull over and dive for cover. At one stop we met a village mayor grasping a shotgun to use against enemy paratroopers.

Except for Lt. Doe, our ragged bunch was a sight as we entered Manila — with beards, torn and dirty clothing, muddy shoes, steel helmets, and .45 pistols strapped around our waists. Manila's streets were almost deserted. Sandbags were stacked near office buildings, and ugly foxholes marred what had been beautiful lawns.

We turned down Dewey Boulevard, on which, it was rumored at Clark, hundreds of planes were taking off hourly and other hundreds that had been shipped from the States were being assembled. The truth was that one P-40 pursuit plane had been forced down there and a mechanic had immediately repaired it. In half-believing this story, my buddies and I had been like drowning men clutching at anything within reach.

After seeing about the supplies we had come for, we looked up one of our pilots who had been sent to Manila for treatment of an eye injury he had suffered when his plane cracked up. He was taking life easy but said he would rather be with us. We wished him luck and left to find a place to sleep.

We checked in at the Soldiers and Sailors Club, which was operated by Chinese. Our group all had dinner together that night — the check paid by Lt. Doe. Then the rest of us left Lt. Doe and Palmer to look for excitement in blacked-out Manila. A few prostitutes, wearing bright dresses and made up with crimson lipstick, had flirted with us that afternoon, but we feared they could be fifth columnists, could roll us, or might have venereal disease.

We finally decided to visit the elegant Manila Hotel but stayed in our tattered uniforms to identify us in case we got caught in an air raid. On the way a car almost ran us down in the blackout. We entered the impressive, dimly lit lobby and walked over to the desk where a dull light glowed, casting weird shadows on the wall. Uncertain, we asked the night manager if we could go into the ballroom. He smiled broadly and led us into the beautiful ballroom where the subdued light mingled with soft romantic music.

Many American and European women were dancing with well-dressed officers, some in uniform and others in civilian clothes. I was surprised because I thought such women had been evacuated shortly after Pearl Harbor. We thanked the manager and soon were sipping San Miguel beer and soaking up the dreamy atmosphere. We stopped a passing waiter to have our favorite songs played by the orchestra — it played my favorite Spanish tune, "La Paloma."

A jovial Air Corps flier joined us. He had noticed our scroungy Air Corps uniforms and figured we had been in combat. He was a leading pilot named Buzz Wagner. Only that morning, he had shot down two Zero fighters over northern Luzon.* A swell guy, Buzz talked easily with us for a while in the way most pilots talk with their enlisted men. After we wished him luck and he did the same for us, he went back to his girl.

Then we were joined by an Army officer who had been in Manila a long time as a civilian in the shipping business. Now, as an officer, he had the job of getting thousands of turkeys to the soldiers for Christmas dinner. Most of the turkeys were stored in Manila, but enemy aircraft had stalled shipment. Nevertheless, he declared, "We're sure going to try to get those turkeys to you boys for Christmas, Japs or no Japs." We told him of our difficulties in getting supplies and that we hoped to get the turkeys. Then we tried to cheer up the conversation with jokes, getting relaxed with more beer.

But Cpl. Hough was getting high — it didn't take much beer to get him under the table because he had just gotten over malaria. Then a military policeman (MP) spotted us and told us that all men in Manila had to have permits to carry guns. Hough hit the ceiling even when the MP showed him the written order. I explained to the MP that we had just come into town and our officer-in-charge would get us permits first thing in the morning. Seemingly satisfied, the MP left, but we took Hough by the arm and bid Manila Hotel goodbye.

Back at the Soldiers and Sailors Club, a Chinese showed us to our rooms, carefully shielding the flashlight in his hand. Entering my room, I beheld a real bed with a Beauty Rest mattress. I touched it to see if it were real and then crawled in and heaved a big sigh. But sleep would not come — any move I made shook the bed and I felt like I was floating. Finally I got up and lay down on the couch, which was more solid and more like the bunk I was used to. I fell asleep immediately.

Early the next morning a knock on the door awakened us. We ate breakfast by candlelight — it was still dark and the city was blacked out. Soon after dawn, an air raid siren sounded. My first thought was to run for a foxhole, but here we were ordered to the ground floor. The civilians gathered there seemed little concerned — we thought their mood odd, having seen the casualties and destruction of the air raids on Clark Field. Still, we did not wait for the "all clear" signal before joining the crowd outside, who were jostling to see the enemy aircraft bomb Cavite Naval Base. The

*Boyd D. "Buzz" Wagner was the first Air Corps ace in World War II. After shooting down the two Zero fighters that morning, he caught twelve enemy planes on the ground and left five burning. Six days later, he shot down three more enemy planes. In April 1942, he shot down three Japanese planes over New Guinea. Sent back to the U.S. to train pilots, he crashed to his death on a routine flight on November 29, 1942.

planes were still in perfect formation after passing over Manila
without challenge. I watched
them until they disappeared —
they had mocked the claim I had
once heard that no enemy planes
would fly over Manila without
being shot down.

Later that day on our way
to Ft. McKinley to pick up the
supplies we had come for, our
group passed by a slum area that
had been completely demol-
ished by enemy bombers — they
were trying to bomb Nichols
Field at night but had hit this
section that was full of poor
people living in wretched conditions. I was told that burnt
human flesh could be smelled
for days afterward. Then we
came to Nichols Field. It had
been easy for the Japs to find the
first day of the war because fifth

Lt. Boyd D. "Buzz" Wagner, the first U.S.
fighter ace of World War II. (*Courtesy Edward
Jackfert.*)

columnists had sent up flares to guide the attackers. Now piles of junk that
were once planes dotted the field. Among the wrecks, soldiers had dug foxholes. We had nearly reached Ft. McKinley when a squadron of enemy
planes drove us under the lip of a riverbank.

After returning to town, I wasn't able to change my pesos into dollars,
or cash in my postal savings bonds. My only choice was to keep the pesos
and bonds rather than deposit them in Manila for the Japs to confiscate. I
strolled by the Panama Café, where Forsythe and I had met the pretty girl
before the war started, only three weeks ago, but the place was closed. Then
I stopped at the Poodle Dog, famous for its Singapore Slings.

The owner's son, a mestizo, wanted to see my prized M-1 rifle that I
had found at deserted Ft. Stotsenburg, but I refused, not trusting him.
Insulted, he declared he was as much an American as I was. Then I began
to like the guy, and he told me to make myself at home so I ordered a drink
and listened to the nickelodeon. Two girls came over, and one of them,
quite pretty, sat on my lap. She wanted a drink and anything else I might
give her.

Sometimes a girl's soft touch and sweet words can make a guy pour his heart out to her — especially if he's been living in the jungle. A fellow has to watch himself or he might get into complicated circumstances. So I drank slowly and listened to the music while trying to talk to her — wishing she were my girl and that we were back in the good old United States of America. Something hard that I felt around her waist made me curious. I asked her what she was hiding. She smiled grimly and quickly pulled out a very wicked-looking dagger. She said she was prepared to use it when the Jap soldiers marched into Manila. Then the siren wailed again. I went into the street and watched the planes pass overhead. Most of the people didn't even glance up — their lack of concern somehow made me more relaxed than I had been in the jungles at Clark Field.

I left the Poodle Dog and met my friends for our return to Clark Field. They were loaded with cameras, whisky, and other items for themselves and buddies. But we still had a few hours before starting back so we visited the hospital to see some of our wounded friends. We found a 14th Squadron man in pretty bad shape from shell shock. The hospital was crowded with boys from Clark and Nichols Fields; some had lost limbs and some had internal injuries. As we talked with them, one question arose again and again, "When is help going to arrive from the U.S.?" We could only look at each other and slowly shake our heads. We ate at the hospital and went over to the Jai Alai Palace, which had been converted into an emergency hospital. The huge courts had been turned into wards. I understood it was bombproof — at least the wounded felt more secure there.

We headed back to Clark Field in silence, each of us keeping his thoughts to himself. I was thinking about all that we had done and seen in the city and was sad to realize I might not see Manila again for a long time.

4

Retreat to Bataan
December 22–29, 1941

On December 22, the day we had gone to Manila for squadron supplies, the main enemy invading forces came ashore on Lingayen Gulf, about 65 miles northwest of Clark Field. General Wainwright's forces could only slow the invaders' drive toward Manila. At first General MacArthur wanted to challenge this drive but changed his mind next day when another major Japanese force landed 60 miles southeast of Manila. To avoid entrapment by the two enemy forces, MacArthur returned to the earlier American plan for a strategic withdrawal of all forces on Luzon to defensible positions on Bataan Peninsula. MacArthur's forces consisted of 15,000 Americans and 65,000 Filipinos, but many of the Filipinos had not been organized into units long enough to be effective against the enemy soldiers — veterans of Japanese warfare against China in the 1930s. It would take an effective command structure and skillful direction to conduct an orderly retreat and avoid a rout of the green troops.

Still camped in the jungle around Clark Field, the 14th Squadron wanted to celebrate the birth of Christ in some way. Our cook, Sgt. Palmer, decided to put together a dinner that would remind us of home so the day before Christmas he and I searched for food among the ruins of Ft. Stotsenburg. Our driver was Aldo P. Maccagli, a short, swarthy New Yorker from Brooklyn who had driven his truck during the air raids when no other would try. Today we drove over to the Stotsenburg ice plant and found plenty of beef — a good replacement for the turkey that had never reached us despite the best efforts of the Army officer we had met in the Manila Hotel.

On the way back we passed a circle of soldiers near the 192nd Tank

Battalion Headquarters. They surrounded an enemy pilot who was being interrogated. One Filipino soldier recognized him as a civilian who had lived in nearby Sloppy Bottom village before the war. But he had returned to Japan to lead the enemy raids on Clark Field.

Back in the kitchen with the beef, we learned the 14th Squadron might withdraw from Clark at any time. During the evening meal, reports of enemy advances trickled in and a half-dozen radio operators left to join the 192nd Tank Battalion, which was moving north to bolster the retreating forces. The roast beef for Christmas Day dinner was almost done when I was ordered to get the chow truck rolling — we had accumulated a large truckload of food to move with our outfit.

I turned off the range under the roast beef, hating to leave the inviting smell as I threw tarp over the supplies we were hauling and climbed aboard the chow truck. I took my place just behind the cab as lookout, loaded down with a steel helmet, gas mask, bayonet, and belt of ammunition for my M-1 rifle. I hated giving up Clark Field. Our role in the war was the fox, and our only chance of survival lay in outrunning the hound and finding a refuge until help arrived.

Others assigned to the chow truck were sergeants Palmer and Murdoch and Lt. James Kale, a pilot. Kale had a crude map that showed the route of our retreat south. As we pulled out, I was wide-awake, every organ and muscle of my body alert. The latest news had the Japs closing in fast. Everything was on the move — the tanks with our radio operators had already roared off to the north while men, trucks, and guns from the north were joining our strategic retreat south.

We moved slowly ahead in the total blackout. As we rounded each curve, I strained to detect any sign of danger so I could alert our driver, Sgt. Murdoch. I knew I made a great target standing and looking out over the cab and half-expected to have a bullet find me at any moment. Other convoys joined the retreat and slowed us down. To keep the bulk of the vehicles moving, broken-down trucks had been abandoned and now littered the sides of the road. Our truck narrowly missed men and vehicles and once almost got bogged down on a soft shoulder. When we hit a couple of trucks parked on the road, they toppled into the ditch. No one was hurt so we continued on our way.

When Sgt. Murdoch got tired of driving, Lt. Kale took over. The big truck groaned as if something was dragging, but we kept going. I noticed smoke that smelled of oil. I banged on the cab with my rifle butt and yelled to Lt. Kale, "Is the emergency brake on?" Kale released the brake — only to trigger a fire under the truck that lit up the whole road. We jumped off the truck and used the fire extinguisher and sand to smother the flames, but the drum underneath was still red and smoking as we hurriedly climbed back on the truck and drove onward, letting the column behind us move on again.

Now we could make good time because the traffic ahead had moved out of sight after our breakdown. However, with no truck ahead to detect obstacles, our increased speed left us little time to stop or veer aside for obstacles. Straining my eyes in the darkness, I soon saw a huge object in the center of the road that looked like a wall. I banged on the cab and yelled, but Kale kept going. Finally I grabbed my flashlight and switched it on. Lt. Kale saw the object just in time to swerve aside — it was a big tree. An officer in the staff car behind reprimanded me for showing a light. But when I explained the reason and pointed out that ours was the chow truck, he apologized, saying, "Don't let anything happen to it — it's priceless." We had escaped the big tree, which stood like an island in the middle of the road, but it caused a number of collisions and injuries that night. Beyond the tree, we passed clouds of fireflies that glowed in the darkness, hovering around trees like tiny lights on a Christmas tree.

About midnight we passed through a town where a number of civilians were coming out of an old Spanish-type church, apparently from a midnight mass in celebration of Christmas. A couple of candles flickered inside. How I would have liked to attend that service! The people passed us silently, apparently in dread that the Japs would be coming soon. In the early hours of the morning we came to a fork in the road at another church that had been camouflaged with palm leaves. We stopped to check our map. Then, "Merry Christmas, soldiers," rang out in a voice clear as crystal. Stunned, we peered toward the church. A Filipino boy of 12 or so came out of the darkness with a smiling face and asked us if he could help. He told us which road to take. His friendly greeting had softened the bitterness we felt at being abandoned by our country in a far-off land. Later I learned that the Filipino lad, who was a Boy Scout, had greeted many other retreating Americans that night before Christmas. Although repeatedly urged to leave for his own safety, he remained a beacon at the intersection for about three weeks. But finally, a flying fragment killed the brave boy when a bomb hit the church and neighboring buildings.

The fork in the road was near the base of Bataan peninsula. As we drove on, fog rolled in from the sea and made visibility even worse. Some trucks were turning their lights on and off; but when we tried it, a guard with a submachine gun swore at us and threatened to shoot. Alone after stopping for directions, we again came to a fork in the road, but no one was there to guide us. We decided to wait for daylight before going on. My job as lookout left me no place to sleep — the rest of the party already filled up the cab and there was no room in the back of the truck. So I lay down on a rock pile and immediately fell into a deep sleep. My dreams took me around the world to the Holy Land and back 2,000 years. Then, suddenly, the sun was shining in my eyes, and Lt. Kale was yelling at me to wake up. Sgt. Murdoch was shaking me — he told me to get the hell awake because the Japs might spot us at any moment. We stopped the first staff car that came by and got directions. Daylight had found us and other outfits nearby in an open area. Now everyone had one thought in mind, "Get hidden before the Japs find us."

We drove off as fast as we could and were able to reach the assigned Air Corps area by mid-morning. Major O'Donnell, recently promoted to CO of the 19th Group, came by and told us to guard the food and use it wisely. Then we unloaded the truck so it could be used for something else. It was time for Christmas breakfast, but since our men were very thirsty, I decided to get some water first. Having no containers, I asked the outfit next to us if we could borrow some of their 10-gallon milk cans to haul some water. Their cook growled at my request and said, "You ought to look out for yourselves." I was angry but asked a couple others about a can. Their answer was, "Get the hell out."

I returned to the 14th Squadron camp and told what had happened — the men said they would make out somehow. I opened up the cans of food with my bayonet, and we all ate without saying much except for crusty, old Sgt. Palmer, already a ten-year veteran. Unhappy about the lack of kitchen equipment, he vowed, "I'm going back to Clark and pick up the kitchen gear we left there." We tried to talk him out of this crazy idea, but Palmer pleaded with Major O'Donnell and got permission to go. Palmer insisted that I go with him. We made good time in daylight even though enemy planes were now active and forced us off the truck several times. Upon reaching the banana patch, we loaded everything we could, even the roast beef, which was still in the field range, well-done and still good. I also loaded the small mattress I had been using. On our way back we picked up some of the boys who had worked all night loading bombs on trucks and trains at San Fernando. Back with our squadron, we used the food and equipment from Clark Field to fix Christmas dinner. The men of the 14th devoured it, unconcerned that it was a day late.

The fellows who had refused to lend us milk cans came over to borrow a pump for their stoves. When they saw our food and equipment, their eyes bulged. Suddenly polite, they asked for some of our store of food. We refused at first but relented when they apologized for their earlier attitude. We were also influenced by there being fellow countrymen in the war with us.

The next day, December 27, I volunteered to go back with a group to look for more equipment at Clark Field. Dodging enemy aircraft, we reached San Fernando, where the last men to leave Clark were resting. Major O'Donnell was there and ordered us to turn back. On our return to camp, I thought I would choke or catch pneumonia because of holes in the truck's exhaust system and the dry, bumpy road. The wrecked cars, tractors, tanks, and ragged Filipino refugees contrasted with the serene rice fields that stretched into the distant countryside on both sides of the road.

On Bataan, the men were tense because of reports that the Japs were closing in from every direction, that Manila might become an open city, and that the Philippines were being cut off from the outside world. We felt that our last stand would be here — perhaps as famous and tragic as General Custer's. (The general and his detachment had been wiped out by the Sioux in 1876.) On the other hand, there was a rumor that the largest convoy ever to sail from the U.S. was on its way to the Philippines.

That night, Maccagli and another man didn't come back from the supply dump with the other trucks. Major O'Donnell asked for volunteers to look for the missing men and truck. Murdoch and I got into a staff car and headed for the dump in the darkness. We found their trail several times, but each time we expected to find them around the next turn, we were disappointed. On the way back, the moon came up, but it only changed the darkness to cheerless, black landscapes of empty farms and deserted towns. Upon reaching camp, I lay down on a blanket under some trees, still wearing full field equipment, and fell asleep.

The next thing I knew, Sgt. George Scott awoke me with, "Get up, Mapes. Get some chow to the boys as fast as you can 'cause we're getting the hell out of here as quick as possible. Our ships and the Nips [Japs] had a battle last night and you know who came out on top." Scott walked along with me and continued, "Geez, you shoulda seen it. I guess you're the only one that didn't. The sky was lit up like the Fourth of July, and I thought the ground was going to come right up and smother me, the way it shook." Scott explained that the Japs had attacked a British ship anchored offshore — the crew had taken to boats or jumped off. Several Americans on shore were casualties from falling trees and shrapnel from American anti-aircraft fire.

I had barely started getting breakfast when a bearded soldier called, "Hey, Sarge, when's chow, or did something happen to it during the night?" I yelled back, "In a few minutes, soldier. Keep your belt pulled tight, you'll get something eventually." When we started serving chow, Maccagli and his buddy showed up. Knowing Maccagli, I figured they didn't want to be found the night before. They had sneaked back into camp ahead of Murdoch and me as sort of a game.

That day the squadron moved to a new sector not far away, where we set up our kitchen. When night came I was determined to sleep on the mattress I had retrieved from Clark Field and had left at our recent campsite in the hurry-up move that morning. I struggled along with it until I reached the river I had to cross to reach our new camp. But I was so tired I dropped it right there and fell on top of it. I was almost asleep when a grouchy sergeant barked, "You get the hell out of here, buddy. Your outfit is camped across the river." I considered taking a punch at him, but instead waded across the river, somehow keeping the mattress mostly dry. On the far side, I threw it down again and immediately fell asleep. The mosquitoes feasted on me all night — by morning, huge welts covered me from head to foot.

With daylight came more Japanese planes, which tried to knock out the 200th Anti-Aircraft Regt. at Cabacon Field and also bombed the ships and docks at Mariveles. We were in the midst of the action but could do nothing about it — our men were trained to put planes aloft but had no anti-aircraft guns. One raid caught three of us washing clothes by a stream. We crawled under a clump of bamboo on the bank. As I lay there, I started shaking for the first time in the three weeks of war. I said, "I must be getting soft because I can't stop shaking." One companion replied, "Hell, the whole goddam world is shaking." Just then a large piece of shrapnel broke off a big limb near us. The tree was left shaking. I answered, "I guess you're right."

As morning became afternoon, smoke blocked our view of Corregidor, but the flames leaping above the smoke showed its location. A few enemy planes were hit and crashed into a mountain or the sea. Still, wave after wave loosed their loads of destruction on the island. Heretofore, it had been known as the "Invincible Fortress," but now our boys were up against serious odds. Our squadron moved again — to a mountainside where we hoped the jungle would give better cover and we would not be in the lines of fire that threatened us on lower ground.

The thought that we were in a safer location lasted only a few hours. Then bombs and shrapnel shattered trees and limbs all around us. We were ordered to pick up our blue barracks bags and get to the port of Mariveles as soon as possible. Low-flying planes frequently forced us off the mountain trail, where we crouched in the brush until the enemy had gone. We finally reached a main road and boarded trucks that joined a large convoy heading for the port.

In Mariveles we found most stores and movie theaters closed and a few cabarets still open — a real serviceman's town until recently. I went down to the beach where fishnets were drying and outrigger canoes were pulled up on shore. Then I looked across the water to flaming Corregidor and ruined Cavite Naval Base. I clenched my fists and with a curse kicked one of the canoes. I felt helpless to stop the onrushing Japs.

Later, a couple of my buddies and I heard singing through the open doors of a good-sized home. Inside we saw American and Filipino soldiers grouped around a piano, singing "God Bless America." We talked with the friendly Filipino family who lived there — they were busy packing and about to leave for a safer spot. We walked on and came to an old mission built by the Spanish fathers. It was still used, but its walls were crumbling from the humidity and lack of care. Even though I was a Protestant, I entered and knelt with my Catholic friends to pray for our safety and for our comrades in combat and also for our loved ones at home. We returned to the house, where everyone was singing. The Filipino family had already gone.

Our time to rejoin the convoy came in a few minutes. We reached the dock as it grew dark. The place was a mass of men and vehicles, crowded into a small area. Everyone was irritable because of loss of sleep, hunger, and shattered nerves from incessant bombings. Furthermore, we realized the terrible danger of an air attack on the congested dock.

I noticed some of the Fourth Marine Division out of China trying to direct traffic. In the confusion, we were herded like cattle to our assigned ship, the inter-island steamer *Mayon*. A nearby explosion scared us but did not interrupt boarding. We couldn't see its source or any damage. At 8 P.M. on December 29, 1941, our Filipino skipper cast off all lines, eager to get underway and find safety in the growing darkness. I didn't know where we were going but was glad to be moving, although I was thinking it could be to a worse place.

5

An Interrupted Voyage to Mindanao

December 29, 1941, to January 1, 1942

We had less space on the steamer, *Mayon*, than we had had on the crowded dock of Mariveles. Our 14th Squadron, and the 28th and 30th squadrons, made a total of 600 Air Corps men crammed on the ship — the *Mayon* normally carried half that number. The close quarters and the tension that had built up in the past few days caused some men to lose control whenever they heard a loud voice or were even touched by their neighbor. Some went into fits of anger and threw fists at whoever jostled them. Calmer men grumbled for food but were more disagreeable about it than before. But it wasn't easy to improvise a regular chow for so many in such close quarters.

The job of feeding us fell to Lt. Kelso, the large pilot who last fall had met our ship in Manila and led the way to Clark Field on his motorcycle. Now Kelso became a mess officer. In a few hours, Kelso's helpers were dispensing food to a line of men that stretched the length of the ship. Chow consisted of canned food that was dumped directly on our mess kits. Nevertheless, the food had a magical effect — there was less bickering, and once in a while someone had a good word for his buddy.

In the uncertainty and confusion on the *Mayon*, Sgt. John Murdoch, my good friend from Philadelphia, and I stuck together. After chow, we sneaked away with a few cans of food and canteens of water. We lay down topside near a lifeboat and used the lifebelts as pillows. We could still see the glow in the sky from fires on Corregidor when we ran out of talk and fell asleep. During the night Murdoch was roused to go on watch. When he reported a distant submarine, the *Mayon* skipper changed course. The submarine headed away from us.

Morning dawned bright and clear, and another chow of canned food kept our spirits up. We helped the crew spread a canvas over the deck to hide the human cargo from enemy air patrols and shade us from the intense sun. Later in the morning we dropped anchor off the town of Romblon on the small island of Romblon that lies 50 miles east of the large island of Mindoro. We were partially hidden in a small cove. Our officers told us we had little to worry about because friendly planes from nearby air fields would protect us. Nevertheless, they ordered us to clean our guns and be ready for any emergency. Being away from the roar of Japanese planes, bombs, and guns made us feel once again that life was worthwhile.

In our relaxed mood, we heard a hum in the distance, which grew louder and louder. We thought it must be one of our escort planes coming to see how we were getting along and then saw that it was a large flying boat, apparently a Navy PBY. It flew directly overhead, lost altitude, and came back over. Finally one of us yelled, "Run for cover! That's a goddam Jap!" We had been fooled because we did not know the Japs had such aircraft. I was standing by Murdoch and Dick Beck, a small blond friend from Indiana. We flattened ourselves on the deck, hugging the side of the cabin as a bomb came whistling down. There was a deafening roar and blinding flash that knocked me almost senseless. Yet I felt water splashing over me — the bomb had dropped so close to the ship that the explosion had thrown water all over the deck. More serious, the bomb had blown a hole in the hull: The ship was taking in water. The explosion had knocked down the railing and broken the cabin windows, causing some cuts from flying glass.

As I came to my senses, I saw our veteran, graying Master Sgt. John A. Wupperfield leap over the side. That was a surprise because during the retreat from Clark Field, Wupperfield emphasized to us the importance of staying calm during emergencies, speaking from experience that went back to World War I. Now, just one bomb sent him off the ship — the first to jump. But others followed him — some throwing their guns before them without a thought of the danger to others who had already jumped.

Meanwhile the ponderous plane had banked and came over again at a still lower altitude. This time the bomb hit the water near the ship's stern. The bomber was flying very slowly and was within easy range of our .30 caliber rifles, but nobody fired. It circled and bombed the *Mayon* again — this time completely missing the sitting duck.

We figured the pilot intended to bomb until he got a square hit. That would blow us to kingdom come since the ship's bow was loaded with ammunition. At the same time, we feared that more Japanese planes might come at any moment to help finish us off. Nevertheless, during each bomb run, 1st Sgt. Scott and Tech. Sgt. James McIntyre joked with the men crouched down on the deck.

I was thinking I might be safer off the ship, even though the Japs had been known to strafe men in the water. My friends advised against leaving, but after studying the currents and shoreline, I felt I could make land. I took off my shoes and pants and tied a small knife to my waist in case of sharks. Then I stuffed my money and a few pictures in my shirt pocket. Finally, I hid my M-1 rifle under some canvas.

Again the flying boat came in. It was another miss and again the exploding bombs shot huge geysers into the air that mushroomed like palm trees. The water had not yet settled when I bade my protesting friends goodbye. I took a deep breath, and a running start took me into the water 30 feet from the ship. Without breaking the surface, I swam underwater as far as I could. When I came up for air, soldiers were bobbing on the surface around me — some scared because of the enemy plane and others in a state of shock. My lifeguard training made it hard not to help the men floundering in the ocean. But I decided to head for shore, thinking I would be at least one survivor to keep on fighting the Japs.

I swam as fast as I could for a quarter of a mile. Then, concerned about sharks, I took off my white undershorts. I had lost my knife but still had the money and pictures in my shirt pocket. The flying boat lumbered still lower for yet another bombing run. I swam like mad to get farther away. But when I paused, the plane was between me and the ship and then it looked like its bomb would fall close to me. My first instinct was to dive under the water to hide, but my mind told me to float on top to lessen my body's exposure to the jolt from the exploding bomb. On my back I watched the bomb strike in the midst a group of soldiers swimming slowly with their equipment and life belts. The explosion jarred every nerve in my body, but there wasn't much pain except a little stinging in the groin. I couldn't tell if I was ruptured but could still swim all right so I continued toward shore.

The *Mayon* sounded its alarm for sinking. The bomber came over once more, very low, but only for observation. Then it flew on and disappeared over the horizon. Soldiers crowded into life boats; others jumped overboard and swam for shore. Unbelievably, the Filipino skipper would not give up his ship. His crew continued to pump water out of the hold — the ship had been taking in water from the hole blown out by the first bomb.

By this time I was closer to shore than anyone except Sgt. Wupperfield, who had been first to jump. He still had 50 yards to go when I overtook him. But I kept on going because he seemed to be doing all right. I was 50 feet past him when I heard a surprisingly loud, "I need help!" I turned back and pushed the old sergeant toward land until we could wade ashore.

We had reached land near a little fishing village of thatched huts, chickens, pigpens, and outrigger canoes. When a Filipino came ashore in a frail canoe with a grass sail, I suddenly thought about my buddies still out in the water. As the Filipino walked away, I called to him several times before getting his attention. Then I talked him into letting me use his canoe with him as crew. It took some forceful language — I believe he feared Japanese attacks and thought his craft could not stand a heavy load. But we got aboard and shoved away from the beach. He operated the sail while I paddled and bailed with a coconut shell — waves splashed in and the craft leaked. I paddled hard to reach the first man I noticed and yelled for him to grasp the canoe quickly for we were traveling at a fast clip, pushed by wind and a strong current. We got him aboard, but I was disappointed because he was a civilian Filipino who had abandoned the *Mayon* from fright and was not injured. Now I had a rescue craft with two Filipinos as a crew — one paddled and the other handled the sail.

Hundreds of yards away I spotted a soldier with his head barely out of water — he looked like he was either dead or dying and only being held up by his life belt. I shouted at my paddler, "Paddle like hell or me paddle you." When we got within 75 yards of the man, the two Filipinos began to jabber and pointed in the opposite direction. At first I thought they might have seen a ship, plane, or sharks, but then I saw something golden in the water that turned out to be a two-foot fish, which they called Lapa Lapa. Our canoe headed for the fish, leaving the helpless man behind. I raised hell with the Filipinos, but they just kept going toward the fish. Then I jerked the paddle away and demanded, "Look, you bastards! This is no time to fish, now get the hell out to that wounded man or I knock your stupid heads with this goddam paddle." But the sail kept us moving toward the fish. The sail man told the other to jump overboard and grab the fish. I yelled, "You can pick up your goddam fish later." I smacked the man on the seat of his pants as he jumped in. But he was interested only in the fish. The other man maneuvered the canoe to get the man and fish aboard — the Lapa Lapa had probably been killed by a bomb.

Now the crazy Filipinos seemed perfectly content to help me. We headed for the motionless body we could still see floating in the water. We found him almost dead — the life belt was keeping his head above water but its neck strap was strangling him. After getting him on the canoe, I loosened his clothes and give him artificial respiration. He finally came to, weak and delirious. I couldn't get his name but gathered he was from the 28th Bombardment Squadron. As we headed for shore, we picked up another GI, who was in better shape — he helped me with our sick comrade. Now I noticed many others in the water, but we had no room for more. Back on shore, I left the stronger soldier with the weaker one and persuaded the owner of the canoe, who had handled the sail, to take me out to pick up some more soldiers. The paddler had disappeared with the fish.

For our second rescue effort, we sailed beyond the floundering *Mayon* because the current was washing some of the boys out to sea. We pulled in three fatigued GIs and headed for shore. A few hundred yards from land we came alongside a large bamboo raft that was manned by two Filipinos and two soldiers. We left our three soldiers with them and turned back for more. This time we headed for the ship. Drawing nearer, I saw a lot of water being pumped out and a rope hanging down from topside. I told a Filipino sailor to hold the rope while I climbed up. I nearly upset the canoe when I grabbed the rope and then was engulfed by water being pumped from the ship. But I managed to hold on and finally reached the deck — scratched, bleeding, and near the end of my strength.

I found the ship in pretty good shape. Most of the crew were still aboard — they had broken open the whiskey and wanted me to join the party. I joked with them and then looked around for my pistol among the debris scattered on the deck but couldn't find it. I didn't disturb my M-1 rifle that I had hidden under the tarpaulin. I did pick up a pair of usable pants. Looking toward land, I saw that most of the men who had abandoned the ship had nearly reached shore. But some men were still drifting out to sea.

Hoping to save them, I climbed back down to the water, where the Filipino was waiting with his canoe. We found three more GIs helpless in the water and took them to the large raft closer to shore that we had used before. Then we sailed farther out into stronger currents to look for others. The wind and current almost capsized our little craft. Fearing for my life, I bailed like mad. The Filipino protested so vigorously against staying out there that we turned back, although I could still see several men drifting away. On the way back, I picked up a second man from my squadron — the other from the 14th was Sgt. Wupperfield.

We sailed close to a group on the beach — among them I recognized buddies from the 14th and our former CO, Major Emmett O'Donnell. He shouted that I should sail along the shore and tell the scattered men to assemble where he was. We did this and joined the group around him. I introduced the Filipino to the major, who thanked us both for our rescue work. For the first time since I jumped off the *Mayon* that morning, I felt tired. Nevertheless, I donned the dry pants I had found on the ship and spread out my paper money and postal bonds on a large flat rock to dry. Then I sat down to rest while guarding my damp money. As I rested, passersby asked if I was trying to start a poker game.

Close by I noticed Murdoch, Knortz, Charley Butterworth, and the veteran, Richard Hough, standing over our small buddy, Dick Beck, who thought he was still on the ship being bombed by Japanese planes. Now, no matter how hard the boys tried to convince Beck he was safe, he would not believe them. He couldn't recognize anyone except Butterworth, whom he called "Buttercup."

I learned later that Hough had smacked Beck over the head with an oar to keep him quiet as they rowed away from the *Mayon.*

Meanwhile, the men scattered along the beach had gathered around Major O'Donnell, who announced the ship was ready for us to go back on board. The Filipino crew had pumped out most of the water and patched the large hole. Outrigger canoes took us back to the *Mayon*, which was soon filled with tired, anxious soldiers — it was a madhouse. We couldn't get the delirious Beck to a doctor — they were busy treating the wounded. Once when Beck overheard mention of the "friendly" flying boat that had attacked us, he headed for the side of the ship and would have jumped if we had not grabbed him. We finally got him below deck to the sick bay, where the medics eventually calmed him.

The crew got the ship underway, but it pitched heavily in the rough sea while the pumps worked laboriously. However, we weaved confidently among the coral reefs that skirted the shore, missing them all. I was thirsty, so I headed for the water Murdoch and I had stored away before the attack. I made slow progress among the boxes scattered about because of the dark and seawater sloshing across the deck with each pitch of the ship. I had nearly reached the water when I stepped on something soft. It felt like a man. I called out, "Hey Joe, did I hurt you? You sure picked a hell of a place to go to sleep." He didn't answer, I knelt down and talked some more, hoping to wake him, thinking he was sick or injured. I touched his face but got no response. I reported the man's situation to the corporal I had passed, who was directing traffic through the passageway. He came and looked but told me to leave the man alone. I stepped over him, got my water, and returned to where I had left Murdoch. He muttered, "He'll probably be in the water before morning. There's nothing we can do for the poor devil. Who knows, he may be better off that way. We might all be better off if something like that happened to us." We dropped the subject and crawled under a tarpaulin to get some sleep.

During the night the wind became a gale that brought heavy rain. Murdoch and most others on deck went below, but I wrapped the tarpaulin closely around me and stuck it out until early morning. Then I went below to find sloshing water and loose boxes that slid and banged against each other. I stretched out on top of a big box. By daybreak the storm had subsided, and we pulled into a small, hidden bay.

The water was calm and the shore lined with palm trees — only beautiful native women were needed to complete the picture of tropical paradise. But we were uneasy when we noticed oil patches on the water and floating wreckage. We hurriedly lowered boats and headed for shore. Behind the beach was a small fishing village, where a few civilians and Filipino sailors sat and watched us. When we asked about the oil patches and wreckage, their answer stunned us — the Philippine inter-island passenger steamer, *Panay*, had been sunk the day before, almost where the *Mayon* was now anchored in 50 feet of water. The *Panay* had been carrying arms and ammunition and had been attacked by seaplanes about when the *Mayon* was under attack off the island of Romblon. We were now off the southwest coast of Negros Island, about 30 miles northwest along the coast from Basay. The place was called Maricolum.

The *Panay* had still looked like a passenger ship, but the fifth column had betrayed her. The Japs dropped 27 bombs before putting one down the *Panay*'s smokestack and exploded the ammunition. She was carrying weapons to arm the 76th Regiment that was to defend Negros against the Japs. But the 76th was not organized then because the *Panay* did not get through; later a guerrilla 76th Regiment, supplied by submarine, was formed and harassed the Japanese occupation of Negros. The *Panay* crew got ashore safely, but the skipper, Clemente Sumcad, was killed by the final bomb.

Major O'Donnell ordered us to go up into the hills and stand by until nightfall. There I spent most of the day resting and reading my pocket Bible. Several of us got together and discussed religion. Our situation seemed marginally better. We could tolerate the flies and mosquitoes because we were so glad to be on terra firma instead of being part of an easy target aboard ship. In the coolness of the evening we gathered on the beach. I was elected to climb a palm tree to pull off coconuts — I had done this often in Florida. I dropped them to the boys, tossing a few to make them dodge. Then we boarded the *Mayon* again, rowing out in some of the *Panay*'s lifeboats. We realized later that a member of the 14th had stayed on shore. He would join the guerrilla forces that formed to resist the Japanese occupation.

Now we steamed southward toward the large island of Mindanao.

There was a high wind that night, and once we thought we spotted a submarine. In the early hours of the first morning of 1942, we made out a few lights flickering here and there on the horizon. At dawn wrecked warehouses and a pier came into view. Beyond was a town surrounded by palm trees. As the *Mayon* tied up to the pier, everyone crowded to that side to get off as soon as possible. Air raids had damaged or destroyed many of the buildings in the town, which was Cagayan, located on the north coast of Mindanao, an island about the size of Indiana and the second largest of the Philippines. Only Luzon was larger.

6

From Cagayan to Lake Lanao
January 1–18, 1942

The 14th Squadron disembarked hastily but took care to land the all-important GI chow truck safely on the dock. We assembled by the warehouses but felt vulnerable there so we moved through town. Filipinos standing along the way formed V's with their fingers and called out, "Victory Joe." They were all smiles, mistaking our bedraggled group of Air Corps men from Clark Field for the long-awaited reinforcements from the United States.

After a pause at a coconut grove, we continued and camped in another grove close to the Bugo River. There I helped Sgt. Palmer set up the gas field range and unload food from our truck. We were about to serve when a GI truck came along to issue kitchen equipment and meager rations. The rations officer was wide-eyed at seeing our gear and the ample meal we had prepared. He asked how we had done it. We answered, "The Fighting Fourteenth is always on the ball, sir!"

After chow I bathed in the Bugo River — my first real bath since leaving Clark Field. Then I crawled into a pup tent that my buddy Murdoch had found for us. I slept peacefully — no longer rocked about by the Mayon and free from air attacks. We enjoyed a few quiet days by the river until the Japs began to fly over. The third day we moved up on a ridge and camped in the jungle near an "S" turn in a road leaving town. A lieutenant drilled us in jungle and infantry fighting for a few days. Enemy aircraft drove us to cover frequently, but we were not discovered. We broke camp on the morning of January 8 and followed the road inland. Within hours the Japs bombed our old camp site — perhaps alerted by fifth columnists.

The rest of the 600 Air Corps men who had arrived on the Mayon now joined us. The rutted road climbed higher, narrowed, and led past steep ravines before we reached the high plateau overlooking Del Monte Air Field. There, half of the 35 B-17 bombers in the Philippines had been withdrawn before Pearl Harbor and escaped destruction since they were out of range of Japanese bombers based on Formosa. However, by December 22, 1941, the remaining B-17s had been flown to Australia. From a distance Del Monte Airfield now looked deserted.

We climbed off our trucks and stretched out side by side along the road in the growing darkness, too tired to unload the equipment or put up tents. The next thing I knew, the sun was glaring into my eyes. When I gazed about, I suddenly realized our danger — all of us still asleep in a line along the road. Before I could spread an alarm, I heard a distant roar that awakened the men better than I could. They ran helter-skelter for a coffee grove only a couple hundred feet away. It was only 40 feet wide, but the coffee trees were six to ten feet high and underneath were grass, weeds, and vines growing to three feet. Yet the space for 600 men was limited — the narrow grove extended only 1,000 feet. The planes appeared briefly at a distance but did not head our way — our luck held again. Now we moved our equipment under the coffee trees and carefully camouflaged our camp.

We called our hiding place the Suicide Strip. There was not space to dig enough foxholes or provide us with adequate cover. Retreat would be suicidal — on one side was a low-growing pineapple grove and on the other was an open, dry river bed. Nevertheless, we prepared to stay for awhile. We had to locate the foxholes carefully so as not to disturb the camouflaging brush. Sgt. Palmer, several others, and I set up the kitchen under the largest tree I could find. We rubbed the bright stoves and utensils with dirt and grease so their reflection would not betray us. Several men went some distance to the nearest spring and brought water while others arranged the food stores so they could be reloaded on short notice.

The first meat we served came from fresh-killed Brahma cattle. The men dived in with gusto and also filled themselves with the fresh pineapple that was all about. But the fruit made our gums sore and our teeth ache, and soon we were running to the latrine pits. We craved vegetables, bread, and hotcakes to go with the glut of meat and pineapples. Our request for help from nearby Del Monte Airfield brought a supply of baking powder that we used to cook hotcakes and biscuits to replace the rice and gravy we had been living on.

One morning a tall GI came walking toward us from the airfield. As he got closer, we recognized our old friend, Walter "Doc" Haddock of the 14th Squadron — a slow-talking Alabaman who had been sent to Del Monte earlier. After swapping stories with his old buddies, Doc wanted to rejoin us. Next day he returned with his transfer orders and stayed — another cook to help Sgt. Palmer and me.

One day a formation of enemy planes headed directly for us at a low altitude. We were certain we had been discovered, but instead the Japs bombed and strafed some Filipino soldiers who were working on a nearby road and bridge.

In the following days, an ex-infantryman in our outfit taught us how to stalk, bayonet, and shoot with greatest effect. We were attentive students because of the bad news that came over a battery radio in the house of the caretaker of the coffee grove. I listened to a fireside chat by President Roosevelt and concluded that it would be a long, hard wait before we got aid from the U.S., if ever. The president explained the difficulty of sending support because of the Japanese-held islands between Hawaii and the Philippines. But my buddies didn't want to hear about our bad prospects — they still believed aid would come soon and told me to shut up. I knew others shared my opinion, but they kept quiet.

Only a few American planes landed at the airfield. We learned about a P-40 fighter flown by Lt. Brown. He flew up to Luzon and back with messages and occasionally shot down or chased enemy aircraft that challenged him. One evening soon after Lt. Brown's return, a Jap plane flew slowly overhead, searching for Brown's plane. But Brown had already taxied into a hiding place. The Jap winged slowly back and forth for a time before turning away into cloud cover. But in five minutes or so the Jap emerged from the clouds and headed our way, this time with a companion. Brown, however, had not fallen for the scheme. The Jap pilot had hoped his apparent departure would entice Brown to get into the air and face the danger of being shot down before he could reach fighting altitude. Instead, Brown just stood in the brush while the two enemy aircraft made another search. Then he grinned as they flew away. We watched the game from Suicide Strip with fascination and then glee.

We felt still more uneasy when flares in the mountains made us fear that fifth columnists would report our location. But the 14th Squadron's outlook changed when orders came for us to pack up 14 days' rations for a trek into northwest Mindanao. There, near Lake Lanao and supposedly far from the enemy, the 14th had a secret assignment. We would make our last stand there and hold out — if possible — until aid arrived. Furthermore, the lake was full of fish and ducks, and vegetables and fruit thrived in the cooler climate. We eagerly loaded our trucks and could hardly wait for darkness — the only safe time to leave Suicide Strip.

We retraced the dark mountain road toward Cagayan very slowly,

The Agus River, four miles north of its source, Lake Lanao. The river flows north to the Mindanao Sea. This image dates from the early 1900s. *(Photo by J. D. Givens, courtesy Jane Doner Frederickson.)*

remembering the steep slopes that dropped from the roadside to deep ravines below. After daylight we kept moving but had to drive the trucks off the road several times when we heard enemy planes. We turned west at Cagayan and followed the shore, which was dotted with coconut trees. A few villages and groups of huts lined the beach, where fish nets and outrigger canoes lay unattended except for a solitary figure here and there.

I sat cross-legged on the front fender of a half-ton truck driven by Aldo P. Maccagli, the short New Yorker we called the "Kid from Brooklyn." I had a two-inch beard and wore my dented helmet. A gas mask hung from one shoulder and an ammunition belt from the other. While keeping watch for enemy aircraft, I noticed monkeys, a wild boar, and lizard-like creatures that turned out to be iguanas. Most striking, though, was a man who strode along the road like he owned it. At his hip hung a kris, a sword with a wavy, double-edged blade, and over his shoulder a shotgun. He wore a dark green, silk shirt and tight-legged pants. His head was topped with a fez and tassel. He was chewing something that smeared his mouth with red stain. From a book I had read at Clark Field, I realized he was a Moro who was chewing betel nut, a mild narcotic. (The Moros had settled on Mindanao centuries before the arrival of the Spanish in the 16th century. Thereafter the Moros had resisted all Spanish attempts to subdue them and retained their Moslem religion. Neither had American rule since 1900 changed the Moros' independent way of life.) Farther on, the houses and gardens were neater and looked more prosperous. We noticed several women with raven-black hair loosely knotted behind the head, and men in large straw hats like those worn by Chinese coolies.

On the evening of January 16, we stopped at Iligan, a port on Iligan Bay. An American infantry officer asked where we had come from. After absorbing the story of our retreat from Clark Field and Bataan, he told us his troops had seen little action. They regarded us as combat veterans and wanted to help. I asked a young lieutenant where I could get some shoe laces — mine had broken and been knotted many times. We got into his car, and his Filipino driver took us through the town of mostly boarded-up stores. Camouflage covered many roofs, including a church's tin roof that was overlain with palm fronds. Along the docks soldiers had dug fox-holes and stacked sandbags around gun emplacements. We stopped at a shack where the young officer kept his guns and ammunition as well as some shoe laces. After he helped me thread my new laces, we told stories of what had happened to each of us since Pearl Harbor, puffing contentedly all the while on his stateside cigars. He gave me several, and then we drove back to our convoy. We were staying all night at Iligan so there was time for the boys to shop, but they found nothing except cheap gin.

The next morning Sgt. Palmer called me over to meet Captain Gary Lane, a tall, recently commissioned officer who had been a missionary in the region. He looked like an officer now even though he was in ragged civilian clothes. In a quiet, sensible manner he used a large map to point out the rest of the route to Lake Lanao. We bade the Iligan soldiers good-bye and turned south, away from the coast. Most of the day our convoy climbed steadily over winding mountain roads through dense jungle. In late afternoon we reached open country and soon drove into Momungan, a small town surrounded by fields of corn, beans, and sweet potatoes, as well as pastures where cattle and carabao (domestic water buffalo) grazed.

At the edge of town vegetable gardens grew, and in the center stood a good-sized open-air market.

Filipino soldiers greeted us, as well as some Moros who wanted to trade. Our boys bought knives and swords — the largest weapon was an old two-handed sword that Maccagli fancied enough to pay a dear price. He made quite a spectacle with the old relic — it was taller than he was. The blade had been used to behead people. Also at the market were ears of cold, boiled corn that cost very little. They were a real treat — we hadn't had fresh corn since leaving the U.S. and our appetites amazed the bystanders.

We returned to our trucks and traveled higher into the mountains. We stopped to gaze at a waterfall that splattered next to the road. Plunging off a cliff far above, it made a steady roar and produced a fine spray and hovering mist. It was the Maria Cristina Falls on the Agus River, which flows northward out of Lake Lanao and carries its water from an altitude of 2100 feet to sea level at Iligan. We ascended through lush rain forest toward the lake. This was paradise — but one did not carry weapons in paradise, nor did he look ragged and beaten. It was almost dark when we reached level ground by the shore of Lake Lanao and camped for the night.

7

Malabang

January 18 to February 1, 1942

On the morning of January 18, I stood at a fork in the road to direct our convoy toward Camp Keithley. A town of attractive buildings shone in the sunlight between me and the lake. Surprisingly, there was no sign of bomb damage. From passersby I learned that the town was Dansalan, capital of Lanao del Sur Province. They pointed out the governor's house, a schoolhouse, a missionary home, and an elaborate market building. Everyone asked for the latest news. I noticed a general cheerfulness and then realized the people took us to be the reinforcements from the U.S. they hoped for. I hated to tell them the truth and I decided not to.

A suspicious-looking fellow, part Jap and part Filipino or Moro, started asking all kinds of questions. I was careful not to tell him anything of importance. Nevertheless, he answered some of *my* questions. He said the Japs had bombed Camp Keithley about December 20 and flown low over Dansalan. There, instead of bombs, they had dropped leaflets saying their forces would take over but no harm would come if the people behaved themselves. This man also reported that thousands of Moros were willing to fight the Japs. But their weapons were limited to some homemade water pipe rifles, a little ammunition, and bolos — two-foot, straight-bladed knives used for cutting sugar cane and brush. The local people had already formed a bolo battalion — members remained at home but were on call to support regular army and guerrilla units with supply, communications, and intelligence.

I motioned the last truck toward Camp Keithley just as the sun set, bringing on the sudden dusk of the tropics. Just then some Filipino constabulary officers came by in a truck and picked me up; constabulary forces were Filipino units made up of local men organized into army formations. Excited by our arrival, the officers greeted me warmly. At Camp Keithley they pointed out the modern buildings that had been used by the constabulary troops, who had vacated the camp after the December 20 raid. Now only members of our 14th Squadron could be seen.

I started the fires on the kitchen range but then took time out to join the rush to the showers, which still operated in the abandoned camp. The cool, clear water poured over us and put us in exuberant spirits. One of us yelled, "Take cover." We dashed out to look for planes but found none. The false alarm did sober us up. I hurried back to help get chow in the old constabulary kitchen — practically at the spot where a Jap bomb had hit the mess hall in the December raid. The debris of cement, sheet iron, glass, and pots made an ugly sight that was hardly new to us. Nevertheless, the wreckage unsettled our men — they were ready to leave right then. Despite their mood, they ate heartily of the roast beef, gravy, rice, coffee, and jam, which Doc Haddock and I set before them. After chow, the officers announced that all but 30 of us were moving next morning. That was not very relaxing because we didn't know which 30 of us had to stay. I got up in time to cook breakfast for an early start. Sgt. Scott called out the names of the 30 who were not going, and the rest of us said goodbye to our buddies, not knowing if we would see them again.

We rode southward along the western shore of Lake Lanao, drinking in the natural beauty and breathing the cool morning air. We passed Moro farmyards full of chickens and sometimes a goat or carabao. Women in brightly colored sarongs stared sleepily from doorways. Several Jap bombers forced us off the road. We hastily covered our trucks with leafy branches and then scattered to separate cover in case the trucks were detected. We had to do this several times before we reached the large Moro village of Ganasi at the south end of Lake Lanao. Here, Jap bombers were overhead again — we drove under bamboo trees and spread out in the pastures and gardens around the village. Above the roar of planes I could hear the ominous sound of gongs, which brought Moro warriors with homemade shotguns and knives running toward us. We didn't know what to make of this strange charge. Were the gongs urging attack against us or giving a late warning of the Jap planes? The Moros suddenly dived into the nearby ditches and brush. One landed close to me. Hardly expecting he would understand, I asked why he had run to hide. But he came back in broken English, "For same reason as you." We talked a little, and I found these fierce Moros feared the air attacks just as much as American GIs. But there was no attack, and the planes flew off.

We assembled at the edge of Ganasi. There again was Captain Lane to give us directions, being knowledgeable in this area as well as the region north of Lake Lanao. After leaving him, we continued southward barely a mile when Jap planes came looking for a target. Heavy jungle growth saved us from attack although we scattered away from our trucks. Then we headed upward on a winding mountain road. After passing a few villages and crossing several streams, we entered an uninhabited region of small lakes surrounded by steep mountain walls. In late afternoon we descended to a town — from there coconut plantations stretched into the distance. Past the town, we looked for cover where we could wait for orders in relative safety. The only spot we could find didn't look good, even after we hurriedly covered the trucks with palm leaves. We sought cover for ourselves in thin underbrush that was some distance from the trucks. We hoped our uncanny luck in eluding the Japs would continue as we waited in the brush, hot and anxious to get going. I sat in the scant shade with my Alabama friend Doc Haddock, who had arranged his own transfer from Del Monte Air Field to be with his buddies.

Our luck held. We had not been there an hour before our orders came. In a couple of miles we reached Malabang, passed through it, and entered a dense jungle. We came to a turnoff that quickly brought us to a small opening in the jungle, harboring a few crude shacks.

Huge tropical trees with large twisting vines and dense foliage prevented sunlight from reaching the ground. This shadowy place did not depress us — we would be hard to see from the air. Captain William Horrigan, a pilot, gave instructions on how to build a camp. He was a large-framed, easygoing man who had been in the Philippines for several years. His warnings not to cut down any heavy foliage or congregate on the road were not necessary. As I helped set up the kitchen, I thought about the dangers facing our buddies who were left at Camp Keithley. Before we could finish, the kitchen crew was called together to listen to Major Luther Heidger, a flight surgeon from the 19th Bomb Group who had just joined us. With a beaming smile he stressed the need for wholehearted cooperation to keep the men healthy in body and mind in the days ahead. His mood rubbed off on me, and I felt better.

Our jungle surroundings enchanted me — in particular, an ice cold, crystal clear spring that bubbled out of the rocks in the middle of our clearing. It filled a natural basin in which two of us could bathe at once. The overflow from our bathtub trickled down a series of rocks to a winding stream that flowed into the Matling River, a short distance away. Directly above the spring, a large patch of blue sky could be seen, surrounded by the jungle's dark canopy. A simple bamboo hut with a palm-thatched roof stood by the spring and was reflected in the pool of water.

A sign announced something in crude Arabic writing. I learned later that the Moros in that region considered the spring to be sacred — hence the Arabic writing that was associated with their Moslem faith. Moros came many miles to bathe in the spring's pure water and then pray to Allah inside the sacred hut. A variety of animal tracks appeared in the moist sand by the pool, showing that denizens of the jungle also enjoyed the spring. Once we realized the significance of the spring, we took care to keep it clean, and stayed away from the ceremonial hut. All of us sensed our good fortune to be safely hidden there.

Now the men relaxed, and we cooks began to hear the usual gripes about the food — there were only two meals a day, and the rice and hash were boring. We said to ourselves, "A GI wouldn't be happy unless he had something to gripe about." The men dug a latrine and garbage pit and then turned to building their own quarters. Their ragged clothes, beards, and mustaches made them look like seasoned pioneers, and they looked ready for Indians with .45 pistols and knives. The soldiers usually paired off to build shelters of all kinds. Generally each pair hacked off poles to make a lean-to, which was tied together with vines and roots. We had been issued shelter-halves, which were prized possessions because, used as a roof, they kept the huts fairly dry. But there were not enough shelter-halves to go around so many huts were covered with leaves, grass, bark, and mud to shield them from rain. Many men weaved vines into beds that were attached to trees and suspended above the ground. To fend off insects, we used tattered remnants of mosquito nets, which we camouflaged with wet coffee grounds and covered with dead leaves and juice of green leaves.

Captain Horrigan and Major Heidger hired some Moros to build shelters for a sick bay/hospital and a kitchen that included storage for our precious food. The Moros used their wicked-looking bolos to cut poles, vines, and palm leaves from which they soon constructed sturdy shacks. The first day we used the new shelter to cook, we gave the boys hash, sweet potatoes, and coffee. After chow, Captain Horrigan had just stood up to give us instructions when the roar of planes interrupted him and almost destroyed the brief sense of security we had felt at Sacred Spring. But the planes flew on. Then Horrigan told us we would be the maintenance crew at the nearby airstrip. Next day he sent a couple dozen men over to begin work. We hoped the airstrip would be used to bring in reinforcements.

I was enjoying a bath in the spring one evening when a rustling made me look closely into the jungle. A flock of wild chickens was going to roost. The birds were a tasty treat I had been told about by Spanish-American War veterans when a boy. Another evening I was digging a drain ditch around my tent when a roar in the jungle startled me — like a plane but on the ground. A short time later my buddy Murdoch rode a motorcycle into camp.

We had not seen him since he had decided to stay at Del Monte Airfield. Before that he had been my buddy aboard the *Mayon*. Now he could barely stand up and was covered with grime and dust. He called for me, and I told him to crawl into my tent. When I settled down beside him later, he seemed dead to the world. But he soon stirred and wanted to talk about his ride from Del Monte. He groaned, "I ache all over ... Jesus, I think I'm going to break into pieces. I rode that goddam motorcycle all the way from Del Monte, and them damn slant eyes kept trying to send me to hell. I was bombed and strafed ... but I just rubbed my lucky leg, picked myself off the road and here I am." I told him he would feel better in the morning. But he kept moving around all night and was still shaky on his feet after low-flying Jap planes awakened us soon after sunrise.

Despite nagging fear that the Japs would discover our retreat, life at Sacred Spring settled down. There were regular hours for chow and camp cleanup, and the sick bay and motor pool were in operation. Palmer, Haddock, and I improved the chow with purchase of local food, such as corn, beans, tomatoes, squash, chickens, pork, and occasionally some fresh beef from a plantation owner nearby, Major Schroeder.

The mess crew would do anything to keep from being bored — a couple went over to help the boys assigned to repair the Malabang airstrip, where they might come under air attack at any time. One job there was to fill up huge bomb craters, some 50 feet long and deep enough to hide a big truck. For this job we had a small bulldozer on which a small machine gun was mounted. Everyone knew that the repairs could bring greater Japanese efforts to find and attack us.

Another way to break the boredom was an evening in the little river town of Malabang. There the boys could buy cheap drinks, boiled eggs, and coffee as well as tuba, an alcoholic drink made from coconuts. The boys' spending drove up prices, and I couldn't believe their exciting tales. Yet I was eager to find out for myself. When my turn came to go, I washed, patched my clothes, combed my beard, and joined the group riding into town. Our worn-out truck rumbled down the jungle road, kicking up clouds of dust. With darkness near, we no longer feared enemy aircraft. We passed bamboo shacks, thatched with palm leaves, which had yards with pigs, chickens, and dogs. Often several children would run out and stare at us. Farther on we passed houses that looked better and had no pigs about — an almost sure sign that Moros lived there, faithful to their Moslem religion. As we entered town, buildings loomed up that looked like

Old Spanish Fort near Malabang, as it appeared in the 1930s. *(Courtesy Jane Doner Frederickson.)*

medieval castles or forts. That's what they were — the Spaniards had built the sturdy fortifications long ago to defend against the savage Moros. More recently, the U.S. had used the buildings to house the Filipino constabulary troops. Close by, Filipinos and Moros were bathing in a stream of clear water. Some Filipinos smiled and called out "Victory Joe," but the Moros were silent. We went by a modern school and then stopped in front of the hotel. Its bar was the extent of nightlife in Malabang, and the boys hurried in.

I lagged behind to observe the smoky, dimly lighted room filled with a boisterous crowd of Filipino soldiers, civilians, and my companions. But I stepped back into the street, wanting to see more of the town before full darkness. I walked down a deserted street toward the waterfront past the familiar sight of shuttered stores. Then I came to a neighborhood of Moros, who could be seen in their shacks built over the water. The poles holding up the shacks had canoes tied to them. Nearby were two motor launches tied to a dock.

Beside one launch an American in Army uniform was straining to load something aboard. While I watched, my friend Bill Knortz suddenly appeared beside me and said that Captain Charles Wyatt, an engineer in the 81st Filipino Division, was loading homemade depth charges. He was taking them down the Matling River a short way and into the Moro Gulf, which lies south of the western end of Mindanao. His plan was to drop the depth charges on the Japanese submarine that was thought to be lurking nearby, coming up at night to send out fifth column messages. Wyatt hoped to be seen as a harmless fisherman until he got close enough to blow up the submarine. His large athletic build, wavy red hair, and air of determination did not make him look like a Filipino fisherman, even though he wore his khakis without insignia and with collar unbuttoned and sleeves rolled up. He stowed his depth charges, refueled, covered up the mounted machine gun, and started the motor. As he chugged down the river, he waved to us. Knortz exclaimed, "Boy, I wish I was with him. What an adventure." Knortz did ride with the captain one night, but they found no submarine.

On the way back to the hotel, I hurried past the open-air market, which reeked of dead fish and attracted a cloud of flies. At the bar I found the boys eating boiled eggs, peanuts, and downing several kinds of drink. There were efforts to "snow" the Filipino soldiers about the war we had seen. But I was sleepy so I took off for camp on foot with a couple of friends rather than wait for the truck. We bought some peanuts at a little store along the way and continued in the darkness. We had reached camp and fallen asleep before the noisy return of the others awakened us.

The next few days continued as before — normal routines at Sacred Spring and filling in holes on the Malabang airstrip. Now more Jap planes were flying over Malabang than ever. One morning three of us were filling our ten-gallon cans with water for breakfast when the roar of aircraft made us look up through the canopy of trees. Almost immediately our patch of sky was filled by a Jap plane flying so low we could see the red ball, symbol of the Japanese Empire, under each wing and even the pilot's face — he looked directly at us. We just froze and stared back. He had just gone when we heard an explosion and rattling of machine gun fire. We ran to get under the largest tree around the spring as the firing at the airstrip continued. Then the plane returned, now strafing. The fighting 14th had scrambled out of its shelters and headed for foxholes filled with water. Sgt. Chandler joined the mess crew under the big tree. The plane circled around, trying to spot us, but the pilot could see only one side of the tree's large trunk at any one time. When he maneuvered to see on the other side, we had time to dart around the trunk and stay hidden from view. Chandler exclaimed, "Isn't this a hell of a note — playing 'hide and seek' with a Jap pilot." Sgt. John Chandler was a lanky, blond from Mississippi who was the top noncom of the 14th at Malabang. His ability to manage the men

Camp Keithley, where I needed all my ingenuity to feed 30 men. (National Archives [SC-315919].)

had brought him rapid promotions since we were at Hickam Field, where he had been a corporal.

After the Jap had given up and flown away, our men at the airstrip hurried into camp and reported they also had been caught unaware. But some had dived into dugouts and manned the machine guns that Captain Wyatt had concealed there ready to fire. One of the boys had run to the tractor and fired the machine gun mounted there. The pilot, surprised at drawing fire, climbed out of range just in time. Although we all were left with the sickening feeling that the pilot would return with companions for a real attack, none came that day.

The next morning, January 21, 1942, we moved. Lt. John Doe, not a pilot, now commanded the 14th Squadron in place of Captain Horrigan, a pilot who was going to Australia to fly in future operations. As we hurried along across more open ground, I noticed Filipino soldiers drilling and washing clothes. Others with slingshots tried to bring down monkeys swinging high in the trees. Soon our convoy crossed the Matling River on a crude, wood bridge, 100 yards long. Unbelievably, it was intact although it could have been easily destroyed by aircraft or sabotage. Relieved to be across, we moved toward higher ground. Then our road, the Sayre National Highway, utilized an unusual underpass-overpass construction to gain a quick ascent. First we drove under the overpass and then climbed steeply to cross above. When the last truck had rolled across, we finally relaxed. Beyond the overpass we rounded a sharp turn and stopped under the welcome canopy of heavy jungle growth. We located our camp on the lower side of the road. Looking down through the trees, we could barely make out the shiny, winding Matling River. We were only a few miles from Sacred Spring and supported the same airfield near Malabang as before.

After Lt. Doe warned us to keep everything concealed from the air, Major Heidger, our medical officer, took charge of laying out the camp. In succeeding days the motor pool crew improvised pulleys for lifting vehicles for overhaul. They salvaged parts from wrecked vehicles and even airplanes. Officers from the 81st Infantry Division, composed of Filipinos and a few American officers, came to have their staff cars and trucks repaired. The motor pool also helped the radiomen build a radio from salvaged equipment — we used the radio to send and receive coded messages. The radio operators would not tell anything about the contents to us or even to curious officers. Every night at dusk we gathered to hear the news broadcasts, but the news was seldom good. For no logical reason, we still hoped for reinforcements from the U.S.

Major Heidger had few sick men to treat but malaria would later strike many of the boys. A current problem, though, was Dick Beck, the intelligent radio operator, who was still distraught from the bombing of the *Mayon* en route to Mindanao and the subsequent rap on the head he took from Cpl. Hough. Now Beck's fright had been replaced by abnormal dependence on his buddies. Major Heidger tried to shake Beck out of it by bluntly urging him to take care of himself. I offered to use Beck in the kitchen. He did light work such as spraying the numerous ants with water from a bug sprayer. His confidence improved, and he felt better still when I let him handle my M-1 rifle.

As the days passed, the squadron settled into a regular routine. We had rigid inspections every day. Yet there was spare time for improving shacks, washing clothes, playing cards, swimming in the Matling River, and the favorite GI pastime of all — sleeping.

About this time I heard from my buddies left at Camp Keithley that things were really nice there. The idea of moving back appealed to me then because some of the fellows here had gotten malaria and one of the noncoms was giving me a hard time. I asked my good friend Sgt. Chandler for assignment to Keithley. He tried to talk me out of it, but when I persisted, he said he would try to arrange it. In a few days I was riding toward Keithley in a rusty civilian truck with my duffel bag and M-1 rifle — Chandler had learned that Camp Keithley needed a mess sergeant.

8

Camp Keithley
February 1 to March 20, 1942

At Camp Keithley Sgt. George Scott and two kitchen workers were overjoyed to see me. The camp was located on Lake Lanao just across the Agus River from Dansalan. The camp buildings looked good to me because, even with bomb damage, they seemed "permanent." Sgt. Scott escorted me through the barracks, which had debris strewed around as though it had never been cleaned up after the raid of 20 December 1941— in fact it hadn't, and I was told to leave everything as it was. Sgt. Scott told me the place was kept messy because Jap pilots flew very low and could look through the broken windows. So far they had concluded that no one used the barracks.

Our boys got up early to get chow, and leave for their secret work before daylight. Then they did not return for supper until dusk — thus giving the camp a deserted appearance throughout the day. At night there was a total blackout. During the day only Sgt. Scott, who did the paperwork, two KPs, and Lt. James Kale remained. Kale, a pilot with no plane to fly, had charge of the mess. But there was no cook at Keithley, little kitchen equipment, and few supplies.

I realized why everyone was so happy to see me — the mess situation was in a deplorable state. I took the huge job of providing food for the 30 men even though I would have liked to be on the work detail with them. It seemed ironic that I should have to start from scratch because when we left this group at Keithley, I had taken as much equipment and supplies as I could, leaving little for them.

The first thing I did was to get the help of my old friend Rosselle, who had jumped into the foxhole on top of me at Clark Field. Another helper was Bob Becker, a boisterous Polish lad who liked to argue — the work detail was glad to let me have him. The third helper was Couch, who could not do heavy work because of his health. But he was good with figures and a professional card player. He entertained us with his sense of humor, often expressed in rhyme. The last of my helpers was Walter "Chick" Gardner, a mere lad who had lied about his age to enlist and was one of the last to join the 14th Squadron in Hawaii. Now, he was still timid and the men did not accept him, in part because he was not strong enough to help them much. I took him under my wing anyway. We all got to work immediately as there was not much time before the workers would return — they hadn't had anything but a few bananas and peanuts since daylight. After a very busy time, we had supper ready just as I heard their motorboats.

Before I knew it, all the friends I'd left behind here crowded around. As I shook hands and exchanged greetings, my eyes misted over at being with them again. They wore Philippine constabulary uniforms and carried bolos and knives as well as rifles and pistols. During supper, Lt. Richard Carlisle, the CO, called the noisy eaters to attention. He welcomed me and was confident I would be a good mess sergeant. I stood and told them I was happy to be with my many friends. I would do my best to please them. I would welcome any useful equipment of supplies for the kitchen that they could find. When I had finished, they applauded and cheered.

Rosselle and I got started the next morning at 3:45. Several small animals about the size of rats rushed by our legs and almost knocked me down. Rosselle told me they were cats left behind when the Filipino constabulary troops had evacuated after the December raid. I lit a lantern — the kitchen did not let out any light — and saw the cats' work that night. They had turned over a pot of boiled potatoes in the middle of the floor and gnawed on most of them. The pancake batter I'd mixed the night before was tipped over, and the cats had gotten into some fresh meat. Rosselle cursed, and I said we may have to exterminate them before they exterminate us. But for the time being we cleaned up the mess and prepared hotcakes, coffee, and some salty, stateside bacon.

The boys ate hurriedly, said it was wonderful, and wanted more. But it was getting late and they had to be gone before the sun came up. After rinsing their mess kits and making their sleeping quarters look unused, they boarded motorboats and outrigger canoes that took them to the large, camouflaged structures they were building along the lake. These shelters were to hide large Navy PBY flying boats that would fly in.

The work details' departure that morning left us feeling lonesome in the large, deserted camp. Still, we had plenty to do. We scrubbed everything thoroughly and straightened things up. In the afternoon I wandered

Dansalan Hotel in Dansalan, provincial capital on Lake Lanao. Despite the dire situation, I discovered and was able to use the hotel's refrigerator and stove. This photo was taken in 1945. (National Archives [SC-316472].)

into nearby Dansalan and found that the Dansalan Hotel had a large, expensive refrigerator that burned kerosene, as well as a gas and kerosene stove. I immediately thought I could make good use of them. Sgt. Scott and Lt. Kale approved of the idea so Couch made a list of the items we were taking and Kale signed it to show the Army's financial responsibility. The list also included a large store of liquor at the hotel, but the officers took charge of it and the men saw it no more. Some of the boys who had to help us move the refrigerator were angry about the liquor — I told them, "Rank has its privileges."

Chick Gardner, the youngest member of my mess crew, needed some friendly supervision to be useful. On my second morning at Keithley, Chick was alone with me in the kitchen when he suddenly disappeared. I continued hammering some shelves together, thinking he had gone to the latrine. But I didn't hear the roar of the Jap plane until it was too late to dive into our nearby shelter. Chick, however, had heard the aircraft early enough to find his own hiding place some distance away. He came back a half hour later with no excuse for not telling me except that he'd been in too much of a hurry. I gave him hell, but more than once afterward he disappeared without a word — a sure sign of approaching aircraft. I came to think that Chick's unusually large ears gave him an acute sense of hearing. One afternoon I was napping in the deserted barracks when a low-flying aircraft jolted me awake. I thought it would take the roof off and was so scared I gave up sleeping in the day. But these sporadic patrol flights must have satisfied the Japs that the barracks were deserted because no attack followed.

Among the belongings of the Filipino troops left in the barracks was a beautiful dagger with a silver handle, and a clean uniform, which I put on to replace my worn-out clothes. Among the many books of interest, the most fascinating told the story of Private Keithley, for whom the camp was named. In the early 1900s he had served in the 28th Infantry Division, which had established a camp near here to subdue the local bands of Moro guerrillas — the U.S. had acquired the Philippines in the Spanish-American War of 1898. One night Keithley, two other privates, and a sergeant were standing distant guard near the Moro stronghold. In the early morning hours about 20 Moros crept close to the four soldiers and killed all but Keithley with their long, sharp krises. Despite serious wounds, Keithley grabbed the rifles of his dead comrades and retreated slowly, keeping the Moros at bay by firing the rifles from time to time. This went on for three-quarters of an hour until he reached the main camp, still carrying the four rifles. Keithley aroused the camp, but that was his last act.

When I arrived, our work detail had depended on the Filipino constabulary to supply fresh meat. But we were getting discarded and sometimes spoiled meat. Our complaints did no good so I told them not to bother about it any more. Seeking a better supply of meat, I commandeered a staff car with mess officer Lt. McClune (a replacement for Lt. Kale, who had replaced Lt. Carlisle as CO because Carlisle was being sent to Australia), and we drove to an open-air market at Momungan, 10 miles to the north. There we found some fresh carabao meat and got it for a fair price after promising we would be back for more. So McClune and I drove up to shop twice a week. Besides meat we bought small tomatoes, cow peas, roasting ears, squash, and sweet potatoes.

Often I crossed the river to visit the Dansalan market, where colorfully-clothed Moro merchants sold a variety of goods and snacks. At the end of the day they loaded family and goods on large outrigger canoes and sailed on to another Lake Lanao market. They knew how to display their wares — spread in seeming disarray on grass and palm-thatched mats but inviting to the customer.

Every member of the family had something to do — I noticed one child not old enough to talk who was serious about his job of shooing flies off rice cakes, made by his feeble old grandmother while she chewed betel nut. She dipped dull, gray batter made of rice meal from a dirty five-gallon oil can and dropped it into a container half-filled with coconut oil that was suspended over fire. She was getting many customers, but I hung back despite the enticing odor. The grandmother was surprised when I finally asked for one. But she took pride in filling my order after wiping the red betel nut juice from around her mouth.

My rice cake was delicious. The rice batter was mixed with fermented coconut blossom juice, called tuba, which took the place of baking powder. Native ginger, cooked into the coconut oil, and brown sugar sprinkled on top gave the cake a wonderful flavor. My comrades didn't like the cakes at first but came to relish them when food became scarce. They did like the fried bananas at the market. The Moros' outrigger canoes interested me, but I didn't ever linger on the shore because of the sickening odor of the fish being sold there.

As a child I had been fascinated by missionaries and their adventures in far-off places. I'd even known a few in my hometown. In Hawaii I had helped in church work while in service. So on my first Sunday morning at Camp Keithley, I looked forward to worship at the small white mission church. My friends and I were late, but a neatly dressed Filipino ushered us to our seats. We followed in single file — we had taken off our helmets, but they clanked against our guns. At first everyone stared at us and we felt self-conscious. Soon, however, the congregation turned its attention to the service, and I observed the members. There were Filipino officers, clean Filipino children with combed hair but sometimes barefooted, attractive young ladies with flowers in their hair, civilians with their families, the pretty organist, and the missionaries, who conducted the service. When the organist began to play the old familiar hymns, I realized how much I missed going to church. The singing united everyone and made us feel at home. A motherly, middle-aged woman preached the sermon. Afterwards she greeted us with a radiant smile. I can't recall her name, but admired her dedication — her three young daughters looked like a handful even with her husband's help.

Rev. Downs, leader of the missionaries, had served in Japan many years and had left for the Philippines just before the attack on Pearl Harbor. Rev. Abbott and Miss Clark had come down to Dansalan from their work in the hills because of unsafe conditions. Rev. Mears had a pretty Irish wife and small child. Finally, there was Mrs. Spencer, who had adult children in U.S., and Miss Woodward, an elderly, crippled lady who had served in many places. I admired the missionaries for doing their job cheerfully and trusting in God to protect them. I returned to my job with greater determination to do it well.

Lt. McClune and I found a Chinese baker at Momungan who baked bread for us every other day from yeast and cassava flour (made from starchy cassava root), mixed with a little wheat flour. We got enough to provide each man on the work detail two slices a day. But then we had the problem of making sandwiches. I thought I could make pineapple preserves from the canned pineapple we had salvaged from the Del Monte plantation near Suicide Strip. Boiling the pineapple with brown sugar gave the desired result. Then I boiled the plentiful local peanuts and ground them with coconut oil to make peanut butter. Now the hungry men had a least one sandwich every day to break the fast between early morning breakfast and after-dark supper.

For variety in our meals, I learned how to prepare a number of tasty dishes from Miss Amelia Pitco, a large, handsome domestic science teacher who lived with Mrs. Spencer. To make gingerbread, she showed me how to extract ginger from the roots and then bake with cassava flour and brown sugar. I also learned how to make sweet potato pie, banana cream pie topped with grated coconut, and preserves from a fragrant wild fruit, as well as a substitute apple sauce from green mangoes and fruit salad from chopped papaya, grapefruit, bananas, and brown sugar. The boys went for all of this in a big way, and I enjoyed making them happy even though I would rather have been on the secret work detail with them in a man's world instead of being in charge of the kitchen.

One day some of the missionaries invited 10 of us, including officers, to visit them. We took pains to look our best and in the dusk walked to their well-constructed home. We filed into the dimly lit parlor, determined to repress our usual profanity. But it was hard to carry on a polite conversation after months of talking only to each other. The missionaries tried to make us feel relaxed, which only made things worse at first. Then after some punch and cake and listening to the radio for a while, we loosened up. Before the evening was over, we were excitedly telling them about the bombing of Clark Field, Bataan, and our hectic ride on the steamer *Mayon*. Sometimes we lapsed into profanity, but they seemed to understand. As we were leaving, they asked us to come again. We invited them to visit Camp Keithley. When we were out of earshot, we began to point out our embarrassing moments to each other. Then a voice interrupted us with, "You sound as though you were having a grand time." It was Miss Woodward, leaning out of a window in the house where she lived with Mrs. Spencer and Amelia Pitco. We quieted down but hurried to the Dansalan Hotel, hoping to resume our loud discussion of the evening. Inside we had to cut short our eager talk again when we recognized General Guy O. Fort standing at the bar — senior officer in the Lake Lanao region and CO of the 81st Division of Filipino troops.

The general had been waiting for some time and probably had overheard some of our conversation. Nevertheless, he didn't seem upset. The officers found a good bed for him, and before retiring he insisted on joining our mess for breakfast. I went to bed wondering if he would like creamed beef over rice — one of our better dishes. I got up early to trim meat from carabao bones, grind it up with onions, and mix it into a batter of cassava flour and powdered milk. The general sat down with the officers and seemed pleased with breakfast — he complimented us on our kitchen setup.

In the weeks that followed, several of us often spent evenings at Mrs. Spencer's house, listening to "Voice of Freedom" on the radio. There was little good news and lots of propaganda. But Amelia Pitco cheered us up with ginger cakes and punch. Other evenings Sgt. Scott and I climbed a knoll that overlooked Lake Lanao to watch the sun set. For a few minutes I would forget the war and imagine peacetime life around the lake. Even after the sun had disappeared, I stood almost in a trance until mosquitoes drove me off or Rev. Mears, who lived nearby, would find me. I could well understand why people such as General Fort and elderly Governor Heffington, civilian leader of the province, had made the region their home. And the Moros had fought the Spaniards for over 300 years to maintain their way of life around Lake Lanao. Even the U.S. had given up efforts to subdue them and left the Moros to do much as they pleased.

We also got acquainted with Filipinos living in Dansalan. Almost every evening some of us would visit a Filipino home near the docks along the river. The mother welcomed the boys and made them feel at home. There were always a few attractive girls there — daughters and relatives. One of them was Milly, a slim girl with black hair and a roguish smile. She had a kind word for everyone and could sing beautifully. Our boys roasted peanuts and usually got pretty high drinking tuba. Some of the Filipino soldiers joined the drinking party and played musical instruments while everyone sang and danced — it was almost like a USO party. Very little trouble came of this. Only twice did I hear of Americans drawing .45s on each other, and in each case a girl was involved. But no shots were fired, and word of the altercations did not spread.

The gathering at Milly's house also led to invitations by Filipino soldiers for Americans to join them in serenading a "beautiful lady." After a few drinks and songs, we were off in the darkness through narrow streets, singing in low voices accompanied by music. When we reached the home of the beautiful Filipino girl, a "Nelson Eddy" in the crowd would step forward and sing or someone would play music. In time there would be candlelight and a stir in the house, and the girl would come to the porch. She looked romantic standing there in the moonlight, trying to look surprised and pleased. We sang a few American, Spanish, and Filipino love songs, and then "Nelson Eddy" would give a flowery speech about her beauty. She replied by asking us to come in, and we did so. The family apologized for the appearance of the house and offered us coffee, ginger tea, cookies, bananas, and tuba. We ate, joked, and sang some songs before thanking them and heading for camp. But we stopped for peanuts and more beer so we did not get back until midnight. Next morning some of the party looked sick and didn't eat much breakfast.

One day a broken-down bicycle lying in a school yard caught my eye. I thought I could fix it so I carried it away. I was riding it a few days later when a Filipino constabulary enlisted man handed me a note from the Superintendent of Schools, requesting that I sign for the bike, agreeing to a value of 150 pesos ($75). Lt. Kale said it was worth only $5 and warned me about having to overpay if I lost it. So I turned it back to the school but didn't give up the idea of finding some transportation. Right at hand were some horses roaming loose around the camp. They had been left by the constabulary troops who moved out of Keithley after the December 1941 raid. I bought some field corn and put some out for the horses every day. I stood at a distance and watched. Each day I moved a little closer while they got accustomed to coming at a certain time to feed. Eventually I had them eating out of my hand and letting me pet them. It took longer to get a rope and halter on one of them. Then after a bit of a struggle, I got a bit in his mouth and rode him around camp. That accomplished, I turned the pony over to one of my crew.

I had my eye on a pretty, stocky roan. He liked corn but didn't like being ridden. However, I won his friendship and finally got a bridle on him. One evening I crawled up on his back and rode out to the parade ground where the boys had gathered to watch my first ride. I knew they wanted a little excitement, and the horse did, too. A little slack on the reins was all he needed. He bucked once, threw his head down, and whinnied. I locked my legs around him, crouched over, and loosened the reins some more. I had never ridden such a horse — the ground was a blur. We rushed toward a large ditch, but I couldn't slow him. I saw myself landing in the ditch with him on top. But then he gave a mighty leap and landed us safely on the other side. The boys yelled in excitement.

I was ready to stop for the day so I talked to him quietly, hoping to slow him down. But when I tugged on his reins, they broke. I grabbed his mane and held on during an even greater burst of speed. This time we headed for a thick clump of trees at the end of the parade ground. What should I do? Jumping off would mean broken bones if not a broken neck.

If I rode into the trees I could be slammed against a tree trunk or knocked over the head by an overhanging branch. It flashed through my mind that I should have jumped off earlier. Getting nearer, the trees looked bigger and closer together. At the last moment I jumped — landing on my feet but falling forward on my left shoulder. I slid along the grass on my shoulder and side of my face — I thought it was curtains for old "Hopalong Mapes."

Then I found I was able to move the different parts of my body and realized the fall had only shaken me up and given me bruises and a skinned cheek and ear. The boys ran up and said I had put on a better show than the rodeos they'd seen. They asked if I would ride the horse again. "I might," I answered, feeling my bruises, "but the next time I'll charge admission." Then I noticed the horse standing a short distance away, eyeing me. I thumbed my nose at him and walked away.

Later that evening my horse came up to the barracks and whinnied. He ate the corn I brought him and let himself be tied up — I used a strong hemp rope. The next day I spoke with the constabulary veterinarian, who approved our feeding and using the horses. He told me that my roan horse had belonged to a Filipino officer who had been killed by the Japs. The horse had Arabian blood and was a good polo pony — that explained his jump over the ditch. His name was Calio, which meant fire. Calio and I had great times together. We took a ride nearly every day, up a mountain trail or along the lake. He stepped along at a good clip with his ears pricked up.

I took Calio to the market to shop for food. Occasionally, we met an elderly, distinguished man who always greeted me cheerfully. He was Mr. Heffington, former governor of Lanao del Sur Province. I would also be greeted by a muscular Catholic priest, who had a ruddy face and kindly countenance. Noticing my beard, he said, "Sergeant, why don't you come out from behind that bush?" I learned that he and the nuns with him took care of sick and illegitimate children. He was of German descent, but I didn't believe the rumor that he was a spy. One of my mess crew, the boisterous Becker, went to the German priest for confession, and I sometimes went with Becker to Catholic services.

After I had finished shopping, I was loaded down with an armful of packages as well as my usual weapons while behind me, tied to Calio's saddle, were larger purchases. As we rode back toward camp, everyone stared and some Filipinos called out, "Hello Joe, have a drink with us." I would answer politely, "Another time." After I had rebuffed them a few different times, the Filipinos accused me of breaking my promise. I thought I should stop to keep up friendly relations. One drink was fine, but I ran into the same thing after a block or two. A few drinks later in the tropical sun and

I was pretty drunk. I would have passed out right there except for a couple of Filipinos who got me back on Calio. My horse took me to the barracks, where some of my crew helped me off. I did the same thing several times and Calio always brought me back. And at night Calio could always find the way to the barracks when I lost my bearings.

The wild cats continued to be a terrible nuisance. Whenever I got meat out during the day, we had to fight them off and sometimes they would fight back. They always seemed to get in at night. They looked sickly and were mangy, making me afraid of germs. I gave my crew orders to kill every cat on sight. One morning Rosselle held a mosquito net at the cats escape hole and snagged several. The noise awakened the boys, who thought the Japs had come. In time we must have killed 150 of them until only one was left, which we kept and fed. I even used my M-1 rifle in the cat war until Lt. Kale told me to stop because I might hit someone.

I broke rules to improve our diet. Two beautiful Angora goats grazing on the parade ground made me think about our dwindling supply of powdered milk. I fed the goats regularly and finally coaxed them up on the high-railed porch. One day we closed the porch entrance behind them and put ropes around their necks. They bleated in protest, but we pulled them to our barracks where there was room underneath to tie them. Some corn quieted them down. I was pleased — one goat would be ready to milk in a week, the other in three weeks. The boys would be happy with milk in their coffee, and they'd get some much-needed calcium.

In the next few days I fed and watered the goats and even petted them and felt their udders. But the day before I planned to begin milking, a Filipino sergeant brought me a paper to read. It said I had stolen civilian property and must release the goats at once. I argued that we had never seen an owner. Nevertheless, the owner soon appeared — an ex-schoolteacher and nice sort of fellow. I offered to buy the animals, but he refused, saying he had several children who needed the milk.

Despite the goat fiasco, it wasn't long before I was trying something else. We were getting short of meat when I chanced to see several pigs on the parade ground, scrounging some corn that Calio had left. Lt. McClune read my mind and told me to leave the pigs alone. But later I said to myself, "To hell with that order." A couple days later, I enticed one of the pigs into a noose with corn and tightened the rope. I was sure its squeals would be heard by everyone for miles around — someone, an officer or Filipino official, would catch me and my helper Rosselle. My agitated helper told me to "kill the bastard or turn him loose." I hit the animal on the head with a machine hammer and stuck him with a dagger to bleed him thoroughly. We lit all the stoves to boil some water and moved the carcass to an empty garage, where we scalded it. We were feverishly scraping off the hair when somebody called from outside. I peered through a crack, expecting to see the Filipino owner. But instead, I saw two beady black eyes, a swarthy, grinning face, and a tall figure in constabulary clothes. I recognized "Chief" Blanche, a Choctaw Indian in our motor pool. I let him in — he had heard the pig squealing and wondered who had killed it. He claimed he was a butcher, and I handed him a knife. The Chief swung the knife to and fro and had the pig butchered in no time. I had my boys clean up all the hair and burn it. We dug a hole for the entrails. The porker had just been shoved into the oven when the owner came looking for his red pig. We invited him to look around, but he could find no sign of it. After he left, we rendered all of the fat we could get from the carcass since we had been short of lard for a long time.

That night the boys really enjoyed the roast pork, candied yams, and gravy. The officers enjoyed it too, and asked the mess officer where the pork had come from. McClune came over and asked me about the pig. I said I'd thrown a knife at a stray cat but hit the pig instead. He warned, "Well, don't kill any more pigs without my approval." But when I saluted, he winked and walked back to the other officers with a grin. I had finally gotten away with something.

9

Master Sgt. Manook —
Farewell to Dansalan
February 1 to March 20, 1942

I had heard about Master Sgt. Manook of the Philippine constabulary force from Sgt. Scott soon after my arrival at Camp Keithley. Manook liked to come by with his two Moro wives and visit with Scott. Manook had been stationed at Keithley before the constabulary troops had vacated after the December 1941 air raid. Now two of our boys back from the Momungan hospital told me Manook was there, undergoing treatment for a stab wound inflicted by a civilian Moro. Manook was a Moro himself but independent-minded. In a short time Manook appeared at Keithley — none the worse except for a wicked-looking scar on his face that had barely healed. He was a large, powerful, six-foot man in his fifties, who had a beer belly and raven black hair with silver streaks in it. Over his uniform, he wore laced riding pants and well-polished cavalry boots. At his hip was a .45 Colt and over his head a bright handkerchief. His ruddy face and clothes made him look like an Indian. He was chewing a large wad of tobacco — unusual for a Moro or Filipino. I invited him to supper and he ate heartily, saying he liked American food; he had lived in America for a time before he joined the constabulary 29 years before. When he invited me to visit his home at Lumbatan on the south end of Lake Lanao, I was eager to go.

But it was weeks before I made the trip. Finally, as Manook's men paddled us across the open water toward Lumbatan, he related how he had gotten his recently healed scars. More than a month before, Manook had taken a short leave from his constabulary outfit to see his wives and children, as well as to arrange for their evacuation if the Japs continued to advance. He was just sitting down to a sumptuous dinner when a neighboring Moro slipped into the dining room and glided directly behind Manook without being noticed. He raised his long Moro dagger and struck toward Manook's heart with all his might. But Manook saw the plunging dagger just in time to hunch forward and lower his head. The dagger slashed Manook's cheek, went through his lower jaw, and penetrated his chest, just missing his jugular vein and windpipe. As the dagger struck him, Manook grabbed the Moro's leg and yelled for his wives. The youngest one had just stepped into the kitchen but now was the nearest. She grabbed a large bolo and rushed to help. The Moro had not broken loose yet. For an instant she had a clear shot: She hacked the Moro's head off in one blow and threw it out the window. Then the two wives tossed the body out. The crazed man was not known to have a particular grudge against Manook. One speculation was that since Manook did not follow all the Moslem beliefs — for instance, he enjoyed eating pork — the Moro thought that to kill a sinner might bring rewards in heaven.

As Manook was finishing his account, his hometown of Lumbatan came into sight at the end of the lake. Several outrigger canoes came out and escorted us for the last several hundred yards to shore. There, half the town greeted us, and Manook gave a short speech. The crowd closed in and followed us into Manook's yard, where they finally broke away after he told them he didn't want to be bothered. Inside the house, Manook's two wives, a daughter of eight, and his orderly greeted us while a little son ran into the younger wife's arms. She had shiny black hair, light olive complexion, soft brown eyes, rosy cheeks, and regular white teeth. Her lips only added to her beauty. She was just about my age — young enough to be Manook's daughter instead of his wife. It was hard to believe that she had struck off the Moro's head. The other wife was about five years older and looked Chinese. She was smart and liked to talk a lot. The wives brought us delicious Tom Collins drinks and sat with us before excusing themselves to prepare dinner. Manook showed me a picture on the wall of his son, a lieutenant in the Filipino army, who was now in the combat area — the son of Manook's first wife, who had died ten years before. We were about to eat when we saw from the window several soldiers from Camp Keithley who had come in a launch to recover two boats that had broken loose and blown across the lake. Manook insisted they have dinner with us. They hesitated because they were on duty, but one joined us while the others watched the boats.

The tablecloth, napkins, and silverware were the equals of any at the Manila Hotel. The wives had prepared American-style fried and fricassee chicken, beef, all kinds of vegetables, and many Filipino dishes, as well as the large bowl of rice in the center of the table. Manook explained that his wives had learned American cooking in high-school Domestic Science classes — it was a qualification for becoming his wife.

Manook realized his own educational limits and felt he could learn something from me. Nevertheless, he could have been commissioned in the Philippine Constabulary because of his leadership qualities. But he decided to stay an enlisted man because he had two wives, while his fellow officers would be Filipino and, being Christian, have only one wife apiece.

I pointed out the difficulty in America of getting along with just one wife while Moros had two wives and got along with them fine. Manook explained he had paid a large dowry for his older wife after his first wife died. The investment had been wise because she had run his store profitably and brought up his eight-year-old daughter. Manook couldn't resist paying a large dowry for his third wife because of her beauty. At first his Chinese wife resented her a great deal. Manook finally persuaded them to stop quarreling — I didn't find out how. Yet now they seemed content; one ran the store and one the house. There was some jealousy, though, about which child got the best clothes and which the father favored. Manook and I drank one last gin together before I returned to Camp Keithley, relaxed and still wondering about Manook's wives.

Next morning I noticed Lt. Doe having breakfast with Lt. Kale, our new CO at Camp Keithley after Lt. Carlisle's transfer to Australia. Lt. Doe had come over from the main group of the 14 Squadron at Malabang. I soon learned that Doe was trying to take me back with him to Malabang. He planned to put me in charge of baking bread for all American troops and civilians in the vicinity of Malabang. But no troops were stationed in the town where the bakery was located — it could be lonesome duty. I didn't want to go, and Kale and the other officers told me they would try to keep me — they were well satisfied with my handling of the mess. Lt. Doe continued to insist on taking me, and as CO of the 14 Squadron, he prevailed.

During my last few days at Camp Keithley I made preparations to have a dinner for the missionaries — we had promised to have them over after our dinner and evening with them. Rosselle and I ordered steaks in advance — they were so expensive we had to use some of our own money. I found canned corn, olives, grape jam, and fruit cocktail in the Dansalan Hotel and baked a chocolate cake and rolls. Lieutenants McClune and Kale helped us get a tablecloth, napkins, silverware, glasses, and china from the hotel.

That night after feeding the men, we set the table, decorated it with flowers, and lit candles. We found a high chair for Rev. Mears's small child. I waited table for the missionaries and officers, causing Mears to remark that he had never been served by a headwaiter. Lt. Kale apologized for the food because we hadn't received supplies for some time, but the missionaries praised our efforts as wonderful and unbelievable.

The day before I was to leave, I tried to persuade Lt. Doe to take someone else. But he told me I would like the new assignment. I insisted I wouldn't. Finally he promised he would let me return if I worked hard and broke in a man to operate the bakery in my place. That evening I made a farewell visit to my missionary friends and Miss Amelia Pitco. I gave her an elegant handkerchief to show my friendship and appreciation for teaching me how to make tasty dishes for the men. Next morning Lt. Doe and I drove by Milly's house in Dansalan, where my friends and I had spent so many pleasant evenings dancing and drinking tuba. Milly had learned I was leaving and now stood outside her home to give me a wave and a wonderful smile.

10

Starting Up the Bakery at Malabang

March 20 to April 10, 1942

On the way to Malabang we stopped to meet Major Louis Schroeder, a planter who had been recently commissioned and now served as procurement officer for the Malabang area. Schroeder greeted me heartily, and Lt. Doe explained I was to take over the Chinese bakery. Near Malabang I greeted my 14th Squadron buddies, including John Chandler, James Palmer, John Murdoch, Bill Knortz, Ben Ferrens, Walter "Doc" Haddock, Charley Butterworth, and Frank Puppario.

After lunch, Butterworth and I met with Captain Harry Katz, an intelligent-looking officer with General Fort's 81st Division. We drove up to the large, unpainted hotel in Malabang and scrambled out. Katz shouted for Yang Ti, a Chinese civilian, who soon came out of the store in the hotel. Katz brusquely told him he was a profiteer and a suspected collaborator. Furthermore, Yang Ti and the owner of the hotel had been hoarding and selling baked goods at outrageous prices. Katz declared the Army was taking over the bakery and shutting down the store. He demanded an itemized list of the bakery equipment for the Army to sign for, and warned against any over-evaluation. None of this scared Yang Ti, and he showed little resentment.

Katz left us with Yang Ti, who led us to the back of the hotel, where we stopped at a rusty door fastened with a large corroded lock. Yang unlocked the door and shoved it open. We entered a dimly lighted room that smelled of fermented yeast and rotted potatoes. Yang's small lamp showed everything covered with dust and soot. Cobwebs hung from the ceiling, and rats and roaches scuttled about a floor caked with flour, dust, and meal. I wondered how this space could ever be converted into a bakery.

The first item to inventory was the large, shapeless baking oven made of brick, cement, and clay. Yang explained that one had to build a hot fire of hardwood and keep it going until coals could be banked on one side. When the oven was too hot to keep your hand inside, it had reached the right temperature to bake. Now you put the dough in — with protective padding for your hand and arm. Square five-gallon oil containers served as bread tins for baking six- to eight-ounce loaves. We also listed a filthy, wooden dough trough, shelves, tables, glass cases, dough knives, and a gasoline motor to roll out the dough. After Yang priced the items on a list for Major Schroeder to sign, Charley Butterworth and I were alone.

Charley agreed with my disgust with the bakery and thought it was as dirty as I did. But he was a bit amused. There was nothing to do except clean the place. After three days, we were still cleaning. Continual feeding of firewood had made the oven hot enough to bake. By that time, I was taking the job as a challenge to produce satisfactory bread.

A couple weeks later Yang asked me if I would haul a truckload of cassava roots to a secluded field a few miles up in the hills. He explained that he wanted to plant the cassava — tubers similar to sweet potatoes and a major source of starch in the tropics — to help feed his family after their resettlement in the mountains to avoid the Japs.

I felt sorry for him because we had taken his property. Yet I hesitated to help because Captain Katz or Major Schroeder would forbid it if I asked and would reprimand me severely if I did it without asking; I thought of Captain Katz's harsh criticism of Yang's reported black market activities. When I talked to my partner at the bakery, Charley Butterworth, he said, "Go ahead and help Yang. Katz and Schroeder will never know, and I'll keep mum." Early next morning, Yang and I filled up the bakery station wagon with cassava roots and drove up to his hidden field. We were back before noon, and no American was wiser except Butterworth.

Meanwhile, we had sent Major Schroeder a list of items needed for baking bread. He came with two Filipinos to deliver the requested flour, salt, sugar, yeast, powdered milk, and Irish potatoes. It was the last of the sugar, lard, and potatoes so we were to use them sparingly. Schroeder looked up Yang Ti and gave him a hard time for overpricing the bakery equipment — Yang was again made out to be a greedy profiteer. Schroeder arranged with Captain Jay Navin to assign two Filipino soldiers to help in the bakery. Navin was an officer from Los Angeles who commanded a regiment of General Fort's 81st Division at the edge of town.

Butterworth and I had the use of an old Model "A" Ford station wagon to deliver the bread. For quarters we had a large room on the second story of the hotel as well as rations to cook for ourselves. Butterworth knew a lot of people in town and liked his new situation away from camp discipline. But I was unhappy because I missed Camp Keithley, where I was well-acquainted in town and loved the beauty surrounding Lake Lanao. Furthermore, I believed Malabang would soon be a ghost town because every time an enemy plane flew over, more people left. Yet my outlook improved as the days went by. One reason was Charley Butterworth, a tall blond of athletic build from South Bend, Indiana — one of the swellest guys I'd known. He kept saying this was a real deal for us both. But I told him I would be going back to Dansalan when he thought he could manage the bakery — recalling Lt. Doe's promise to that effect.

In our spare time we often drove our Ford a mile to the mouth of the Matling River, where it flows into the Moro Gulf on the south coast of Mindanao. There, we turned off at the ruins of a Spanish fort and parked under high palms by a Moro fishing village. The beach was covered with outriggers and nets. Captain Navin's soldiers patrolled here — it looked like a likely spot to land for an attack on Malabang. Everyone stared as we took off our clothes and plunged into the ocean to wash off the sweat and grime from our work in the bakery. Sometimes our Filipino helpers went along as well as Filipino, Spanish, and Moro children from town. In the water we played tag with the kids, and on the beach volleyball — the boys had made a net out of woven vines and a ball out of bamboo that was crude but had a lot of bounce.

When we got back to the hotel, Charley wanted me to go visiting with him, but I wasn't interested since I wasn't going to be in Malabang very long anyway. I spent time just strolling around and reading or writing in our room. We left town once or twice a day to deliver our bread to the 14th Squadron camp. There our old friends gave us the news that the boys on Bataan couldn't hold out much longer.

In view of the uncertain situation on Mindanao, our officers told Butterworth and me to take off on our own in case of attack if we could not get back to the 14th Squadron. For a possible long stay in the mountains, each of us packed a change of clothes, a shelter half, cans of food, a medical kit, a map, compass, ammunition, and weapons as well as matches and a flashlight. We had two escape plans: (1) to drive our station wagon into the mountains as far as possible, destroy it, and proceed on foot, or (2) to slip away by boat up the Matling River. We always had everything ready to go, as well as the Ford gassed up and pointed in the right direction. We had three plans for getting out of our room: (1) to throw our packs out the window and jump after them, (2) to go downstairs and out through the bakery, or (3) to climb out on the roof and shimmy down the drainpipe.

Without warning the order came down for Cpl. Butterworth to leave at once for a jungle hideaway, called Lanochin, to join a group who were to assemble P-40 pursuit planes under high trees that could hide their activity. He said goodbye, and there I was — still operating the bakery and with no replacement that would let me go back to Camp Keithley. Major Schroeder had more bad news: My station wagon was needed elsewhere so for my bread deliveries I was given a worn-out truck that steered badly.

In fact, Schroeder told me to give up the idea of going back because I was needed at Malabang for reasons other than baking. A few days later, another officer explained that my real job in Malabang was to observe and report any sign of fifth column activity — there were a number of suspects in Malabang. If anyone wanted to know why I was the only American in Malabang, management of the bakery was my cover.

With the loss of Butterworth, I realized I needed other Filipino helpers at the bakery. The original ones had become lazy and then came down with malaria. I went to Captain Navin, who had provided the earlier ones, and told him I wanted some good workers with baking experience. This time he sent me three good men. I told them their jobs and for awhile got results by using kindness and diplomacy. At times, though, I had to pretend I would kill them if they didn't snap to. But my threats came too often to be effective so I had to be on hand to keep them from lying down on the job. Finally I noticed the effectiveness of seeming to be very angry or in a bad mood first thing every morning. Then they would keep on their toes all day and take responsibility for doing most of the work. They never seemed to show any resentment. Yet if I forgot and was friendly when I first saw them in the morning, they turned lazy.

Another problem was that most of our wheat flour had been used. I had to mix in a large proportion of rice and cassava flour, causing the bread to be light. Major Schroeder gave us our last Irish potatoes from his nearby plantation and brought over a large flowerpot to make yeast. I was to be very careful with the flowerpot because it belonged to his wife, who was in the States. He told me she would raise hell if anything happened to it, and then grinned.

The yeast situation became difficult. I fermented sweet potatoes, but the bread didn't taste good and had bad color. Neither squash nor rice worked, either. Then I thought to try tuba, the local drink made by fermented coconut sap. The tuba worked very satisfactorily, but no money had been designated for it so the finance officer refused to provide funds. I was sore but determined to figure something out. The answer was barter.

A Filipino gladly brought me a gallon of fresh tuba every day in return for several loaves of bread. Major Schroeder, who knew I had run out of potatoes, asked me how I was doing so well. When I told him of my scheme, he could hardly keep a straight face as he cited Army regulations that forbade trading government property for alcoholic beverages. Then he laughed and said that that regulation didn't apply in the Philippines. He patted me on the back and told me to keep up the good work. My helpers' liking for tuba was one drawback. Sometimes they drank up tuba that was needed, and one time they all got drunk. I really raised hell and put the fear of God in them; I never caught them doing it again.

When the lard supply ran out, I had no ready answer, but Captain Navin had his men render coconut oil, which Major Schroeder delivered along with rock salt. But the major was not always prompt so I usually requested more salt and coconut oil before I actually ran out. One day I was so short I didn't send any bread out to Schroeder's plantation when his man came for it. I had to tell him we'd been forced to stop baking. The next day, Schroeder himself came to the bakery and searched high and low for some bread while I was at the Moro market, but my men had hidden it well. When I returned, Schroeder almost shouted, "Where in the hell have you hidden the bread and why didn't you send me mine?" I handed him a loaf and explained that his delay in providing salt and coconut oil was close to stopping bread production. The major just laughed and slapped me on the back. He said I was pretty shrewd and doing good work even though I had played a mean joke on him. So with schemes and unusual ingredients I supplied the American troops and plantation owners with bread, as well as quantities of the "pan de sol" rolls that the Filipino troops liked so much.

Despite early difficulties, my Filipino helpers seemed quite fond of me, as well as loyal. The smallest was a Chinese mestizo who was the smartest and, I felt, the most dependable. The three of them stayed in the bake shop all night to guard it, taking shifts. The man on watch also had the job of keeping the oven hot with firewood so we were always ready to bake. If the Japs got close, they were to awaken me in the hotel and the four of us would leave together in the bakery's truck.

Usually I got up a couple times during the night to see how things were going and have a cup of coffee. The nearest American I could count on was Captain Navin with his Filipino troops. I felt I had to trust in God and my three helpers. They might run, but I hoped they would stay with me even if fifth columnists brought a Jap patrol into town or tried to burn down the hotel.

In the morning, after the usual "angry" session with my helpers, I sometimes had one of them fix me breakfast of rice, eggs, and coffee. Then I drove to the spring to get water for the bakery—first taking a quick plunge in the clear pool of water. I got acquainted with the Filipinos and Moros who also came daily to get water, wash clothes, or bathe. Upon my return to the bakery, the boys loaded the truck with freshly baked "Mapes Special Bread," which I then delivered to my buddies at the 14th Squadron hideout where I had been stationed before transferring to Camp Keithley.

There I had to listen to my buddies gripe about our commanding officer, Lt. Doe, who had brought me down from Keithley to run the bakery. I told them they were lucky not to be in the fighting on Bataan. When I asked if anyone would like to trade places with me, no one was interested. Yet there was serious trouble at the camp. Doe was a reserve officer with less time in service than most of his men. But he demanded undue respect in the jungle, like a little king. The men had become mean, irritable, and easily insulted. After drinking a lot of tuba, they would deliberately break rules to challenge Lt. Doe, who threatened them with general court martial as soon as he could find the time and place. Some of his charges were so serious that conviction could result in execution or many years in prison. Those so threatened said Doe would get a bullet in his head during action against the Japs. There might have been chaos if it hadn't been for our ranking noncom, 1st Sgt. John Chandler, who implemented and modified Doe's orders in ways that incurred as little resentment as possible. Major Heidger was busy treating malaria cases with a limited supply of quinine and Atabrine. Each time I delivered bread, more of my buddies were sick.

I would soon get tired of the griping so I'd hurry back to town and stop at a small shack where Everesto, a Mexican-Filipino, was busy frying bananas for his two sons to sell at the market. He served me the fried bananas, black coffee, and coconut milk. Later I would stroll through the large marketplace, pretending to be looking for something although my purpose was to chat with merchants, hoping to glean information that would identify fifth columnists. I would also linger in shops, drinking coffee while talking with customers.

By now I had the bakery well enough organized to have time on my hands. Sometimes I became so lonely that I wanted to get drunk, but did not for fear of sudden enemy attack. I was the only American enlisted man in town and didn't have a girlfriend to keep me company.

I passed some of my time with Mama Godi, a Filipino mestizo, who ran a hotel across the street from mine. I talked with her and her children, and occasionally one of them played the old piano for me. I would just sit there and gaze into space — dreaming of better days and sometimes trying to figure out the future. I let them use my oven for special baking, and they invited me to come and eat at my convenience. The father was an American, so I could enjoy an American breakfast sometimes. He had disappeared when the war started, but the family was doing a good job shifting for themselves. I couldn't help noticing the older girl of 16, who had a light complexion and worried about being raped when the Japs came. The fear preyed upon her day and night until Captain Wyatt, who roomed at the hotel, arranged for the family to retire to a mountain hideout when it became necessary. The girl became much happier and began to spend more time at the hideout and less in town.

Feeling lonely one day, I walked across the street to visit with Captain Wyatt, who was sitting in the bar with a Filipino woman. Two months earlier Bill Knortz and I had watched Wyatt motoring down the Matling River with homemade depth charges, hoping to drop them on an enemy submarine. Now, as I approached Wyatt's table, the woman excused herself and Wyatt invited me to sit down for a drink. With good liquor and a trustworthy companion, I decided to make up for lost time. I poured the captain's liquor into my water glass several times before he noticed his bottle was almost empty. He was taken aback, but before he could say anything I thanked him for his generosity. I explained I hadn't had a drink for a long time and my job was driving me crazy because of the loneliness. Then I quickly excused myself. Afterwards I thought this was one time I had gotten back at the officers who had cornered all the good liquor. Nevertheless, Captain Wyatt and I remained good friends, and I drank more of his whiskey.

At the edge of town another American was as lonely as I was. This was Captain Navin, whose job was to train and equip Filipino soldiers. After working all day with his men, he was eager to visit with me — another American separated from other Americans. Evenings he would invite me to his headquarters for a drink and snack. We talked about everything under the sun except our present situation. We wandered back through the years to our childhood, discussed what we would do after the war, and considered going into business together in California. I learned he had married a nurse in California, but the two didn't get along, probably because the captain was a slave driver even though he could be charming. Here in Malabang he did not get along with Filipinos — they were angered when he shot their pet dogs for practice. He rubbed others the wrong way by meddling in their private business. He tried to order my fellow Air Corps men around even though they were not in his command. He didn't get far directing me because I simply avoided him until he called a truce. Anyway, I wasn't in his command. Then he tried to get me detached from the

Air Corps so I could help command his Filipino troops. He had no luck with this idea, either. Nevertheless, we remained on good terms and helped each other. I baked rolls for his Filipino troops, and they rendered coconut oil to provide lard for my baking.

One morning while coming down the hotel stairs, I heard somebody ask for me in English with a Filipino accent. A Moro soldier in Filipino uniform stood at the foot of the stairs, armed with a gun and bolo and holding a sack of struggling chickens at his side. He held the sack out to me and said they were a gift from a dear friend. When he refused to take any money, I asked who would send me such a scarce and choice present. He replied, "His name is Chicken," and handed me this note:

> Dear Mapes,
>
> I am happy to learn that you are stationed in Malabang and have sent you this present as is my custom to express my friendship to my very dear friends.
>
> I have been stationed at Barira, about eight km south of Malabang and will be glad to visit you in the near future if you will say when and we will have a good time eating chicken and drinking and talking about old times.
>
> Manook

I told the soldier to wait for an answer. I asked Manook to come as soon as possible and thanked him for the priceless chickens. While my helpers were putting together a bamboo cage for the chickens, it dawned on me why Manook had come to be so called. Because he sent chickens to his friends, they gave him and he gave himself the name that was the Philippine word for chicken — Manook.

In a few days Manook sent word he was coming that afternoon. I hurried the caged chickens over to Everesto, who agreed to fry them and prepare a feast at my expense. Manook arrived in mid-afternoon with his Moro orderly, Ricardo, who was his youngest wife's brother. Ricardo was intelligent and looked to be an ideal soldier, guard, and orderly. While enjoying his favorite drink of gin, Manook told me about his new assignment as liaison officer with General Fort's Bolo Battalion, which consisted of scattered Moro clans. Manook was well qualified to be a go-between among Moros, Filipinos, and Americans. He himself was a Moro, a veteran of many years in the Philippine Constabulary, and he had lived among Americans in his early life. His current duties did not let him get home often so he understood my loneliness.

When I asked, he took me around town and introduced me to his

Moro friends, telling them I was his very good friend. On the street all eyes were on us — Manook and Ricardo made a striking appearance. We visited several well-to-do homes where we drank tuba. In late afternoon we returned downtown for dinner, which Everesto and his whole family had prepared. In the growing darkness we sat down to eat in the light of a cotton wick, made from kapok trees and submerged in a bowl of coconut oil. We had just begun to eat when Kukie, the 14th Squadron drunk, came by, full of tuba, and sat down at my invitation. We had talked ourselves out by 11 P.M. Kukie was staggering so I took him part way to his camp and then drove Manook and Ricardo to their camp at Barira. On my way back to Malabang, Bolo Battalion guards stopped me twice, but mention of Manook made them remember me and they saluted as I drove on.

Getting together with Manook had chased away the doldrums of loneliness. In following days, the Moros in Malabang accepted me more and more after seeing me with Manook, who visited often. He kept my chicken cage full so we would dine on chicken and tuba. My Filipino helpers fried the chicken in the bakery stove, and I provided music with records of Al Jolson and German, Chinese, and Filipino classics. We continued the evening with visits to Manook's friends in Malabang.

One day I visited Manook's camp. It was located on a Moro chief's plantation on which sub-chiefs and tenants tended the coconut groves and raised sugar cane. The produce was sold at a nearby Moro market. The camp served as headquarters for General Fort's Bolo Battalion of several thousand Moros, consisting of a number of different clans, each led by a Moro chief. The camp trained the Moro chiefs to work together against the Japs. The headquarters stood at the bend of a large, rocky stream that was convenient for bathing, washing, and fishing. The Moro chiefs in training sat cross-legged on the ground as Manook introduced me to them. My M-1 rifle got their attention so I dismantled it to show the working parts and then quickly reassembled it. The rifle amazed them, and they offered to pay a lot for it in money or valuables. Yet they took my refusal in good grace and accepted me as a friend. My acquaintance with them and Manook's Moro friends in Malabang could help my intelligence-gathering and might save my life when the Japs came.

Now many Moros wanted me to visit them, and I never refused. I always invited them to have coffee with me at the bakery and would take them to where they were going in my truck if it were possible. At times a Moro chief had traveled a long way and needed a place to stay. But I was always a little suspicious. Accordingly, when a tired Moro chief arrived, I invited him to my room and told him it was my custom for guests to leave their weapons in my closet. I explained that my rifle was also there, and they complied. Usually they liked to talk most of the night, but when they went to sleep, I stayed awake with my .45 pistol and bayonet hidden under the blanket.

The visitors marveled at my knowledge of their language and customs, as well as my apparent respect for the Koran, their bible. With a few casual remarks, I led them to believe I was half-Arab — I had been brought to the U.S. as a small child, I said, but when my Arabian mother died, I had been reared like an American. Yet I still remembered Muslim customs and felt at home in their Moro culture. My heavy beard encouraged them to believe me — they said such a beard was typical for Arabs.

The Moro mayor of Malabang had his office across the street from the bakery. He enforced the law and had a number of Moros in the town jail nearby. They peered through barred windows all day except when the guard took them across the street to the toilet. Then the chains holding them together made an awful clanking sound. But it was worse at night when the prisoners chanted prayers to Allah while they beat time with their chains.

The mayor was short, intelligent, and highly nervous. He used colorful profanity to express himself in English, a language he had learned as a small boy from American soldiers after the Spanish-American war. I visited his plantation, which his men worked with tractors and trucks. He had several attractive wives and grown children, including a pretty daughter who taught school nearby.

I was lucky to escape the malaria that had beset our camp, but a wisdom tooth was giving me a lot of pain so I asked Lt. Doe for permission to visit the dentist at Camp Keithley. Since Doe had business in Dansalan, just across the river from Keithley, he decided to combine our trips and ride in style with me as his driver. When we reached Dansalan, Lt. Doe sent me into a hotel to find an Air Corps officer, but a large black guard stopped me at the door and asked my business. He told me the officer we wanted had moved back to Camp Keithley and that Manuel Quezon, President of the Philippines, was staying there. He was on his way to Australia to head the Philippine government-in-exile. Doe impatiently told me to drive him to the officers' barracks at Camp Keithley.

I left him there and went to the dentist, a Filipino captain, who said my tooth should not be pulled because he lacked the medicine to stop infection. The tooth was all right — just irritated because of skin growing over it. I let him cut the skin off, and the pain was excruciating and I bled a lot. Afterwards, I picked up some quinine to take to Major Heidger at Malabang for his numerous malaria patients.

My friends at Camp Keithley told me nobody had ridden my horse

Calio since I had left. Filipino soldiers had moved into the wrecked barracks and started fixing them up. They had made little effort to hide their cleanup efforts, which the Japs would be sure to notice. New attacks would destroy Camp Keithley's usefulness, which had functioned for months because we had made it look deserted. I spent the rest of the afternoon with Mrs. Spencer and my missionary friends. After returning to Camp Keithley, I fell asleep waiting for Lt. Doe.

The next thing I knew, Doe was shaking me. I grabbed my gun, thinking Japs were near, and asked why he was so excited. He snapped, "I have important orders that have to be delivered to Malabang before sunup so get ready to go." Halfway back to Malabang the car coughed and sputtered to a stop. Lt. Doe angrily claimed I was at fault. Because the car had no lights, Doe burned out our last three matches as he tried to see what was wrong. The lieutenant swore some more and ordered me to find a Moro house and get a light. We had to get to Malabang by daylight.

I trudged off across plowed fields and rice paddies until I found a Moro shack. When I approached, cold sweat broke out on my forehead. I imagined Moros lying in ambush in the undergrowth around the hut. But I wasn't able to rouse anyone — either the place was deserted or the Moros there didn't want to be bothered. I found my way back to the road and then followed it for some distance before several dogs barked and a Moro guard called out.

The guard led me to the door of a house where a Moro chief stood and asked in the Moro language what I wanted. But he couldn't understand English or Filipino dialect so I tried pointing to the fire inside the house to get across my need for a light. I couldn't think of the word for fire in Moro. He brought me a dipper of water and some food. But I kept pointing to the fire while his wives and children stood watching behind him. Thinking I wanted one of his wives, he scowled, but I shook my head vigorously. Finally, he pointed to the fire, and I nodded. He had two of his men make huge torches. They lit one and followed me back to the car. I believed the gas line was blocked with dirt, and when all else failed, I tried to blow enough pressure into the gas tank to break up the clog. When I could blow no more, the release of pressure caused the car to jump and throw gas into my eyes and face. I was temporarily blinded but soon could see a little, although my eyes hurt a lot.

When I said, "It looks like we'll have to figure out some other way to get to Malabang," Doe angrily ordered, "Go back to the Wattu motor pool and get another car. Get going!" I didn't like the idea of a trek of three miles in the dark past Moro villages. I knew that some Moros would ambush and kill a man for his rifle, so I decided to leave my M-1 behind. When I asked

Doe if I could take his .45 pistol, he snapped, "No, dammit. I need it myself." So I set out in the dark toward Wattu, fearful that each clump of bushes along the road hid a hostile Moro. Dogs barked as I passed several Moro houses, and Moro guards stopped me twice. But they let me go by, seeing that I was an unarmed American. I reached the motor pool at 4 A.M. and woke Sgt. Elwin Bishop. He got a car and drove me and a mechanic back to Lt. Doe. Still keyed up, Doe blamed me for taking so long. The mechanic soon fixed the car. Then Doe and I drove on in the fresh car, and Bishop and the mechanic went back in ours.

At Ganasi, the lieutenant stopped for breakfast while I waited in the car. I was hungry and my eyes still hurt. A Filipino lieutenant I knew saw me and asked me to eat with him at another place. He ordered and before I knew it, the waiter had brought me black coffee, fried eggs, and rice. I ate heartily and thanked him. I returned to the car just before Doe, who said, "Well, Mapes, it won't be long now before we'll be in Malabang and you can have your breakfast."

When we reached our Malabang camp, I found everyone still excited from early morning explosions that had been mistaken for an enemy attack. It turned out that a fire in our motor pool had touched off some small caches of ammunition. Back at the bakery, people in Malabang were just settling down after the town alarm had started a civilian evacuation. The guards scanning the Gulf of Moro from the watchtower had picked out specks on the horizon that quickly became larger. They sounded the alarm signal for enemy attack. But after they scrambled down, the fast-moving craft turned out to be fishing canoes from Jolo. That scare, plus an unidentified aircraft, had caused Captain Navin to deploy his troops for action. Afterwards Navin put on a dance to relax his men. I danced with a large, attractive girl, who asked me to "come out from behind that beard."

11

Romance
April 10–20, 1942

I continued to drive down past the ruins of the Spanish fort for frequent swims in the surf, just as Charley Butterworth and I had done before he was transferred. After parking, I passed by the house of an old Moro chief who always greeted me from the porch of his plain bamboo hut that stood on stilts high above the ground. One day we started talking, and he invited me to come in. He motioned me under the house where he opened a trap door above me. Then he let down a bamboo ladder. As I climbed up, he gave me a hand as I stepped into the house.

On the walls were hangings of Moro design, a homemade water-pipe shotgun, and wicked looking knives and krises. The chief's erect bearing, I learned later, carried over from service with U.S. forces in the Spanish-American War, in which he lost an eye. He belonged to the American Legion and most of the time wore a legionnaire's hat cocked at a rakish angle. He had had a better home before the war, but when his pension checks stopped, he had sold it.

In the front room we sat down cross-legged on a beautiful mat used only for visitors. His motherly-looking wife brought in betel nut for us to chew. As we talked, I brought up religion so I could show my knowledge of the Koran. My familiarity with the Moro bible amazed him, as it had other Moros. Like them, he commented on my Arabic-appearing beard and believed I was part Arabian.

In a while the chief's fierce-looking bodyguard sat down and chewed betel nut with us. He had left his beautiful wife in the kitchen helping the chief's wife and daughter, Conchia. Something was bothering the guard, and I suspected I had caused his irritation in some way. I stayed alert to his every move while trying to look relaxed.

Thereafter I stopped often to chat with the Moro chief, hoping to catch a glimpse of Conchia, who was even more beautiful than the bodyguard's wife. But the bodyguard continued to be uneasy in my presence. Moro religion and custom prevented me from getting acquainted with Conchia without her parents' consent. The suitor bargains with the parents for the dowry payment before even talking to the daughter. The amount paid by the husband could range from a small sum to several thousand pesos (up to $1,000 in 1941 U.S. money). The girl accepts her fate with little bitterness — one of the customs that make her almost a slave.

I said nothing of my interest in Conchia, but everything I noticed made me more interested — her appearance, manner, and charm while she mended clothes and did other household duties. Although we did not talk, I would exchange wistful smiles with her when her parents weren't watching or seemed not to be. She was of medium height and perfect in figure and poise. She had clear, light olive complexion and long, black hair, loosely knotted in a simple upswept style. Her clothes did not completely cover her body, and only enhanced her appeal.

Her father grew to like me so well that he wanted to adopt me as his son, since his had been killed by the Japs. I tried to pass this off lightly but then realized he was serious and would be offended if I refused. Furthermore, being close to an influential Moro chief might save my life if I were cut off from my outfit — a strong possibility since at the bakery I was some distance from the 14th Squadron camp. In addition, I had seriously thought of staying in the Philippines after the war and becoming a plantation owner. For these reasons I accepted the chief's offer, but did not mention it to any American — to avoid ridicule from my buddies and reprimands from officers.

A day or two after this decision, I got up the courage to tell the chief and his wife that they had a beautiful daughter. I glanced toward the kitchen, where Conchia and the guard's wife were preparing lunch. Conchia's parents showed no surprise, and their thanks amazed me. By chance the guard's wife had heard my praise of Conchia but thought I was talking about her. Her husband noticed the flush of joy on his wife's face and harshly scolded her and scowled angrily at me. Suddenly I realized the source of my earlier unease about his attitude: He was extremely jealous and feared I would attract his wife.

The chief and his wife smoothed things over, but I decided to let things cool off. I had skipped visiting them only a couple days when the chief and his wife showed up at the bakery with two striking Moro rings.

They pressed them on me, declaring they would bring me good luck all my life. Then the old chief invited me to dinner that evening to talk over an important matter. I brought along some brightly colored clothes and two yellow T-shirts for Conchia and her mother — all confiscated from a Japanese store in town.

Before dinner, the chief showed me around his farm. He had an old truck, a couple horses, a few carabaos, goats, and chickens as well as some crude farm implements. He grew corn, beans, tomatoes, and potatoes. When asked, I told him I had thought a lot about staying in the Philippines after the war and would like to work with him to start a plantation. I thought to myself that I might stay, but whether I did or not, I would be safer when the Japs came if the Moros thought I planned to settle there. At my words about staying, the chief patted me on the back and said, "I am proud of my new son."

For dinner, the two of us sat on the mat in the front room, as usual. A short time later the chief's wife sat down beside us — something she had not done before. In a serious way the chief asked me if I were lonely. I knew what he was talking about. I admitted I was lonely and said I liked his daughter very much. In answer, he told me they had decided to do something unusual — to give their daughter to me in marriage without getting a dowry. The wedding would take place in the near future, and then I would be one of them. After the war we would all work together to develop a big plantation. I was struck dumb for a few moments, hardly believing my good fortune. Then I expressed my joy and told them I felt greatly honored. While supper was served, I sat dreaming of future romance and adventure that would replace my present loneliness. It was easy to think about staying in the Philippines because I had no girl in the U.S. and had been gone over three years.

When Conchia served me, she smiled roguishly but seemed a bit nervous. The dish that tasted best of all was rice baked with chopped tuna and highly seasoned with spices and red pepper. The parents told me that Conchia had made it especially for me. My presents overjoyed them. The guard's wife put on one of the T-shirts and paraded around the kitchen — she looked like an American sweater girl. I gave the guard a nice present. Now friendly, he offered to help me gather firewood for the bakery. Conchia's mother asked if I could get some lipstick and perfume for her. I promised to try and then thanked them for a great evening. For the first time, I shook hands with Conchia — a breach of custom even though we were engaged. Her mother gave me a motherly kiss. I saluted the chief and shook hands with the guard.

The next morning I was floating on clouds while doing my work.

Later I drove out to discuss the wedding with the chief. He agreed to my request that, to forestall Army interference, no American should be told about the wedding. We decided that the ceremony should take place soon. But first the high Moro sultan and priest had to grant permission. The family had to invite guests, arrange for music, and buy a whole carabao for the wedding feast. In the following days I became like a Moro, stopping every day to have Conchia cook my meals, mend my clothes, and wash them. I brought Conchia two bolts of fine cloth and her mother the requested lipstick and perfume — all from the Japanese store. As head of the bakery, I had access to its contents.

But Conchia had a request that was difficult to satisfy. It was the custom for the groom to secure a suit of clothes for one of the bride's near relatives as notice of a coming Moro marriage. The request was difficult because a suit wasn't to be had at any price. Then I recalled seeing a white sharkskin suit in the Japanese store — it was beautiful and the only one there. When I took it to Conchia, the family thought there wasn't anything I couldn't do.

The Japs were getting closer as the wedding date neared. Captain Navin, who had been promoted to major to give him better treatment if captured, moved his troops elsewhere. Sgt. Manook also moved with his Bolo Battalion. Navin and I had a few bites together before we bade each other farewell and good luck. Manook and I had a last drink and resolved to get together later to fight the Japs as guerrillas. If I was cut off from my outfit, I was to stay with Moro friends until Manook came for me. At the 14th Squadron camp Sgt. Chandler told me I should be ready to come when the 14th moved. I would be notified.

My talk with Chandler reminded me I was in the Army — I hated to think what would happen if I got married. Also I wondered if I really loved Conchia. Maybe I was just lonesome. If I married some nice girl in the U.S., I would always have this Moro affair on my mind. If I had children with Conchia, they would not have a chance if I left them behind. If I brought them back to the U.S. they would be outcasts. How would God accept my Moro marriage to a girl of another religion?

Yet when I tried to decide to give it all up, it wasn't all that easy. I knew of several incidents in which the Moros had punished or killed for offenses less than mine would be. Another drawback would be the lack of Moro support — or even betrayal — if I were cut off from my outfit during the Japanese advance. I thought of Conchia's feelings too. I needed a miracle.

I prayed for guidance. Just two mornings before the ceremony, as I baked the daily supply of bread for the troops, my mind was churning more violently than ever. That noon I drove the bread up to the camp, as usual. I was surprised to see soldiers loading trucks and dismantling the motor pool repair shop. Sgt. Chandler came over and said, "This is your last delivery, Vic. Get ready to move out with us tomorrow. The Japs are coming." My miracle had happened. Chandler told me to load my truck with essentials, dismiss my Filipino helpers, and return to camp at sundown. I hurried back to the bakery and packed the truck, aided by my unhappy helpers. The young Chinese mestizo took the breakup of our bakery team the hardest, and I hated to say goodbye to him — he had been especially helpful and loyal on the job. But that was an easy farewell.

At 5 P.M. I headed for Conchia's house. At first they thought I had come to get married ahead of time. When I told them the bad news, Conchia's mother began to cry. She held my hand and told me she hoped no harm would come to me. The old Moro chief told me he had been a soldier and understood that duty came first. He wished me luck and hoped I would return soon. He was going to evacuate his family soon and then join the Bolo Battalion to die fighting if necessary. Then I turned to Conchia. She just stared at me. I felt as if her eyes were looking through mine, trying to read my very soul to discover whether I loved her or not. I couldn't stand her gaze any longer so I whispered goodbye and kissed her hand. I got in my truck and started off. As I waved, Conchia waved back with a bright silk handkerchief, and kept staring after me. Her mother was still crying while the old chief saluted. They disappeared in the dust thrown up from my truck. I never saw them again but often have relived our parting, especially the image of beautiful Conchia staring into my eyes.

12

Bacolod Grande

April 20–26, 1942

My next stop was our camp outside Malabang, where 1st Sgt. Chandler greeted me with news that we were heading for an important new assignment to the north, on the west shore of Lake Lanao. After Chandler saw that the squadron was about ready for the move, he told the boys he was taking the squadron records and going ahead with me. That made them laugh. They said, "You'll never make it in that old truck." But Chandler shot back, "I'll leave it to Mapes. He'll make it." Then Chandler climbed in and sat beside me with his sawed-off shotgun. Bertha, the squadron's pet monkey, leaped into his lap. The little spider monkey had been jumping around with excitement, not wanting to be left behind.

At first the road was deeply rutted and upgrade. Then as we drove into darkness and our descent toward Lake Lanao, we had easier going. I liked having my good friend Chandler with me. We stayed ahead of our convoy and stopped at Ganasi to wait for our boys. I drove alongside some trucks that had gone ahead with malaria patients and helped make them comfortable for the rest of the trip. When the rest of the convoy caught up, the boys were surprised to see me already there in my old truck.

Lt. Doe decided that Palmer and I should go ahead to Dansalan for more detailed orders while the convoy followed more slowly. My buddies still kidded that my truck would break down before we got there. But they were wrong again — we had no trouble reaching Dansalan. After getting the orders, we came back across the Agusa River to Camp Keithley and waited until the boys pulled in. Before we all bunked down, some sailors from the Patrol Torpedo (PT) boats dropped by. They had been sent to operate PT boats on Lake Lanao to deprive enemy use of seaplanes on the lake and protect the large Navy PBY flying boats that were expected to come down for refueling. One well-built sailor, Bill Johnson, entertained Palmer and me with sea stories until everyone around us had fallen asleep.

Palmer and I stayed on guard duty all night and then got breakfast for the boys before we roused them at 4 A.M. They hurriedly ate boiled eggs and drank black coffee, and then we headed back south toward Malabang. At daylight we stopped at a large Moro village right on the lake and were ordered to make camp in a coffee grove.

Staying on watch all night may have triggered a bad attack of malaria in Sgt. Palmer, a veteran mess sergeant of ten years' service. That left me to oversee preparation of breakfast in the coffee grove 100 feet from the main road. I had the men set up field ranges and serving tables. Soon all was shipshape — the mess crew knew how to set up a kitchen by this time.

Our campsite stood in the middle of the property of an important Moro chief, who was mayor of the adjacent village. Our CO, Lt. Doe, told us the importance of getting along with the Moros in the village called Bacolod Grande, since we were all soon to be fighting Japs. The mayor would furnish men to guard our camp and equipment. But being close to the village and in the chief's valuable coffee grove brought problems.

The first difficulty arose as we drove our mess truck off the main road toward the kitchen site. Angry shouts stopped our driver but only after he had motored over several ancient graves. We had driven through a grave-yard where generations of the important families of Bacolod Grande were buried. We apologized, but now and then a forgetful Yank would tread on a grave and cause more turmoil. Or a soldier would accidentally damage or destroy a coffee tree. The owner-chief would immediately appear and had to be appeased with an elaborate apology. It happened more than once and caused great embarrassment.

After dark, nearly half the male population of the village carried out the chief's promise to guard the camp. They would stand all night and most of the day a short distance from our kitchen and camp — just staring at us with their mouths open. Neither rain, sun, insects, hunger, thirst, or fatigue bothered them as long as they could watch. They crowded into the kitchen and got in everyone's way. When they tampered with equipment, I got angry and tried to move them back with the help of my boys. We succeeded, but they were resentful and moved back very slowly, each with an awful scowl on his face. But next day they would push closer again.

We didn't trust the regular guards furnished by the chief but didn't know how to tell them we didn't need them. They thought they were quite important and deserved great respect for guarding the camp. They expected more service from the kitchen than our own soldiers, demanding coffee at any hour day or night. Nevertheless, they fell asleep while on guard duty and we missed items from the kitchen.

On the other hand, the Moros let us sleep wherever there was space in the village. It was no longer crowded because many women and children had been evacuated. A large frame building with a tin roof was soon filled with GIs, who had been getting wet daily because we were in the rainy season. Kukie, the squadron drunk, and his drinking buddy burst in one evening after too much tuba and gin and woke everyone up. The complaints that followed caused 1st Sgt. Chandler to declare, "Whoever is close to those soreheads should knock hell out of them when they come in like that." Chandler seldom showed so much aggravation — his responsibility for keeping us on good terms with the Moros may have put him on edge.

Some officers lived in Moro houses while others lived in the command post close to the road. Two men slept in our chow truck as guards. It was full of canned food that we had saved since our arrival on Mindanao. It was our last reserve, packed and ready to go at a moment's notice. Once some Moro kids sneaked up and got a few cans before being noticed, but our guards didn't shoot at them — nothing would be gained by raising the ire of the villagers.

At first I slept in a pup tent near the kitchen. Then I suggested to my buddy, Vergil Haifley, that we make rough beds under a Moro house. Verge, a short and opinionated son of an Army captain, was willing to try anything. Sleeping there among the chickens kept us dry during rain, but the bamboo-strip floor squeaked whenever the Moros walked around over our heads. Worse, loose dirt dropped on us through cracks in the floor, so we spread a piece of canvas over our heads. Yet it was easy for us both to put up with living in the village because we were fascinated by the Moros. However, we did not sleep under the house for long.

At first I had been so busy at the mess kitchen that I put off repeated invitations to visit a nearby Moro house. But one day I finally told the Moro messenger who had again come for me to wait until I finished my work. He was still there after several hours so I followed him to a substantial Moro home. There an old white-haired Moro chief greeted me. Years before, he had been mayor of Bacolod Grande. He asked if I recognized him. I recalled his face but could not remember where I'd seen him, even when he told me I had done him a great favor. Then he reminded me of the time he had stopped at my bakery in Malabang, exhausted and hungry. I had fed him, let him stay in my hotel room, and next morning driven him out to the Bolo Battalion headquarters.

I had forgotten, but the old gentleman insisted he was going to square things. He proudly introduced me to his two wives, son, and a beautiful daughter, who seemed to like me at first sight. Yet he did not seem too pleased at the way we looked at each other. He went on to tell me that while in Bacolod Grande I was to stay in one of his houses. It stood on stilts at the lake's edge and came with a canoe. He promised that each day someone would come over to see if I needed anything.

As I was leaving, he gave me a big bunch of bananas, three chickens, and two dozen eggs. To my surprise, he now seemed pleased by his daughter's smiles at me and invited me to visit again. I thanked him but explained how busy I was as mess sergeant. I said to myself, "Don't get into another situation like you did in Malabang." I thanked the chief wholeheartedly for the gifts and use of the house. Remembering Verge Haifley, I let the chief know I would have a housemate. That day we moved in and found the Moros had cleaned up the bamboo dwelling and neatly patched it. Our outrigger canoe was tied to a stone pier.

As I had told the old Moro, I was really busy at this time. My crew and I set up the squadron kitchen, dug a garbage pit, and provided for sterilization of cooking utensils and mess kits. A major problem was water — twice a day I sent someone to a spring near Ganasi at the south end of the lake. These trips passed through areas that enemy planes patrolled so we had to drive off the road at times. At Ganasi I arranged for the Filipino bakers to give us bread on a regular basis.

The 14th Squadron now gave full effort to receive the Navy PBY flying boats, which we were to refuel for their onward flight to Corregidor, the island off Bataan peninsula to which General MacArthur's forces had retreated. The planes were to deliver medical supplies and take out nurses and Navy officers before the expected surrender there. Our men were building camouflaged hangars along the shore to conceal the PBYs.

Navy PBY flying boats were used extensively for supply runs to besieged Corregidor. (National Air and Space Museum, Smithsonian Institution [SI Neg. No. A-42511].)

Others collected the last of the high-octane fuel and hid it in various places to keep it from fifth columnists.

As the kitchen work began to go more smoothly, Haifley and I enjoyed the comfort of our house. We built rough beds and fixed a place for cooking. When we were off duty, we swam and bathed. Moros would bring us roast chicken and fried rice. When we were full of food, we lay on our beds and gazed through the side window to watch two pretty, half-naked girls pounding rice under the house next door. Their graceful bodies moved rhythmically with each stroke. Then we turned our heads to look through another window and admire the expanse of Lake Lanao. When we became drowsy, we crawled under mosquito nets and listened to the gentle waves lapping against the pier and the sigh of cool wind through overhanging palm trees. Our cares seemed far away. The Moros treated me better than any of the U.S. officers. My earlier kindness to the old Moro had paid off in a big way.

On a trip to Dansalan my missionary friends there gave me a good book on Moro people and their religion. I learned that Bacolod Grande was very old and had been a Moro stronghold against the Spaniards and, much later, against the Americans. The Bacolod Moros had a bloody past and still had reputations as fierce fighters. But they were very friendly and kind to us despite a few differences, which we resolved peacefully. Bacolod Grande now was mainly a permanent resort for Moros of inherited wealth who had large landholdings elsewhere that were worked by dependent Moros. I could understand why the resident Moros had fought so fiercely to keep their village. Because of the lake breezes and abundance of fresh fruit and vegetables, I came to love the place too. I believe that the Moros' religion also helped explain their preservation of a way of life through many generations and their willingness to protect it. In fact, a large mosque stood in the center of the village.

In our house by the lake I was again separated from the rest of the squadron so Haifley and I kept our packs, guns, and ammunition ready for a quick getaway by canoe. If need be, we would join Moro guerrilla forces.

I had less time relaxing in our house after another attack of malaria almost killed Sgt. Palmer, the senior cook. Now as mess sergeant, I had responsibility for feeding our 14th Squadron as well as the 30th Squadron, which was also working on the PBY shelters. The PT boat men were working on the lake as well, and would come to the kitchen day and night with huge appetites. Filipinos stopped to eat on their way southward to the front line. Daily flights of Japanese aircraft kept the mess crew jittery, but no bombs were dropped, possibly because of our location close to the Moro village.

My helpers, Jerry Coty, Ishmael Gudgeon, and a man we shall call Pvt. Kilroy did much of the kitchen work while I had to go for water daily and pick up bread at different places. The boys worried about me when I was late getting back. I often went to Dansalan to get more of the items rationed by the Army Supply Depot there. I said I needed more than enough for the 14th and 30th Squadrons because of Filipino soldiers passing through. On this basis I succeeded in drawing some extra supplies, which I took to the food market with the idea of trading them for food we needed more.

At the market I had already become acquainted with Mr. Lutz, a shrewd, friendly merchant who was half-German and half-Filipino. His prices for vegetables were too high so I tried to buy directly from the little farms. But the farmers informed me that Mr. Lutz had already contracted for their crops. Hence I had to deal with him directly. As we became friendly, I got some good trades for sugar and meal in exchange for some of the less desirable items I had drawn form the Army Supply Depot. The Army inspected Lutz's records so I signed for only the amounts of food he was permitted to sell me. We both stuck out our necks to feed my men.

Mr. Lutz invited me to elaborate dinners with 15 guests or more — young men, girls, and merchants from the community. Servants brought Chinese, Filipino, Spanish, and American food while musicians played background music. After dinner the host passed out expensive cigars — a great treat. But the fear of the approaching Japs pervaded the town — many residents had already evacuated. Lutz had chosen and supplied a hideout for his family. He invited me to join him there. While in Dansalan I also visited my missionary friends. They always tried to help me, and I used their money to buy meat for them from Mr. Lutz, who had cornered the supply and sold mostly to the Army.

My job as mess sergeant became more hectic because of our all-out preparations to service the PBYs on their rescue mission before Japanese forces reached Lake Lanao— they had already landed 35 miles to the south, near Parang in Cotabato Province. Everyone was busy and hungry, and it was becoming more difficult to get food at Dansalan, even with the help of Mr. Lutz. The hungriest men I fed were the PT-boat sailors who were fixing and operating launches on the lake. Sadly enough, they seemed to use their "control of the sea" to divert food I sent out to our work details at the hangars. I believed the sailors were satisfying their own huge appetites rather than delivering the food I sent. But I had no proof, and our workers who claimed they didn't get their chow could have exaggerated. Nevertheless, there was a lot of ill feeling. The food shortage reached the point where we had to decide whether or not to use the emergency rations on the chow truck. Some wanted to eat it all up while others, including the officers, wanted to hold it for battle situations. In the end, we used supplies from the truck sparingly.

One evening after dark, not long before the PBYs were to arrive, Lt. Doe received a puzzling phone call. The caller, apparently a senior American officer, ordered Doe to have the lights turned on at the Malabang airstrip. The 14th Squadron had moved from Malabang some days before, but we had left Lt. Jacques Jamal and a few men at the airstrip. Lt. Doe said he would turn on the lights and hung up. But Doe hesitated to contact Jamal because the caller had not identified himself, although he sounded confident and authoritative. Lt. Doe told me his doubts. I insisted he should do nothing — the call must be an enemy scheme since an authentic order would come from a known superior. Doe was convinced, and the airstrip remained dark.

At this time our pilots at Bacolod Grande were sent to the Del Monte Airfield south of Cagayan to be flown to Australia because of their value as flyers. Lt. Doe was not a pilot and had to stay with us.

13

PBY Flying Boats

April 26–29, 1942

We still needed more fuel for the PBYs that were soon expected, so I volunteered to make a run to Dansalan for gas. My Filipino companion and I took turns driving and looking out for low-flying planes, which forced us to drive our old plantation truck off the road several times. When we reached Army Headquarters in Dansalan, a GI in a well-pressed uniform escorted me upstairs to the office of Major Samuel Forte, an infantry officer, recently assigned to the Lake Lanao area. I walked up to his desk, saluted, and handed him my requisition.

Forte didn't say a word but looked me over from head to foot. I wore muddy, scuffed-up shoes and a patched uniform. I had a shaggy beard and carried my prized M-1 rifle. Fort kept staring and then asked to see my rifle. He barked, "Why haven't you given up that rifle to the infantry by now?" I told him I had found it in a deserted barracks after the Japanese attack on Clark Field and that Major Emmett O'Donnell had permitted me to keep it. Then he growled, "Why don't you keep it clean?"

When he read the request for gas from our commanding officer, Lt. Doe, he raised hell and declared we could "rot" before we got gas from him. I left in a hurry and returned to Bacolod Grande. Lt. Doe was furious. I learned that he and Major Forte had had several heated arguments about what the Air Corps should do. For one thing, Forte, an infantry officer, believed that camaraderie between pilots and enlisted men was bad for discipline and should be stamped out. But time was running out for servicing the PBYs.

The Japanese forces that had landed south of us near Parang were stalled for a time by Filipino soldiers, but there were no American planes to oppose enemy aircraft. Filipino soldiers continued to pass through Bacolod Grande on their way to the front.

The day after I returned from Dansalan, two PBY flying boats settled down on Lake Lanao and taxied into the docking spaces we had built along the shore. Our men brought large branches out of the jungle and covered the great planes with greenery, working quickly because of the possibility that enemy aircraft might chance by.

As we began to refuel the PBYs, the increased boat traffic irritated a Moro chief. He stationed himself on his canoe with loaded gun in the path of our boats and threatened to fire if we did not stay off his private fishing grounds. Our men wanted to shoot him but finally decided to simply avoid that stretch of water. On shore Moro landowners threatened our men who were setting up machine guns to fight off Japanese ground attacks. When we had to transport the high-octane gas across Moro property, we had to pay large amounts of emergency money or take a long way around. The men disliked the Moros more and more, but they had strict orders to avoid any confrontation because of the PBY effort.

While we refueled the planes, the pilots retired to the Dansalan Hotel for rest. I was sent after them to deliver a heavy briefcase that a pilot had left behind. I told the bellboy that I had something important for the pilots so he took me to them even though they had asked not to be disturbed. But the pilot was happy to get the case and asked me to sit on the bed and chat. I wished them luck on their flight north; and they said they'd need a lot of it. They were all volunteers because of the danger of landing and taking off in the waters off Corregidor. As I drove back to camp, I prayed for them and determined to do my part in preparing for their return to Lake Lanao.

After dark on April 28, the pilots warmed up the engines. The Navy launches towed the flying boats into deep water and churned up the placid surface so the aircraft could take off more easily. The planes struggled into the air after a long run, circled to gain altitude, and headed north. That day the Japs were celebrating the Emperor's birthday by continuous bombing of the American holdouts on Corregidor. The attacks left fires that were still burning when the waiting evacuees heard the friendly hum of the approaching PBYs. As usual, the Japs were not flying after sunset.

At 11 P.M. the ponderous craft swooped down close to Corregidor and taxied to shore in full view of the Japs on nearby Bataan. In 30 minutes, the cargo for Corregidor had been unloaded and 46 Navy officers, Army nurses, and a few civilian women had boarded. Then the PBY pilots gunned their engines and lifted off from the water with a roar. Not a shot was fired by the enemy. Flying south, the pilots encountered fog and were lost for a time. But when they flew clear of it, they recognized land forms under the starlit sky and were able to establish their location and take a new course.

The PBYs had not reached the lake by daybreak, as expected, so we began to worry. Then we heard a steady roar. They soon skimmed along the lake's surface and settled in the water short of their hidden hangars. I prepared food for the lucky passengers, who were being brought to our camp in outrigger canoes. We had coffee, coconuts, fried bananas, and hotcakes with weak syrup ready when they came ashore. Most were nurses in weak condition. There were also a few Navy officers and General Seals with his sick and elderly wife. We had forgotten that the women would need a little privacy, but we quickly screened off some space for them. They all enjoyed breakfast and said how glad they were to be there. Some noticed the dwellings of Bacolod Grande and remarked they hadn't seen Philippine village life before. Most were dressed in coveralls that were too large for them, but none seemed to care about appearance now. They were driven away to where they could rest while we prepared the PBYs for the flight to Australia.

After hours of intense effort, we had the planes ready, and the canoes took the passengers back to the flying boats. The long flight ahead required a maximum supply of fuel so the crew encouraged the passengers to discard all but essential belongings. Some of our men persuaded passengers to part with items such as candy, canned foods, and silk ladies' underwear, as well as captured Japanese flags and hara-kiri knives.

Finally, the first plane warmed up its engines while the Navy launches churned up the water. The heavily loaded plane lumbered along at full throttle but seemed stuck to the water long after the time needed for liftoff. I could only watch and pray until it broke water. Then the bulky craft seemed to take forever to rise more than a few yards. At last it circled higher and headed for Australia. Later we learned it carried two enlisted stowaways — one from Corregidor and one from Lake Lanao.

The second PBY soon headed toward the churned-up water for its takeoff, but it abruptly slowed and veered off course. A submerged rock had damaged one pontoon. The scared and downcast passengers disembarked. Among them, unbelievably, was our commanding officer, Lt. John Doe, who had stowed away in hopes of reaching Australia instead of staying with us to face the Japs. Now, even while griping about Lt. Doe, we bent all effort to get the second PBY airborne. We took the pontoon to our motor pool, where the men worked all night. They didn't even break for chow so I sent them food.

The next day, after the pontoon had been reinstalled, there was still some water in it so Doe went ashore for a pump. But just as he reached the water's edge with the pump, the plane roared down the lake and headed south. I rushed out of the kitchen — we had not expected a takeoff so soon. Lt. Doe stood gazing after the plane, pump at his feet. I have never seen such a bewildered and disappointed man. At that moment I couldn't help but feel sorry for him. I learned later that the plane had taken off in a hurry because the crew feared an immediate Japanese air attack — only the crew and a few officers were aboard, making for a relatively easy liftoff. The passengers from Corregidor, whom they had left, had a nervous and bumpy ride to Del Monte Air Field. From there, they hoped to be flown to Australia.

Our men working on the pontoon returned to Bacolod Grande exhausted and almost starved — they had gone without food for 36 hours. I had been sending meals out to them, but again we suspected the PT-boat men of satisfying their voracious appetites at the expense of the Air Corps. Some of our boys couldn't even eat right away, and did not recover for a day or so.

We discussed the two stowaways. Many thought "good riddance" because they couldn't be counted on in battle. As for Lt. Doe, some wished he had also escaped. But we all felt proud that the "Fighting 14" Bomb Squadron had gotten the two flying boats up to Corregidor and back to Australia.

14

A New
Commanding Officer
April 29 to May 3, 1942

We expected Corregidor to fall at any time, and close to us the Japs were occupying Malabang after their northward advance from Parang. At Malabang they had landed tanks near to where I used to swim, and where Conchia and her family lived. But I was sure my friends had evacuated into the hills. Japanese foot soldiers reached our airstrip soon after Lt. Jamal's detachment left — he and his men straggled into camp the day after the second PBY flew off. We learned that Major Navin's Filipino troops had been withdrawn from Malabang while some Filipino constabulary troops had faded into the hills. An artillery officer of the Filipino 81st Division, Captain A. H. Price, had fired at the enemy with two ancient 2.95 guns, but the Japs had outflanked him and almost captured his men; they escaped with weapons and ammunition but some men were killed.

In the confusion at Bacolod Grande, we almost shot one of our own men, a medic named McGuire. He had risked his life to drive a slow-moving bulldozer up to our camp from Malabang and was mistaken for a Jap when he suddenly came into sight. But he had not been a prime target for enemy aircraft. Instead Japanese pilots concentrated on automobiles, which were likely to carry officers. They had strafed several cars and almost killed several of General Fort's staff officers. Fort commanded all American and Filipino units in the area, including the 14th Squadron.

The second night after the last PBY had flown off, Haifley and I again went over plans for escape from our house by the lake. We talked with a few Moro friends about joining them in the village or paddling across the lake to meet them. Next morning I prepared breakfast for the camp and readied the kitchen equipment and food supplies to move on quick notice.

Meanwhile in Malabang the Japs took over American supply trucks. Disguised as Filipino drivers, they got past the defending Filipino guards. The sudden appearance of the enemy forced another withdrawal to a line near Lake Dupow. It was a small body of water, surrounded by steep mountains through which the road from Malabang followed a narrow pass northward. Captain Price had tried to slow the enemy below Lake Dupow by mining some bridges. But the charges were too damp, and the Japanese tanks lumbered across. Price was again almost cut off but withdrew safely to the new line.

More Filipino troops streamed southward through our camp to join the Filipinos trying to hold at Lake Dupow. At the same time wounded soldiers from the front reached us and were treated by Major Heidger. Some wounded arrived by boats manned by PT sailors, who were also busy hauling supplies on Lake Lanao.

Although I was in charge of the always-busy kitchen, I was sent south on an errand to Ganasi, close to the front, where I found the medics working beyond the limits of normal fatigue, seeming to draw on supernatural energy to treat the many wounded soldiers. I had hardly returned to camp when I was sent in the opposite direction, to Dansalan. In case of a sudden move, I instructed my mess crew on how to load the kitchen equipment and pack food supplies. I told Haifley to lay out my belongings at our house by the lake.

As I drove away, I sensed an end to the camp at Bacolod Grande and wondered if I would see my buddies again. Riding with me were my lanky, slow-talking kitchen helper, Pvt. Kilroy, and a wounded Filipino soldier who was going to the hospital in Dansalan. En route we met the usual enemy planes, which forced me to drive off the road a few times. We overtook Moro and Filipino families, leaving their homes laden with bundles of belongings. None asked for a ride. Some even gave the "V" sign. We met trucks of weary-looking Filipino soldiers, heading for the front.

I stopped at the Wattu motor pool for gas, where Major Heidger had set up a hospital with two medics. He had moved north from Bacolod Grande to be farther from the front and already had some patients. At Dansalan I took my Filipino to the emergency hospital, which was a converted schoolhouse full of badly wounded men, mostly Filipinos. Amputation patients were partially conscious, and they were screaming. It made my stomach turn, and I prayed for everlasting peace on Earth. Some of the 14th Squadron were there with malaria; others had been injured in accidents.

The wounded were glad to see Pvt. Kilroy and me, and devoured the food I gave them — they had not been eating well on Philippine rations. Fearing a Japanese breakthrough, several of them insisted on going back with me to the squadron. I couldn't refuse although I had no authority to take them. I found that the missionaries and local American civilians in Dansalan had all moved six miles into the hills to a refuge near Bubong that General Fort had long planned for them.

I picked up food supplies from Mr. Lutz and with Pvt. Kilroy hastened back down the road toward Bacolod Grande. I also had the malarial boys, but I left them at Wattu with Major Heidger and continued southward with a reluctant Kilroy. He said it was suicide — we would be killed. Nevertheless I pressed southward, bent on returning to camp as ordered.

My companion became more alarmed when we met some of our squadron heading away from the front in cars — they wouldn't even stop to tell us what was happening. Then 1st Sgt. Chandler came up from the south. He stopped and told me that he was now Lt. Chandler and commanded the 14th Squadron in place of Lt. Doe. Doe's old nemesis, Major Samuel Forte, who had recently turned down Doe's request for aviation gas, had broken Doe to the lowest enlisted rating because of his attempt to stow away on the PBY.

Chandler informed us that General Fort's defense line at Lake Dupow had not held. Chandler had orders to withdraw the squadron to Dansalan and await orders. I insisted on continuing south to Bacolod Grande to get my belongings and see about our emergency chow truck. Chandler said that was a good idea so I kept on with Kilroy, who now grumbled more than ever because we were moving toward the front while the squadron was moving to the rear.

At Bacolod Grande our old camp was almost deserted. I hurried to my house by the lake and found my personal belongings laid out for me as Haifley had promised. Some Moros asked if we were coming back to help them fight the Japs. I assured them we would. They insisted I should stay now, but I explained I had to remain with my American comrades. At the old kitchen site I picked up a few items and helped a few soldiers still there load supplies on our remaining trucks and helped get the emergency food truck started. At last we all headed for Dansalan, much to Pvt. Kilroy's relief.

We had hardly started north when we met Lt. Chandler and the rest of the squadron returning southward — General Fort had ordered us back to Bacolod Grande to make a stand because of the Japanese breakthrough at Lake Dupow. The men dreaded this idea. They had been trained for servicing and flying aircraft, not for infantry combat. The situation reminded us of Custer's last stand against the Sioux. Night had fallen when we reached Bacolod Grande. Chandler told us to be ready to move again soon and ordered everyone except the guards to turn in for the night because this might be the last good rest we would have in a long time.

But we could not sleep. Instead we began talking in low tones. Many promises were made that whoever survived would visit the families of their comrades who had fallen. Gradually talk died down, but I don't think many were sleeping. Each was thinking of what tomorrow might bring. Haifley and I slipped away to our house and found that everything I had not picked up that afternoon had been taken; we had hoped in particular to pick up the mosquito netting. We were just leaving when the friendly Moro chief next door invited us to stop by. We followed him into his dimly lit house, where he and his wife made a great effort to make us feel at home. They were glad to see the squadron back and thought the Yanks could stop the Japs from capturing their beloved Lake Lanao. We learned that more of the village's women and children had been sent to the hills and personal property had been hidden. The men planned to defend Bacolod Grande as long as possible and then burn their houses and retreat by canoe or jungle trails to hideouts from which they planned to wage guerrilla warfare. Haifley and I listened to their brave plans. They insisted that if things got too bad for us, we join them as leaders in their organization.

We finally talked ourselves out. The chief improvised a bed for us and sent for the mosquito netting that had been taken from our house. But our long talk with the Moro family had only given us more to think about and keep us awake. Fighting with the Moros in the hills might be worse than sticking with our outfit. On the other hand, after our outfit had been on the run for five months, we were now supposed to fight a battle we had little chance of winning — we might have a better chance of surviving with the Moros. But we decided nothing. The rest of the men had such thoughts, and Lt. Chandler knew it.

Next morning Chandler challenged us either to get ready to fight or grab our packs and take off with the Moros. In a way, all of us wanted to go, but none of us did. Like American soldiers through history who had stuck with their outfits, we could not desert our squadron. This unanimous decision to stay together gave us courage — we stood ready with weapons and packs to fight the enemy.

Chandler deployed us just south of Bacolod Grande in a line that extended from the lakeside road far back into the jungle toward the nearby mountains. Those near the road dug in and stood by with Molotov cocktails, which Captain Wyatt had passed out. They had been made with beer bottles, gasoline, pine tar, and wicks. Captain Wyatt took Knortz, Haifley, and a couple others toward the advancing Japs to mine the road and construct tank traps.

We stayed in our positions hour after hour, chilled by the damp air blowing in from the lake and under constant attack by mosquitoes. The continuous lapping of waves and sounds of birds and frogs bored us. But we were startled by the sudden rustling of the wind in the tree tops or underbrush, the scurry of a frightened animal, or falling limbs. Finally Chandler had someone relieve me so I could make some coffee for the boys. Working as fast as I could, I worried that the Japs would come before I finished.

About this time my helper, Kilroy, and another private were sent off in a truck to get something at the camp. Kilroy had been shaky during the return from Dansalan. When the two privates didn't return in a short time, we suspected we'd seen the last of them. Later we found the half-ton truck along the road. The two had taken to the hills — one died of malaria, and I never learned the fate of the other. Finally we were ordered to assemble on the road at once. The men were wet, muddy, chilled, and tense — a pathetic group.

Major Schroeder and Lt. Chandler told us they had orders for us to move south as far as we could before daylight to stall the Japs before they reached Bacolod Grande. After the retreat from Lake Dupow, General Fort was going to make another stand at Ganasi, a crucial Japanese objective. There the highway divided: One fork led northward along the west side of Lake Lanao past Bacolod Grande to Dansalan, and the other turned eastward along the south side to Lumbatan.

It was still dark when we climbed on our trucks and headed for Ganasi. Nobody cracked jokes because everybody expected the worst. My old truck seemed to be falling to pieces — it rattled so much the enemy could have heard us ten miles away. Without lights, the jolting made it difficult to stay on the rough road. Several soldiers rode with me, including our recent commanding officer, now Pvt. Doe, standing on the truck bed and holding onto the side to keep his balance — no longer able to sit by me and give orders or blame me if anything went wrong. Nobody would talk to him.

As we chugged along through the jungle, I thought how different war was from what I had expected. I remembered the parades of big guns, roaring tanks, and new GI trucks loaded with well-armed men and ammunition. Then I recalled my 23 months in Hawaii, where pilots flew hundreds of planes on daily practice operations and there were frequent alerts to maintain a high state of readiness. I could not relate those vivid memories to our present situation. Against the enemy's well-armed foot soldiers, some of our men had only .45 caliber automatic pistols with little ammunition while others had outdated Enfield rifles that were dangerous to fire because they might explode in the user's face. Our new commanding officer, Lt. Chandler, had only a shotgun. Worse, we had no planes to attack the enemy and protect us from strafing and bombing. We also lacked tanks to deal with theirs.

15

Ganasi

May 3–4, 1942

As day was breaking, we reached the southern end of Lake Lanao. A group of General Fort's troops lay exhausted by the side of the road. Some were badly wounded. Others were moving toward the front. We drove ahead slowly, expecting the fireworks to start at any time. We felt bitter at the thought of being thrown into a losing battle. Dawn had turned into bright sunlight when we came upon Col. Robert Vesey, who commanded a regiment in Fort's 81st Division, and Navy Lt. Commander Strong. Both stood by the road, covered with mud and badly in need of sleep. In tired voices they ordered us to park at an old Philippine camp at the edge of Ganasi. I had climbed down from the driver's seat to direct traffic just as the firing started. In the excitement, a soldier jumped out of our truck almost on top of me. His rifle smacked my mouth and knocked my gold bridge loose. He apologized but got away so fast I couldn't tell who it was. I put the bridge back — it hurt for a while, but I had plenty of other things to think about and soon forgot it.

That morning, most of General Fort's Filipino 81st Division and assorted Air Corps soldiers had crowded into Ganasi, a small village that was confined on three sides by steep, jungle-covered mountains and Lake Lanao on the northern side. Fort's badly equipped soldiers were hollow-eyed and looked hungry and exhausted. Officers deployed some in ambush and shifted others to new places. Some movements were orderly, some not.

I had barely gotten my bridge back in my mouth when Sgt. John Spruill broke his leg jumping off a truck. Bill Knortz and I ran over and found him jerking around in pain. I pulled some split bamboo strips off a fence, which we used as splints. Knortz and I put him in a car heading north with others wounded from earlier fighting. Some of our squadron, including Lt. Chandler, had volunteered for advance scouting patrols and had left. Captain Wyatt had taken others to blow up advancing Japanese tanks.

Since our outfit hadn't eaten for 36 hours, I started to prepare something before the fighting began. I thought it might be the last meal for some. As I hurried about, we noticed a strange-looking Moro, chanting loudly and waving a kris in a circle. Looking closer, I realized he was the sultan I had met at the Bolo Battalion headquarters at Barira — I had visited there when I ran the bakery at Malabang. The sultan had strong religious and patriotic feelings and told me then he would die defending his country if he had to. This calm, peaceful-appearing Moro chief had become a raging savage. His face was painted, and his eyes looked like he had been taking dope. He wore an odd, brightly-colored costume and moved with slow, jerky steps while loudly praying to Allah — declaring he would die fighting the Japs but would go to heaven. He shouted for others to join him. Even though we had been friendly before, I felt uneasy when he moved closer to my truck. Could he have decided that Americans were the cause of the Japanese invasion? If so, Americans should be punished, and right now my helpers and I were the nearest ones to attack. I told our men nearby to keep an eye on him and riddle him with everything they had, if necessary.

Then Captain Katz, who had installed me as the baker at Malabang, came by and asked, "What are you trying to do, Vic?" I explained, but Katz shook his head and declared, "This is no place for an old worn-out truck. It's a dangerous place to fix food — it's likely to become a bloody battlefield at any minute. Move the truck back and set up a kitchen as fast as you can." I drove back with my helpers, Coty and Puppario, and Sgt. Palmer, who was ordered back with me because of his malaria — he seemed almost dead.

We passed hundreds of Moros from the Bolo Battalion going to the front, armed with homemade shotguns and krises. There were also truckloads of Filipino soldiers moving toward Ganasi. It was hard for me to squeeze back north in the opposite direction. Ganasi already seemed crowded. I thought a general retreat on this narrow road would be impossible — our forces would have to fight to the death or be pushed into Lake Lanao. We had just passed the spring where I got water for our camp at Bacolod Grande when I heard firing and saw Japanese patrols at some distance in the mountains. More Filipino soldiers moved past us toward the front.

I hated to leave my comrades at Ganasi but felt safer where I was. Nevertheless, I was still determined to prepare food for them. Behind a low range of hills I came upon a small stream running through a gully close to a bamboo thicket. I drove the truck off the road, turned it around for a quick getaway and covered it with bamboo branches. My boys and I heated GI cans of water on the gas burner to make coffee and got out the bread that was left. We had eggs ready to scramble. When the enemy planes flew over, we ducked for cover. From the other side of the ridge, we heard firing of small arms, machine-guns, and mortars that was becoming louder and more frequent. Still more Filipino troops passed on their way to the battle.

We sat tight, wondering how the battle was going and not knowing whether we would be sent forward with food, be ordered to fight, or be withdrawn. We feared the Japs would break through and discover us. Ages seemed to pass while we listened to, but could not see, the battle going on close by. An enemy plane kept circling over our heads, but we stayed hidden under the bamboo thicket. The noise of battle grew louder. Trucks continued to pass on the road nearby. I said to my helpers, "I didn't think we had that many troops to fight here." I heard a rifle fire close by, and mortar shells dropped near us. Then we could see Japanese patrols up on the mountainside coming toward us in a flanking movement. I worried that Japanese tanks could destroy our truck or blow up the road and cut off our retreat. By late morning I decided to move, orders or no orders.

We threw most of the equipment and chow into the truck and cleared away the camouflage. Then Jerry Coty ran out to the road and gave me the all-clear signal. Frank Puppario stood by with his rifle while I raced the motor and took off in a roar over the rocky ground toward the road. Palmer was so sick he could barely hold on. The roadway was filled with so much dust I could barely make out the truckloads of troops, which now headed northward away from the battle. Many sweating soldiers were also retreating on foot at a slow, dogged pace. Apparently the Japs had broken our defense line at Ganasi so our men were falling back before the enemy could complete their outflanking movements. Along the way our forces blocked the road and blew up bridges to hinder pursuit, even if some of our men were left on the other side. We were about the last truck to get out before the Japs closed in. I drove carefully but fast while Puppario and Coty watched for planes.

The old truck seemed to be on its last trip — rattling more than ever, sputtering, missing, and heating up badly. It nearly stopped on the upgrades. Japs were advancing on nearby hills while their planes flew over us at will. We climbed to where we could look down on Lake Lanao. It was covered with boats and launches heading for the middle — a sure sign that our troops had been driven out of Ganasi. Launches ran zigzag courses to avoid bombs that enemy planes splashed among them. The Japs were also firing from shore, and it looked like they had captured some boats from which they were firing on our craft, as well as on men in the water. We proceeded, but after coughing around a few more curves, our truck stopped completely. Mortar shells were dropping around us, but I decided to fix the truck rather than take off on foot. Coty stood guard while I unscrewed the gas line — I suspected it was stopped up. Then Puppario blew it out with the tire pump. After we put it back together, the truck started and we were on our way.

We soon entered dense jungle, which deadened the sound of battle behind. We were all alone until we rounded a sharp curve and came face to face with the muzzle of a sub-machine gun in the hands of a swarthy fellow in blue fatigues. He yelled and waved his gun. Was he friend or foe? They boys grabbed their weapons and crouched down. I thought he might be a Filipino third lieutenant in tattered uniform but suspected he could be a Jap in disguise. He told us he was Stephen Laro, an American officer of the 81 Division, who had lost his troops following enemy mortar fire. Some of them had faded into the jungle and others had been killed. Laro was boiling mad. He planned to guard the road at this bend and fight it out with the Japs single-handed if he couldn't rally some men retreating from Ganasi. I reported on what I had seen along the road, and he ordered me to proceed beyond Bacolod Grande to Major Heidger's latest emergency hospital, where I could leave Palmer. Then I was to find all the men I could and to return with them. I greatly admired this brave, fiery officer.

I drove on as fast as the old buggy would go. We rounded the bend where the squadron had dug in the night before to stop the Japanese tanks. Now Filipino troops were putting a 2.95 mountain gun into position under the direction of Captain Price. He told me to take Palmer on to the hospital and return as soon as I could. Then we drove on to our old campsite at Bacolod Grande, where four of our men were trying to start two trucks. One was the emergency chow truck we had left hidden there. After we got it started, I told the three chow truck drivers to take it up to the Wattu Motor Pool and stand by for orders. Then we got the other truck started. Its driver also headed for Wattu with a load of high-octane gas, having already received such orders. I started up again and soon came upon another truck stopped along the road; two of our men were trying to start it. I yelled and waved as I passed. A staff car with several officers overtook us and passed but soon came back and headed for Bacolod Grande. Another staff car soon followed south with several soldiers from our squadron. I didn't know why they were going toward the Japs, but I had little hope the Japs could be stopped after what I had seen.

Soon I arrived at a small constabulary barracks on the lake's edge. Inside, Major Heidger and a few medics were changing it into a rough hospital, having relocated from Wattu. After I brought in Palmer, Heidger ordered me and my boys to help him — to forget the orders Captain Price had given us. We worked hard with the medics, who told us we were much needed. Casualties were coming in and hundreds more were expected. Explosions sounded from the direction of Bacolod Grande, and we saw bomb splashes out on the lake among more fleeing launches. Observation planes were slowly flying over our scattered troops to signal enemy troops where to direct their mortar fire. Then a formation of bombers flew directly overhead — we were certain they had noticed our trucks and would destroy the place. We fled into the brush and watched several formations drone by. They paid no attention to our trucks and makeshift hospital and flew on toward Dansalan. Soon we heard dull explosions and saw smoke rising to the north. The Japs were probably going after Camp Keithley, which had not been disturbed since the December 1941 attack.

Major Heidger ordered me to get on the truck and watch for the enemy with field glasses. I had not scanned the hills very long before I spotted Japanese patrols advancing with light machine guns. Shortly, our bedraggled troops came up the road and struggled on toward Dansalan. I climbed down from the truck to help settle the wounded, who were coming by truck and on foot. Major Heidger told me to stand by — he wanted to move the wounded to Dansalan. Meanwhile some of my comrades from the 14th Squadron were trudging by. I called to them to stop for a bite to eat — I still had some chow I had fixed that morning. Some kept going, saying they had no appetite for anything. But others stopped and gulped down some food. They said we'd be lucky to come out of this mess alive. A few of the retreating men told me I had better leave while I could. This advice hit home — I had waited long enough.

I motioned Coty and Puppario to get in, and I drove off, feeling a little guilty about not following Heidger's orders to stand by. On the way to Dansalan I picked up a few exhausted Filipino soldiers who didn't even have guns. In the growing darkness I failed to see a large rut in the road. The jolt killed the motor, and I couldn't get it started again because a short had run down the battery. While I was fussing under the hood, the Filipino soldiers I had picked up took off. I was about to give up when another Filipino came along and offered to help. He was barefoot and his only weapon was a bolo. I didn't recognize him at first but then realized he was the neat, well-equipped officer I had known at Malabang. He didn't know me either, then we both remembered each other at the same time.

He told me that Japanese mortars and machine-gun fire had killed most of his men. His rifle had been knocked from his hands, and he and others had run for their lives. He hoped the Japs wouldn't be able to occupy the interior mountains of Mindanao because that was where he was going. He suggested I come with him. I wanted to go but couldn't — feeling I would be deserting my friends. He had been working with me as we talked, but we had had no success so after a friendly farewell the Filipino officer walked on.

I was still trying to start the truck when I heard a vehicle approaching from the south. It came to a full stop beside me. In the darkness I didn't know who it was but then recognized Captain Price and his gun crew, whom I'd run into earlier in the day. They still had their 2.95 mountain gun. Price was a ghost of his former self — his clothes torn, his eyes bloodshot, his beard dirty and stubby, and legs swollen and cracked. He smelled of powder and seemed to exist only by supernatural power. In a low and hollow voice he told me he had almost been killed or captured several times. He had lost some of his best men and his other big mountain gun. It was the most humiliating time of his life to be shoved around by those yellow so-and-sos. He hadn't slept for so long that he felt numb. I got some food off the truck, but he wasn't hungry — he had gone so long without eating that his stomach had shrunk. I insisted, though, and he ate a little. He thanked me, and then I asked him how I should handle being stalled on the road with Puppario and Coty. The captain was on his way to General Fort's mountain headquarters above Bubong to get orders but insisted on towing us as far as Dansalan. I told him to go along without us — his efforts were too valuable to be slowed down. Nevertheless, his crew took a gun tow-rope and hooked his truck to mine. While under tow, it was a job steering on the winding road in the darkness. Once I nearly tipped over.

It was just getting light on the day after the retreat from Ganasi when the wreckage of Camp Keithley came into sight. All that remained were smoldering ruins of barracks and other buildings. Across the Agusa River, beautiful Dansalan looked even worse. Blackened heaps showed where shops had been. The big building owned by Mr. Lutz was gone — only his safe had defied the fire. Captain Price left me where some of my buddies had gathered near the missionary houses and continued on to General Fort's headquarters in the hills. I joined my friends, and enjoyed seeing them as much as if we'd been separated for two months rather than 24 hours. I found Lt. Chandler, Bill Knortz, and others from the 14th Squadron, as well as a few from other outfits.

In a short time I learned what had happened since I had left them at Ganasi to fix chow. The Japs launched a heavy offense with tanks that fired on our troops crowded into the level space at Ganasi. Next, Japanese patrols with light machine guns and rifles fired down from the hills and lobbed mortar fire as directed by a light plane. Our troops held for a time but scattered when they realized they were being cut off. During this time, ex-Lieutenant, now Private Doe took off and hadn't been seen since.

I learned the fate of the Moro chief who had changed into a mad warrior in Ganasi. He had climbed on top of a Japanese tank that was firing on our troops and swung his kris on the tank's turret until the blade shattered into pieces. Then he beat on the tank with the handle until gunfire knocked him to the ground. Yet he still crawled after the tank on his hands and knees until he fell down dead.

My friends told me that our emergency food truck I had recently sent to Wattu with three men had been lost. They were not the best men for the job — the squadron drunk Kukie, Kukie's drinking buddy, and a big, fat, lazy Texan. They had not stopped at Wattu but took off for Del Monte Airfield. Fate had mocked us by letting us keep our valuable chow truck until we really needed it and then having it taken away by our own men.

It was late in the afternoon when Lt. Chandler told us we were going to leave at once for General Fort's mountain headquarters near Bubong. I asked what I should do about my wreck of a truck. Chandler decided to tow it with his big GI truck — my kitchen equipment could be useful. As we moved out in the growing darkness, rain came hurtling down on us.

16

Major Heidger

May 4–5, 1942

Lt. Chandler's little convoy headed in the pelting rain toward General Fort's mountain headquarters. We followed a road that switched back and forth above the lake for two miles or so before we turned and climbed steeply among the hills and left the lake behind. Chandler led the way in a Ford Model A station wagon with a few men riding with him. The rest of the party rode in the GI truck that was towing my truck in low gear. I had a hard time staying on the muddy, slippery road. I ached all over and was dead-tired from lack of sleep. I had bad scares twice when I almost plunged off rickety bridges, but the sturdy GI truck pulled me back from the edge and the dark void below. The wet, chilly air made me shiver.

We finally came to a wide clearing where many trucks, some broken down, were parked facing in all directions. A large army house trailer loomed through the darkness and drizzle. Filipino officers and Moro guards stopped us and asked for our orders. Chandler explained that we were going to see General Fort. They told us how busy he was but decided to let us go on. However, the road ahead was one-way so we had to wait for traffic that was coming down from headquarters. While waiting, I was struck by the proud bearing of the leader of General Fort's Moro guards. This Moro, barefoot and in soaked clothes, strode back and forth at his station with a huge bolo at his side.

Soon an old commercial truck came sliding down the road toward us. It was loaded with dynamite and explosives. Sitting on top of the cargo were several of the PT-boat sailors who had been part of the Lake Lanao navy. They had made several trips with explosives to be used in demolition work to stop the advancing Japs. Even though they had been recent targets of gunfire and bombs, they laughed about riding on the explosives truck. We wished them good luck as they proceeded down toward Dansalan.

A little later downhill traffic ended so Lt. Chandler led the way upward in the station wagon. I joined the rest of our party in the GI truck that followed; we left my old truck with kitchen equipment and food supplies behind. It was still raining, and torrents of water were rutting the one-way road. We halted several times to repair bridges and fix the road before we could proceed. Then Lt. Chandler's station wagon slid along a muddy embankment and lodged against a big tree. After a struggle we got it back on the road and proceeded to a point where the road ahead seemed to have disappeared. When we came closer, we realized that General Fort's men had stretched chicken wire over the road and covered it with vines. Banana trees and shrubs that overhung the single lane added to the illusion. We carefully passed by the camouflage and climbed upward some distance before reaching a large clearing. At the edges stood trees with heavy foliage that branched over many cars and pieces of equipment. Among the trees we could see a number of thatch-roofed huts that would be invisible from the sky. Officers and Moros, all wet and muddy, stood around a large shack. They were waiting to report to General Fort and get instructions. Captain Price passed our truck on his way to report, but I didn't get a chance to speak to him. He and the other officers who went in seemed more dead than alive. Then it was Lt. Chandler's turn. He came back out shortly. The general had gruffly demanded, "Who gave you orders to bring your men up here?" General Fort just shook his head when Chandler explained that there was no one to give him orders back in Dansalan. Fort ended the conversation with, "Return to Dansalan immediately and stand by for orders."

Tired, wet, hungry, and downcast, we hastily started back down the hill. Chandler and others led the way in the station wagon while the rest of us followed in the GI truck. We left my provision truck where I had parked it at the beginning of the one-lane road. Everyone felt adrift, wondering what would happen to us. A phrase kept running through my head: "Blessed is he who endureth to the end." Every man prayed during that dark, jolting ride back to Dansalan. The sight of the town's wrecked houses and shops depressed us still more. Enemy bombing had ruined the attractive town that had glistened in the morning sunlight when I had first seen it a few months before.

We drove on to the yellow schoolhouse, where some busy medics and Major Heidger welcomed us. He had removed his patients from the lakeside where I had left him yesterday. Here in Dansalan he had joined two Filipino doctors who were tending patients at the schoolhouse. He was happy to see me because he needed help. When I explained that we were exhausted, he told us to stay and go to sleep. Nevertheless, he might need us at a moment's notice to help evacuate wounded Filipinos and Americans.

I found a vacant cot in one of the wards and collapsed on it, fully dressed and my gun at the ready. I worried that the Japs might attack while I was asleep but did not finish my prayer before I was dead to the world. I was awakened by an explosion that rocked the earth. I jumped up. After looking around in the faint morning light, I heard the hospital stirring and realized where I was. I wondered whether the Japs would capture us or kill us on the spot, as was rumored to be their practice.

Major Heidger called me to one side and told me he had his hands full with the wounded. I understood his concern for them — brave men who had fought against an enemy that had aircraft and tanks while our side had none. Heidger wanted me to stay and help him, assisted by two or three others I would choose. The rest of us who had come down from General Fort's headquarters would be sent to the front.

While we slept, the enemy had been slowed down. Our troops were mining bridges and roads and building tank traps. They planned to ambush the Japs along the western shore of the lake. Meantime, I would care for the wounded men. Heidger thought there was a good chance that the Japs would spare the hospital. He recalled that in World War I the Germans had treated the wounded and medics of captured hospitals with consideration. I was skeptical of the idea, but I understood how Heidger felt about his patients. I promised to do all I could to prepare food for them. They told me they hadn't had a hot meal for days.

With the help of a few buddies who had come back from General Fort's headquarters with me, I found oatmeal, canned milk, and some stateside coffee that somebody had hidden and not come back for. We cut off the tops of five-gallon oilcans and washed them out with ashes and sand to cut the coating of oil. Soon we had hot coffee and hot cereal for the grateful patients. We enjoyed the cereal ourselves, and the coffee tasted wonderful. We had taken care of the immediate situation but needed more chow and equipment to keep it up.

Meantime the explosions that had awakened me became louder and more frequent. How soon would the Japs be able to break through our troops and roadblocks? Most of my 14th Squadron friends who came down with me the night before were getting ready to go to the front. They weren't eager to go but felt it was their duty — a feeling that had kept them together so far, although many of the 14th Squadron and a few other Air Corps men had faded into the hills in the confusion of the fighting at Ganasi and the subsequent retreat. The Air Corps had been trained to service and fly aircraft. They had never been organized or trained for infantry action. Nevertheless, at least 24 of those missing joined the guerrilla forces of Lt. Col. Fertig and continued the fight.

While I was talking with my buddies, an erect, elderly figure on a nearby porch looked down at us. We recognized each other at about the same time. I hurried over to shake hands with Governor Heffington, whom I had known when I was mess sergeant at Camp Keithley and shopped for food in Dansalan. About 70 years old, Heffington had been in the Philippines since the Spanish-American War and served as provincial governor. I introduced him to my friends and then asked him what he would do when the Japs came. He scratched his head and replied, "I'll just stay home and let them come." He added with a sad laugh, "I can't stop them." I asked, "Why didn't you go with the missionaries when General Fort sent them to the mountains?" The old governor explained, "I hated to give up my home until the last moment. It's all I have left and I've worried that the Moros would ransack the place." He pointed to a nearby building from which the Moros had taken the tin roofing, and another place where they were pulling out nails. The Moros were swarming over the ruins of Dansalan and hauling away the loot to their mountain shacks.

I let the matter drop and told the governor about my problem feeding the hungry patients in the schoolhouse. While I spoke, it occurred to me that his house would be a good place to prepare the food. When I asked, he thought a minute and said, "I don't see why not. Make yourselves at home and use everything you need. The Japs will soon kill all of us and take the house anyway so you might as well." I hurried over to tell Major Heidger of the governor's offer. He was preparing to operate on a Filipino soldier but paused to say, "That's a grand idea!" He asked me to quickly boil a lot of water so he could sterilize his instruments and wash out the soldier's badly infected wounds. I hurried back to the governor's house. He showed us his large, modern kitchen, which had a wood and coal stove as well as an electric one — now useless since the power system had broken down. There were clean pots and pans of all types as well as knives and a meat block. I had my boys start a fire in the stove to provide the hot water that Major Heidger had requested.

Then the governor took us around his home — really a mansion — which was full of books, hunting souvenirs, and fine furniture he had collected since 1900. The tour ended at his bomb shelter. Then one of my boys said in an undertone, "It would be nice to have a drink now, but I guess the officers have cornered it all." The old governor overheard the remark and chuckled, saying, "I know young men like a drink sometimes. It will go good now. Can you keep a secret?" He gave us a key to a wooden panel in the wall that opened to show a large supply of costly whiskeys and wines. We drank with the governor and toasted that we would all somehow live through this mess. Again the phrase haunted me, "Blessed is he who endureth to the end." In spite of all we had seen and the pause for drinks, the tour had taken only a few minutes. But it had made us forget the situation we were in. We felt better even after explosions from the battle and the singing kettles of boiling water brought us back to reality.

We found Major Heidger looking over the kitchen. Its equipment and the ample supply of boiling water made his face light up. He thanked my helpers and me for setting things up, but his smile vanished when I asked about the patients. He and the two Filipino doctors had almost no medicine and little modern equipment. Heidger insisted on keeping my men and me to help at the hospital. One of them asked, "What will become of us and the patients?" The major replied, "I don't know. But if we trust in Christ and do what the Lord expects, God will take care of us." Then he had us all bow our heads, and we joined in the Lord's Prayer, which comforted us.

Heidger stated there was a chance that General Fort might stop the Japs with the help of the Moro Bolo Battalion. Our men were stationed to ambush the enemy near Bacolod Grande. As for himself, the major would stay at the schoolhouse to care for the wounded until General Fort ordered him to retreat. If he had no orders, he would care for his patients until captured.

Governor Heffington walked toward us. Major Heidger said, "We're grateful for the use of your house. It will be a great help to the hospital." I put in, "It's too bad we don't have the emergency ration truck that Kukie and his friends drove off toward Del Monte Airfield." Heidger only said, "Yes, but it can't be helped." Then I thought of the old chow truck that I had left at the base of the one-lane road to Fort's headquarters. The major said we certainly needed the chow truck and asked me to take a small truck and one of the boys to get it. Then Heidger started talking about making a permanent hospital at the schoolhouse. I walked away to find somebody to go with me to retrieve the chow truck. In a short time I rode off in an old truck with a Filipino driver.

We passed many civilian Moros, carrying everything they had looted from evacuated homes. Old cars and worn-out trucks littered the roadside. Quick to swoop down, Moros were cutting off tires with bolos, ripping off chrome, and pulling off windshields to use as windows in the hills. As we headed eastward along the north end of the lake, a formation of Japanese bombers drove us to cover, but they droned onward toward Dansalan —

we wondered if the hospital would be hit. From our hiding spot, we saw smoke across the lake all the way from Ganasi eastward to Lumbatan, where flames and smoke reached high into the sky. Lumbatan was where I had visited Sgt. Manook's home. I wondered whether the Japs were destroying the town or if our men had set it afire to make it useless for the enemy. Many outrigger canoes and a few launches were leaving that side of the lake, but the sound of explosions showed that fighting was still going on.

Suddenly I saw something that made me forget everything else. Three canoes full of Moros were approaching. As they paddled nearer, we could see that the Moros in the front canoe were paddling with all their might to pull the other two canoes, which were joined by a platform that carried a large polished piece of furniture. The bulky object was surrounded by Moros, apparently trying to keep it upright. As the Moros came closer, we could see that they were holding in place a piano so heavy the canoes were riding low and unevenly in the water. The piano would slide toward one canoe and then the other, causing a continuous struggle by the Moros to keep it from toppling into the water. I stared in amazement at the sight and wondered if the missionaries or Miss Pitco had owned the instrument.

Then explosions came from the direction of Dansalan — probably the work of the planes that had driven us to cover. I feared the hospital had been hit. But then excited yells of the Moros grabbed my full attention. The piano was tipping ponderously to one side despite frantic Moro efforts to keep it upright. They sprang away just in time, and the piano plopped into the water and sank, leaving only bubbles and yelling Moros on the surface. The piano had ripped apart and sunk the canoes that carried it — only the lead canoe escaped, and now the Moros in the water were clinging to its sides. The Filipino driver and I were still laughing when we climbed on the truck and headed for the base of the mountain where I had left the truck of food.

We were almost there when Major Hammond, a civilian recently commissioned, stopped us. He had charge of Moro workers who were repairing the road and bridges ahead. He rode on with us. Soon, however, we had to stop for a truck that had slid part way off the road but not far enough to let traffic pass. Hammond jumped out to encourage the Moros there to get it back on the road. They could barely budge the truck until Hammond ordered them to push it out of the way. They did this easily and tipped it over for good measure — probably figuring they could tear it apart and take away the pieces later.

After a few minutes, we reached the parking lot where I had left my chow truck. Its contents were in a jumble. But, looking closer, I realized that not much had been taken except some canned food and my barracks bag. I started to bawl out some of the boys for messing with the truck but calmed down when I thought about the confused situation. However, I couldn't start the truck — the Moros had cut all the ignition wires, hoping to bring up another truck to carry off the food as well as the crippled truck's usable parts. Not wanting to give them that pleasure, I hitched the food truck to the truck the Filipino and I had brought up. He got in his vehicle, and I stayed in the chow truck to steer. We started down the hill in a hurry, reasoning that the parking lot was a likely target for enemy aircraft.

Along the road the Moro workers took their sweet time getting out of our way and then scowled at me as I passed, hating to see the food truck slip out of their hands. The Filipino driver succeeded in steering clear of the loitering Moros until a little later, when my rear wheels locked and began to skid. The driver tried to unlock them with a sudden jerk, but instead of the back wheels unlocking, the front wheels fell off and the front end of the truck fell heavily in the middle of the road. Just then a Japanese plane flew over but continued on toward Dansalan. We were blocking the road for a convoy that carried some tired Filipino soldiers and their officer. The Moro workers stood around grinning, expecting we would be shoved off the road to make way for the soldiers and they would get our trucks to loot after all. Major Hammond appeared, and we decided to have the Moros move the chow truck to one side while keeping it upright. When some Moros started to pick up things in my truck, I yelled at them. A Filipino truck drew alongside, and the Filipinos quickly loaded everything over to their truck.

While they worked, I learned that many of their buddies had been killed or wounded; others had deserted. Their able Filipino officer had kept fighting while retreating around the eastern side of the lake, across from Bacolod Grande. They had blown up bridges and torn up the road into Lumbatan, which they had helped to burn — I thought the flames there might have been the work of our forces. General Fort had ordered these soldiers around the lake to bolster the front at Bacolod Grande. Their route lay through Dansalan, so we joined their convoy with our food and kitchen gear on one of their trucks.

A short distance along the way, a large American ran toward us, waving his officer's fatigue hat. It was Lt. Col. Barnes of the medical corps — he had been caring for wounded men near Lumbatan when advancing Japs forced him to retreat in a truck with his most seriously wounded Filipino patients. The truck had broken down nearby, and since then Barnes had been caring for his patients with only his medical kit. He was so glad to see me he had tears in his eyes. He was overjoyed when I told him about Major Heidger's schoolhouse hospital and Governor Heffington's house. In a short time we had transferred Barnes's patients to a Philippine Army truck and continued on toward Dansalan. Our little convoy of Filipino troops, food supplies for the hospital, and wounded soldiers was beautiful — full of purpose and cooperation. Yet it was sad because we knew deep in our hearts we could not stop the Japs.

At the hospital we found no damage — the bombers had concentrated on Camp Keithley and the steel bridge that linked it with Dansalan. We moved Barnes's patients in and unloaded our food and equipment that the Filipinos had saved from looting. Major Heidger was full of plans to organize his hospital; he told us we'd be so busy we would forget the Japs. He also praised my Air Corps buddies for helping him with the patients — the men who had come down with Lt. Chandler and me the day before. Then he asked, "Vic, would it be possible to fix a nice dinner for the medics and Air Corps men, as well as getting chow for the patients?" I told him I would be glad to and rounded up Puppario and Coty to help. It was a pleasure to fix dinner with the field ranges and gas burners that the Philippine truck had brought down, and with the ample equipment in Governor Heffington's kitchen. As we worked, I remarked how nice it would be to stay here for a long time — Puppario and Coty agreed. But that idea was a dream. All we could do was to live day by day and enjoy what we could.

The Air Corps boys who had been helping Major Heidger all morning were to leave for the front after dinner along with Captain Katz, Major Schroeder, and other officers. I decided to make the dinner a farewell banquet for them all. We hurried to feed the patients and then worked on the banquet with the help of several volunteers besides my regular crew. I found some Australian ham packed in sawdust. My helpers collected an assortment of canned food that the governor had on hand or that was on the truck. Others prepared the spacious dining room in banquet style, using the governor's silverware, cut-glass dishes, and goblets. There would be whiskey and wine enough for all, and then some. After the food was put on the table, Governor Heffington, Major Heidger, Lt. Col. Barnes, the other officers, and Air Corps men sat down. Major Heidger gave the blessing. With good wine, we toasted everyone going to the front. We soon forgot the war with plenty of food and drink, but enemy planes overhead cut short our relaxed mood. Someone said, "Well, if the Japs get us now, we can at least say we had one last good meal in grand style." After we had satisfied our appetites and drunk all we wanted, the boys and officers leaving for Bacolod Grande took some of the liquor and bade us goodbye. As we wished them good luck and watched them go, we wondered if it was a final farewell.

Nevertheless, the dinner was good for our morale. We hustled to clean up the dining room and kitchen, conscious of our duty to support the hospital. Heidger was already busy operating on a poor Filipino soldier who was nearly dead. But Lt. Col. Barnes was getting drunk and feeling sorry for himself. He kept repeating, "It's awful! All of us will be killed by the Japs very shortly." Hearing more sounds of battle, I felt ashamed at not being with my buddies at the front. Barnes's drunken prediction of immediate disaster might come true. But Heidger's effort to save lives and his trust in God crowded Barnes out of my mind. The old refrain came to me again, unbidden: "Blessed is he who endureth to the end." I prayed for strength to carry on. Then louder explosions and gunfire caused me to look down the lake toward Bacolod Grande.

Canoes were racing northward toward us and to the northeast shore of the lake. Trucks of our retreating soldiers approached the steel bridge that spanned the Agusa River between Camp Keithley and Dansalan. The enemy dive bombers that flew over were still trying to destroy the bridge to cut off our soldiers' retreat to Dansalan. Despite the noise and threat to the hospital, Major Heidger was busy operating, but the exploding bombs scared the medics and patients. Although unable to knock out the bridge, the bombers had set several buildings afire, causing billows of smoke to drift over to the hospital. Many of the less seriously wounded men ran, walked, and even crawled from the hospital — some naked and some wearing only white underclothes over their bandages. Some couldn't make it to a ditch or foxhole and simply sprawled in the open while covering their heads to drown out the roar of aircraft. The planes attacking the bridge were flying so low the pilots could not help but see them.

With binoculars I saw a small group of Japanese shock troops moving in the hills across the river to outflank our troops. I pointed them out to Major Heidger. When I trained the glasses on the Dansalan Hotel, I picked out Knortz, Ferrens, and other 14th Squadron boys but could not tell what they were doing.

Filipino troops gathered in the hospital area. They said they were too weak to fight the Japs any longer and fell exhausted at our feet. Yet other Filipino soldiers began setting up machine guns and digging foxholes around the hospital. They had decided to defend the wounded in the hospital, doing what they thought was best. Major Heidger admired their determination but realized that a battle there would destroy all of us. He ordered immediate evacuation of patients and hospital equipment to

General Fort's headquarters above Bubong. The Filipino troops would keep the Japs at bay long enough to complete the move. After the last truck had been loaded, we noticed Governor Heffington standing on his porch. When we urged him to come with us, he again said he didn't want to leave his home for the Moros to loot. But we finally persuaded him to change his mind and promised to take care of him.

17

The Road to General Fort's Headquarters

May 5–6, 1942

After Governor Heffington agreed to come with us, Major Heidger turned to me and said, "I wish I had another truck for you, Vic, to haul some things I'll need." John Clark from the 30th Squadron came running up and asked what we were going to do. When we told him we needed another truck, he reported passing one that had been abandoned near the dock at Camp Keithley. He went on to tell us of the action he had been in near Bacolod Grande. There, Filipino and American soldiers had ambushed a convoy of trucks loaded with Japanese troops. Crossfire had killed hundreds of the enemy, slowing their advance on Dansalan. It had taken them time to bring up artillery, tanks, and reinforcements, and then they had advanced more cautiously. But with close air support they had attacked and scattered our forces. Yet our men had damaged the road and blown bridges as they retreated toward the still-intact steel bridge into Dansalan.

During this period, Clark had escaped in a motor launch and tied up at the Camp Keithley dock. Now he wanted to know what to do with the launch — it contained ammunition and two .50 caliber machine-guns. Major Heidger said he didn't care so much about the launch but wanted us to get the truck and bring all the supplies we could up to Fort's headquarters. He wished me luck, and I saluted as he drove off.

Clark and I walked across the steel bridge and in a few minutes reached the abandoned truck. It had been riddled by bullets, and there was blood on the shattered windshield. Had the driver and passengers fled or tried to take a wounded man to safety? To our surprise the truck started, but it ran very hot — bullets had hit the radiator, and most of the water had leaked out. We added water and drove to the nearby dock where Clark had left the launch.

We jumped into the boat, fearful of being spotted by the Japs. After we broke the machine guns off their mounts, I lifted them and two boxes of ammunition up to Clark, who had scrambled back onto the dock. While bullets whizzed overhead, I threw the rest of the ammunition overboard and climbed up with Clark. He had taken some hand grenades out of one box. Each of us took one, pulled the pin, and threw it into the launch. We fell flat on the dock, but when we peeked over the edge, we found the explosions had done little damage. We exploded two more without better luck. Then we lugged the guns and ammunition off the dock and loaded everything on the truck, which protested with a cloud of steam as we drove off. We found some water for the radiator and hurried toward the bridge, hoping it had not been destroyed.

There was fire and smoke everywhere because Filipino soldiers were burning everything that had not been destroyed by enemy planes. I remarked, "Maybe the Filipinos will burn the launch before the Japs get there. I guess we should have done that ourselves." Soon the bridge loomed ahead, and we crossed into Dansalan, greatly relieved.

But the ruined city made my heart ache. The smoke was so heavy we had to drive slowly to avoid miscellaneous articles strewn in the road. All around were smoldering heaps of buildings, twisted sheet iron, and loose electric wires that dangled in the air and looped on the ground. Plundering Moros were another obstacle. We almost collided with some who were loaded with bundles and slow to get out of the way. They glared at us as though we were intruders. They showed no concern about the fast-approaching Japs.

A few blocks farther our truck again threatened to strand us. It had almost stopped steaming for lack of water, and Clark feared the engine would permanently lock under the extreme heat. Just then I noticed a broken water main up the street. I yelled for Clark to stop and hurried off to the hydrant with a leaky oil can, but when I got back to the truck, I was splattered with water from a dozen holes in the can so there wasn't much left to pour into the radiator. I had to make several trips before we drove on.

At the old Municipal Building I noticed the same strapping Moro guard who had impressed me earlier when we were waiting to make the final ascent to General Fort's headquarters. Now this loyal Moro was taking papers and records out of the municipal offices and loading them in a camouflaged staff car, to deprive the Japs from using them in administering the region.

The Moro's little monkey sat on the front fender with a chain around his neck, waiting patiently.

Then our truck began to cough, now demanding gas. Clark coaxed it along. "I know a gasoline dump just a half-block from here," he said. "Maybe we'll find some gas there." We sputtered to a final stop right by the gas drums. When we climbed down, there was a strong smell of aviation gas and we realized the drums had been punctured and turned over to prevent their use by the Japs. Disheartened, we thought about abandoning the truck and moving on foot to keep ahead of the Japs. First, though, we decided to check the drums more carefully. I saw some distant Moros transporting some full oil drums. Clark remarked, "Those damn Moros will take anything whether they can use it or not." We had checked almost every drum when I kicked one that sloshed and didn't move as easily as the other. I shook it, and sure enough it had several gallons — its puncture was a foot from the bottom of the drum, which had been left standing. Carefully we got almost all of the gas from the drum into the truck's tank. The satisfied truck now seemed to run better than ever.

Then I thought of the guardhouse in town, where General Fort's command jailed its soldiers. Who should I find there but Aldo P. Maccagli, the truck-driving "Kid from Brooklyn." He had been put away for giving up his .45 pistol in a trade with a Filipino or Moro—a serious offense in view of our military situation. Maccagli didn't want to join us, but I later learned that he joined Lt. Col. Fertig's guerrilla forces. Another prisoner I released was a large soldier of the Philippine Constabulary. I never saw him again.

Next we headed for the hospital to pick up the equipment for Major Heidger. Close to the hospital in one of Governor Heffington's sheds we found some five-gallon tins of gas that we piled on the truck. The heavy load slowed us almost to a crawl as we followed the road eastward along the north shore of the lake. I took a last, sad look over the water toward the ruins of Dansalan and Camp Keithley.

Now that we had picked up Major Heidger's equipment and were on our way, we hoped things would go smoothly for awhile. But our overloaded truck didn't let us relax for long. We had not yet turned away from the lake when the engine started to steam again as we were coming down a steep incline that brought us close to the shore. We stopped and turned off the ignition, but the motor kept running and began to smoke. It became cherry-red — the truck would surely burn up if we didn't do something. I rushed to the lake for water. But before I returned, Clark had cut off the gas line, fearing the truck would explode. The overheated engine was stuck in place. The fact that there was still some water in the radiator made us realize that the high octane aviation gas from the dump in Dansalan was more than the truck could handle.

Imagining all kinds of things happening to us in the growing darkness, we checked our rifles and ammunition. We could still see boats coming in our direction. Were they friendly or hostile? Japs were coming around the lake toward us from both directions and getting closer. Now Moros appeared, hovering around like vultures and waiting — patiently, for the moment — to get at our loaded truck. Clark and I were in a quandary — if we stayed to guard the truck, we feared being caught by the Japs; but if we abandoned the truck, its badly needed contents would fall into the hands of the Moros. We stood our ground. Now a new fire leaped up ahead of us about where the road turned away from the lake into the hills. Behind us fires and explosions around Dansalan made us feel surrounded.

Suddenly we heard a vehicle approach from behind. We hoped it was one of ours but we weren't counting on it. An American truck came into sight. Still, we didn't relax — in the past the Japs had driven American vehicles, pretending to be Filipino drivers, to get behind our lines below Ganasi. To our relief, I recognized Lt. Chandler, Knortz, and a couple others from the 14th Squadron — I had seen them through binoculars near the Dansalan Hotel during the day. They were worn out but had a bottle of good whiskey to share with us — some officer had left it at the hotel. We gave a toast that we would survive this mess. Chandler reported that three of the 14th who had volunteered for a dangerous scouting mission were almost certainly dead. They were John H. Martin, Fred Defenbaugh, and Earl Cook — among the bravest men in our outfit. Chandler and the others had been blowing up or burning anything that might help the Japs. They were going to the mountain headquarters for more explosives. Chandler decided to take Clark with him and left me to guard the truck against the Moros until another truck could be sent down from headquarters to bring up the food and gear. Chandler assured me I wouldn't have to wait long.

After my group disappeared into the darkness, the Moros edged a little closer but took a look at me and stopped. Even though I felt more helpless alone, I did my best to put up a good front. They could see my good M-1 rifle, and I looked pretty alert because of the tension I felt. Our standoff dragged on. Luckily, the moon rose so I could still watch them. Still, they showed no sign of giving up the chance for plunder. Then another vehicle approached from the direction of Dansalan. I figured it could be Japs because there had been plenty of time for them to get here since Chandler had gone.

It was an American car, but I was prepared for Japs to be inside until Lt. Col. Robert Vesey and Lt. Commander Strong stepped out. Since I had seen them at Ganasi on the south end of Lake Lanao, they had been at the front trying to stop the Japs. Their dirty and torn clothes, stubbled beards, and bloodshot eyes made a pitiful sight. They moved slowly and talked in subdued tones. They were glad to see me, and I was certainly happy to see them. They told me things looked awful and the only thing left now was to carry on guerrilla warfare. As to the load on my truck, Vesey was definite: "We need those things in the hills." The two officers had not eaten in a long time so I opened a can of salmon with my bayonet. They ate in a hurry with their hands and said how good it tasted. They also assured me they would send down a truck to get the valuable items I was guarding. I saluted as they drove off for General Fort's headquarters.

Now I felt more lonely and exposed than ever. How long would this keep up? Had I been forgotten? Were my orders to stay there sensible? In such a bad state of affairs would this truck make much difference? But it wasn't long before I heard another vehicle coming from Dansalan.

I figured my luck had run out until the truck pulled up beside me. This time I was overjoyed to see my good friend Captain Price and his crew. Like Vesey and Strong, the recent fighting had left Price bedraggled and discouraged. He reported the Japs were advancing everywhere and if they kept on as they had in the last four hours, they would soon reach our headquarters. When I asked him about my truck, Price said he wouldn't countermand the order for me to stay, but advised me to load the most important stuff on his truck and go on with him. His crew helped me transfer the machine guns, ammunition, medical equipment, canned food, a gas burner, and several cans of gas. Then I drove off with Captain Price, leaving some supplies and the wrecked truck to the Moros, whose wait had paid off to some extent.

In a few minutes we reached the turnoff that led into the mountains. We followed the familiar road to the base of the one-lane road where the chief Moro guard was back on duty after securing the city records from the Dansalan town hall. He waved us on — no traffic was coming down. Driving in steady rain, we slid and dodged recent washouts; heavy traffic and the rainy season had stopped repairs. We passed loaded trucks that had slid off the road and were perched precariously on the side of the mountain. After passing through the leafy tunnel that camouflaged the road, we slowed and then came to a halt.

Ahead of us stretched a long line of trucks and cars that had floundered to a stop on the roadway or been shoved to the side. When we got out to move aside the abandoned truck ahead of us, the ground was so slippery we were barely able to stay on our feet. I noticed a long line of Moros moving quietly forward in single file, paying no attention to anyone. We were still struggling to shove the truck aside when we heard angry yells of profanity from the truck behind us.

The voice was familiar, but I couldn't quite place it. He wanted to know why the stupid so-and-so ahead of him was holding up traffic and stopping him from getting to General Fort's headquarters. When he stomped up to us, Captain Price quietly said, "Take it easy." I looked carefully at the excited man, who was covered from head to foot with mud and shaking all over. I finally recognized my friend Major Navin, who had commanded the Filipino troops in Malabang. I had known him well there while running the bakery. After he recognized me, he apologized for being so rude. He was in a hurry to get to a doctor because he was in great pain and almost blind. He had tried to destroy the same launch that Clark and I had damaged at the Camp Keithley dock. As he'd poured gasoline over the boat, he had spilled some on himself. When he ignited the boat, he went up in flames as well, and had to jump in the lake to extinguish the flames. He had been burned so badly he had covered himself with mud to ease the pain.

Since headquarters was not far, I said I would go with Navin on foot to the hospital. Captain Price said okay so Navin and I started up the slippery incline in the same direction the file of Moros was moving. In a short time I saw through the drizzle a large stack of boxes that several soldiers were breaking open. By the feeble light of a small lantern, the men were handing each half-naked Moro an Enfield rifle and ammunition. The heavy, awkward Enfield was left over from World War I and was sometimes dangerous to fire, but General Fort was handing it out anyway, expecting the Moros would use the weapon to ambush Japs who came up the mountain toward his headquarters. I believed the Moros might kill some Japs but worried they might use the rifles against us. Major Navin and I continued on and soon reached Major Heidger's emergency hospital. Heidger told me he would take care of Navin, and then asked me to stay to help.

I was to join others in moving litter patients who were sprawled on the ground in the rain or waited in trucks stuck down the road. I picked up one end of a litter and followed the other carriers toward an opening in the jungle. As we passed headquarters, I saw General Fort inside, walking to and fro in front of a dim lamp and smoking his pipe. Other officers hung around at a little distance, not knowing what to do next. Only Major Heidger knew what he had to do and he was doing it. Entering the darker jungle, we slipped frequently on the narrow, rocky path. The cold drizzle continued. We all had to rest several times.

Finally we came to the worst hospital I had ever seen. It was a long, low, straw-and-thatch building, constructed around trees that came out of the roof — their dense foliage hiding the structure from the sky. Coming closer, we saw spots of light here and there inside. We entered to find the patients lined up in close rows on a bare, bumpy floor made of small poles. There was just space to make another row for the new patients. Some of the wounded already there were very still. Others were crying out in great pain or moaning. Some prayed and asked for a priest. Seeing them made my heart ache, and I felt rage toward the Japs. I prayed for the wounded, and then the haunting refrain again came to mind, "Blessed is he who endureth to the end."

After several trips, I was completely exhausted — my body ached, and I couldn't keep my eyes open. I helped set down a patient on the floor and found a place between two wounded soldiers to lie down for a quick rest, my rifle close at hand. My quick rest turned into a deep sleep. I don't know how long it lasted, but the first thing I knew a medic was shaking me. He urgently warned, "Everyone is getting ready to take off — the Japs are expected at any time. They've completed a circle around Lake Lanao and are at the lower end of the road that leads here." I was so intent on getting out of there that I barely noticed that the man lying beside me had died.

Hungry, cold, and weak, I stumbled back to the headquarters' area, where I found and ate a can of tomatoes. I felt better and hurried to fill one small can with salt and another with brown sugar. I found a trampled bag of rice that I used to fill a small sack. Finally, I wrapped my personal effects in my shelter half and was ready to go. After all the haste, we just stood around waiting for orders. I sat in the back of a truck, waiting for Japs to come or … what?

Sitting there, I thought of all the retreats and losses that had left just a handful of miserable Americans with very few options. The Japs would certainly find our wrecked vehicles and make their way up to us. Would they kill us and the helpless patients or would there be a surrender? I figured I could do little good if killed, and surrender could be worse than death. I looked toward the headquarters' shack and again saw General Fort slowly pacing back and forth. Our leadership was too weary and confused to prepare for a Japanese attack — things could still get worse. I remembered the men who had already struck off into the hills, Maybe I could be more effective waging guerrilla warfare rather than waiting to be captured or killed in this mess.

18

Into the Mountains
May 6 to June 2, 1942

We were still waiting for orders when the first signs of a rainy dawn showed more clearly the ragged group of soldiers scattered around the headquarters shack. I slid off the truck's fender and started up a half-finished road that led into the mountains. Besides my rifle and food, I carried a medical kit, road map, and the New Testament. The confusion I was leaving depressed me. At the same time I felt guilty about taking off because we expected the Japs to attack the camp soon. After hiking for a half-hour, I sat down on a large rock to rest and ponder what I should do next. I had started to read my Bible when I heard voices behind me. Soon two tired friends came up with their rifles and packs. They felt the same way I did about the mess behind us so we decided to stick together. From there the road became steeper and was overgrown with brush. In a few hundred yards, we sank down on a fallen log and talked about our situation.

Even though no one believed that headquarters would organize any resistance to the Japs, we hated to leave the wounded Filipino soldiers and other Americans. But we would be no good dead. We were sick of being chased and wanted to get so far into the hills that we would have peace and quiet for a little while. As we sat there talking, seven other Americans caught up with us. Now we were ten. The road had become a trail. In silence, we stumbled and sometimes fell while the mountain air and rain chilled us. We talked in low tones and had to rest often. Seven more men soon joined us.

We were a motley sight with all kinds of headgear but no helmets. One man wore a dress hat, and others had different straw hats — Philippine and American. Many wore just bandannas. There was a variety of beards —

some big and shaggy and others cut to special styles. Our clothes ranged from civilian to Philippine constabulary and American uniforms, with various mixtures. All of our clothing was wet, torn and muddy. A number of the boys suffered from malaria, sores, and colds. Resting became a primary occupation. Many men were from my 14th Squadron, and I knew them well. Others came from the 30th Squadron, and a few from the PT boats on Lake Lanao.

As we talked things over, most of us worried that we might be considered deserters. Moreover, we would constantly fear being hunted down by the Japs during the many months before American forces came back to the Philippines. We had heard the Japs were pretty rough on guerrillas. Even without Japs, survival in the hills for an extended period would be a tough struggle. During this grim conversation, my inner voice kept saying, "Blessed is he who endureth to the end." I took this to mean that I should have undying faith in God and never give up. I grasped my New Testament. Reading it had helped many times when I was troubled. My Bible would do the same now.

Our discussion turned to practical matters, and the future. Taking stock of our equipment, we found several watches and two compasses, as well as binoculars that belonged to John Clark, my recent supply-trip companion. There was another road map of Mindanao besides mine and a number of New Testaments. We were short of matches and tobacco. But nearly everyone had a first aid kit with bandages, salve, and a few quinine pills. Even better, we had one medic in the group, who had a good-sized first aid kit and medicine.

However, we didn't have much food and it was scarce in the mountains. One man, though, had bought enough Moro rice cakes the day before for all of us. Munching the rice cakes brought us all together — we realized we would have to depend on each other. We liked being away from discipline and officers. We did not elect leaders, but a few would strongly influence the others in making decisions.

The first decision was to move farther away from headquarters. We expected the Japs to capture it soon and come after us. None of us were well acquainted with this region, but several had bits of information that we put together. We believed we were near the planned site for an evacuation hospital that was located in a small valley next to a stream. Beyond lay the Butig mountains, a higher range with fertile valleys that might provide a ready source of food. For now we decided to take a look at the hospital site before heading for the Butig range.

The trail became steeper, and the higher altitude made us short-winded. We covered less ground between rests, and the rests were longer.

An enemy plane seemed to be hunting us and made us scurry for cover. We expected to hear bombs dropping on General Fort's headquarters — the Japs certainly knew by now where it was. But we heard nothing except the fading sound of the plane's engine. The trail ended by a small crater and gurgling stream — probably the site chosen for the hospital. At first we thought it would be a good place for us, but we decided to go on because it would be too easy for the Japs to find.

From the crater we found a faint path that led us still higher. The going was rougher than before. Several men with malaria, including Sgt. James Palmer, our veteran cook, lagged behind, almost at the end of their endurance. We had to help them and go slower. When we came to an abrupt slope that was like a slippery wall, Palmer said, "Boys, I can't make it. You go ahead." Palmer was older than the rest of us, and his malaria had been so bad a few days before that I had taken him back from the front line at Ganasi for treatment — he had been in poor shape then. Now I told him, "Don't talk like that, Jimmy." Then we pushed and pulled Palmer and others who needed help up the steep incline. Even some of the healthier men fell and skinned themselves. At the top we rested with a sense of relief. We believed we were safe from immediate pursuit because the rain would wash out any sign of our passing since we had left the road.

While resting, we noticed several paths. We pondered which one to take — we feared choosing one that would take us in a big circle or one that would lead us quickly into the hands of the Japs. We finally headed up a path that led due east — at least according to our compass — toward the vast, mountainous interior of Mindanao. As we dragged ourselves off the ground, I gasped for air and ached all over. Nevertheless, I was in better shape than most of the party. We had climbed so high we were walking in clouds. Occasionally, the sun broke through to show Lake Lanao far below. Along the shore, flames and smoke rose at Lumbatan, Tamparan, and Dansalan. We were still stopping frequently to catch our breath or hide from enemy aircraft, which never seemed to give up searching for us.

In the middle of the afternoon we came to some sagging, long-deserted shacks made of poles tied together with vines and covered with mats. There was no stream nearby, and the site seemed too open to be good for a camp. However, many of the men were so far gone, they couldn't go much farther. We discovered a lean-to down from the trail that was in better shape than the shacks we had first noticed. The weary and sick crawled in and collapsed on the floor.

Some of us dropped our packs and took our rifles to explore the vicinity. As we circled the camp, we found two trails. One led over a steep embankment into dense jungle — an established trail that had been used recently. The other trail showed even more recent use and ran straight downhill but was not too steep for easy travel. We chose to follow it but first we returned to the lean-to to pick up our packs and tell our companions we were going ahead. They were to follow when they could.

We had not gone far when shadows of the late afternoon and chilly air made us think about making camp, but there was no sign of a good place. I began to wonder if I should have married Conchia and become part of her Moro family, or joined the Moros I knew in Bacolod Grande, or stuck with Sgt. Manook. I prayed for everything to come out all right.

The trail climbed steeply for a short distance. At the crest, we looked down on a little hollow, densely shaded by a canopy of huge trees. Underneath, brush had been cleared away to show a clear, winding stream of some size. On our side of the stream stood a number of shacks that were constructed like those in which we had left our comrades. But these shelters were in pretty good shape. I thought about this secluded, comfortable place — it seemed like God had looked down from heaven and seen some of His sheep lost in the mountains without water and shelter and led us here.

The camp had been recently occupied. The personal effects left inside included crosses, rosaries, photos, and letters — signs of the Catholic faith and a hurried departure by Filipino soldiers. Poles were stacked to dry for firewood, but because they were damp it was hard to build a good fire. Then our comrades straggled into camp, delighted to find not just us but a better shelter for the night. Someone remembered that people in the U.S. enjoyed eating fiddlehead ferns so we started eating the ferns that flourished in the moist hollow — a salad to go with the food in our packs.

Next morning a figure came hesitantly out of the jungle on the other side of the stream. He barely had strength to wade across and clamber up the bank on our side. By the time he reached us, we had already figured him to be a Filipino solider who wanted to escape into the hills. He carried a full pack, which might have something useful in it. In line with what we all were thinking, Bill Knortz offered the Filipino a deal: "You can join us but if you want to go on into the mountains, leave your pack here." The tired Filipino gave up his pack and trudged on. A number of straggling Filipino soldiers came up the same trail that day and the next — they all faced the same deal and left their packs with us rather than stay. They had come up the trail on the other side of the stream that led from the eastern shore of Lake Lanao. These men probably had fled from fighting there. The junction of that trail with ours, which led up from the north end of the lake, caused us to name the place Camp Y.

Our uphill, strenuous hike to Camp Y did not free us from officers for long. In the afternoon of our second day there, Major Heidger and Lt. Col. Barnes appeared, bringing along some wounded who could walk. Heidger wanted to bring up the other wounded men and establish a hospital that we would staff— I seemed to be a favorite part of his plans for hospitals at various places in the past few days. Now he suspected we might fade into the hills at any time. Therefore, he threatened desertion charges after the war against anyone who took off.

The next morning made clear once again that we weren't very far from the American command. Lt. Chandler, new CO of the 14th Bomb Squadron , strode into Camp Y. Formerly the outfit's top sergeant, he had been commissioned and ordered to replace Lt. Doe. The slight, conscientious Chandler had been busy setting tank traps against the advancing Japs. He was so popular with the men that no one disputed the crazy orders he brought: We were to return to headquarters and then go down near Lake Lanao to retrieve the .295 mountain gun Captain Price had been forced to abandon.

The dissent was mostly passive. Suddenly, about half of Camp Y became too sick to move although they had managed the hard trek up there three days before. But ten of us chose to go back with Chandler. I was one of them, even though I resented the crazy orders we were following. I took out my anger on Lt. Col. Barnes, the doctor who had recently predicted disaster for all of us after getting drunk at the hospital in Dansalan. Now I walked over to him and with my bolo slashed off the flask of whiskey he always carried attached to his shoulder strap. I declared, "We're going to need this more than you, Colonel!" I handed the whiskey over to Lt. Chandler, who then led us down the trail. We passed the whiskey around at rest stops, but it didn't last long.

At headquarters there was wreckage all over. General Fort had ordered his Filipino troops to destroy buildings and items of value, even a supply of pesos. But now Fort had decided to stick it out on a day-by-day basis. When the officers noticed my return, they realized I was just the one they needed to run the rice mill and mess for General Fort and the dozen American officers of the 81st Division, who commanded the Filipino troops. As to the rest of the men who had come down with Chandler, they soon started back to Camp Y, carrying ammunition and records to bury there. So much for the idea of bringing up the abandoned mountain gun from Lake Lanao!

I didn't mind staying at General Fort's headquarters for the time being. General Wainwright's surrender of his forces on Corregidor on May 6, 1942, ended formal resistance on the largest Philippine island, Luzon. But I wanted to be near General Fort to find out what would be in store for us on Mindanao Island if we didn't go into the hills. Meantime, word of my food and rice pancakes brought visitors.

Even Pvt. (formerly Lt.) Doe showed up and demanded fried bananas. I reminded him, "No bananas grow in the mountains." He looked well-fed and wore good clothes. We didn't know where he had been since he disappeared during the fighting at Ganasi. Now he was acting as though he were still an officer. But the officers didn't welcome him — in fact, they sent him over to stay at the missionaries' camp.

One day Captain Lane, the former missionary, stopped by for chow and poured out an angry account of a Moro's theft of his wife's purse. He had not been present and now vowed to find and kill the guilty Moro and bury a dead pig over him — a flagrant insult to a Muslim. I feared for Lane and told him to take it easy. But he was still keyed up when he left to look for the culprit. That was the last I saw of him. I learned later that he found the Moro in his village but was no match for him and was killed.

One day a slim American major, about 40 years old, rode into camp on a bicycle, perspiring from riding up the last steep section of road. But his uniform was neat and clean. More unusual, he wore a white armband with red Japanese letters on it. I learned that he was Major Pritchard from the staff of General Sharp, who commanded all Philippine and American forces except those on Luzon. Sharp had dispatched Pritchard to work out the surrender of General Fort's command to the Japs in Dansalan.

General Sharp had the sad task of carrying out General Wainwright's orders of May 7, 1942, to surrender all forces in the rest of the Philippines. However, Wainwright had no such authority since he was already a prisoner himself, having surrendered his command on Corregidor the day before, on May 6, 1942.

Yet it should be noted that Wainwright acted under the threat of Japan's General Homma to execute the Corregidor prisoners if Wainwright did not order the surrender of all other units in the Philippines. The Corregidor prisoners may have been saved from execution, but many of them lost their lives during the Bataan Death March or later in prison camps.

General Fort initially rebuffed Pritchard and the order to surrender. Fort had long planned to continue the fight in the hills with the help of the Moros. While providing and serving food for General Fort and his officers, I heard their discussions about surrendering, carried on quite openly around a large table. Lt. Col. Vesey said very little and looked tired and discouraged. Major Schroeder, who had provided needed supplies at my Malabang bakery, had plenty to say and would yell at me for coffee. A Filipino millionaire, Lt. Louis Rosario, who owned sugar plantations on Cebu, was miffed because he hadn't shot a Jap yet. General Fort hated to surrender because of his earlier plans to keep fighting. Yet now he had a direct order that was coupled with the threat of Japanese retaliation against the American and Filipino soldiers captured on Corregidor. It was not until ten days or more after General Wainwright's surrender on May 6, 1942, that I was convinced General Fort would follow suit. I headed back to Camp Y to see if my friends were ready for us to strike out on our own. I sent a reluctant Sgt. Palmer back to the heavier workload at headquarters to replace me. He didn't want more work, but he was no longer interested in breaking away.

A day or two later Major Heidger and Lt. John Stephens of the 81st Division appeared at Camp Y. Heidger called us together and said Lt. Stephens had an important announcement. The young officer's sad look told us the news before he spoke. We were ordered to surrender to the Japs with our arms and equipment within three days — part of the Japanese terms brought back by Major Pritchard. The Japs had warned that we should surrender at once or the men who had already been captured elsewhere would be punished or killed. If we did not surrender, they would hunt us down and kill us as spies and guerrillas. But if we surrendered, we would be treated fairly; in fact, they would guarantee we would not be POWs, but hostages of the empire. The lieutenant concluded by saying that he and Major Heidger were going back to headquarters now, and we were to come down the next day.

I walked out through the trees, hitting the trunks with a large stick, feeling sick to my stomach and shedding tears of anger. Even if the Japs wanted to take care of us, how could they feed us? It had been difficult for us to obtain food from a friendly Moro population. Now we would surely die of hunger, if not from tropical diseases; I had no confidence in the Japanese ability or desire to provide medical treatment. The others at Camp Y had similar worries, and we all wrestled with what we should do. We walked over to a nearby Filipino camp to ask the advice of Captain Phil Cadiz. He looked us over and told us of a good hideout elsewhere on Mindanao. He wouldn't go himself since, as an officer, he had to obey orders. He wouldn't order us to take off but would not blame us if we did. Also, Major Heidger seemed to have left the door open for anyone to leave by not repeating his earlier threat to bring desertion charges against anyone who broke away.

Yet Lt. Chandler, the popular leader of the 14th Squadron, now believed we should carry out the surrender — for a brief time he had wanted to stay in the hills. Our hopes for a leader were dashed further when Sgt. Herbert Zincke and other rated men likewise decided to surrender. Later, some of the boys came to see me because I knew the people and country better than most. I had to tell them I had not made up my mind. What nagged at me, though, was that my good friend Sgt. Manook was only 40 miles away in a well-fortified place.

That night I couldn't get to sleep. First the idea of escape and then of surrender ran through my mind. Both had so many drawbacks I kept going back and forth. Escape could bring later desertion charges that could wreck my future. Yet if I surrendered, I might starve or die of disease. Then the future wouldn't matter at all. None of us slept much that night.

The next morning Major Heidger appeared again — I felt he was surprised we were still there. When we brought up the questions of taking off, he repeated his threat to bring desertion charges, but less emphatically than before. Then he told us he had some triple serum for smallpox, cholera, and typhoid fever that he wanted to give us before we became prisoners. The serum was old, but he believed it was still effective. We all accepted his offer, and then turned to the sad task of destroying Camp Y.

We worked in a daze, feeling that our old world had come to an end. We carefully hid our ammunition. A few of us hid personal things in case we escaped later. Knortz and Bill Johnson, the PT sailor, buried some dismantled guns and ammunition. Lt. Chandler buried the daily muster sheets of the 14th Bomb Squadron he had kept since the beginning of the war as sergeant and then as CO. To frustrate the Moros we dug shallow holes and buried items of little value near deeper holes that were well hidden and held guns, ammunition, and valuables. I destroyed my letters, pictures, and documents — some men kept theirs. A heavy downpour began as we left, adding physical discomfort to our misery of spirit. No one said a word as we strung out on the slippery trail to headquarters. Our years of discipline made it difficult to do other than obeying General Fort's order to surrender. Yet many of us were determined to make an early escape into the hills where we would be free of our blundering officers as well as the Japs.

By the time we were sloshing through the mud at General Fort's headquarters, everyone was hungry. But Sgt. Palmer, whom I had sent down from Camp Y a few days earlier to handle the mess, told Lt. Chandler, "You'll have to get your food elsewhere." Chandler asked me to see what I could do. I borrowed some rice from the Philippine kitchen nearby and got some cans of tuna from General Fort's stores. With the help of volunteers, I fixed some food for the men. The food and hot tea relaxed us, and we soon fell asleep even though we knew that next day would bring our surrender.

On the morning of May 30, 1942, 45 to 50 Americans* and 300 Filipinos assembled on the open ground. A sergeant called out the Americans who were leaving at once with General Fort for Dansalan. Five names,
including mine, were not on the list. General Fort told me we were to come
along in two or three days with the trucks of material to be turned over.
I'll never know whether or not he was giving us a chance to take to the hills
by the loose way he gave the order. I waved to him and his soldiers as they
marched away, some barefoot and each with a whipped expression on his
face. Some were so sick they could barely keep up. My main job was to feed
a few American and Filipino officers left behind, as well as my group of
five GIs. There wasn't much food left so I tried to bargain with the Moros
for more. But now I had to pay a high price — their previous good will had
vanished when they realized we were surrendering. Yet one Moro, Ganasi
(same name as the place), proved to be a friend. He and his men had taken
the job of maintaining the trucks that were transporting surrendered supplies to the Japs in Dansalan. Ganasi helped me obtain chickens, eggs, and
potatoes — even paying for them himself.

Besides handling the mess, I was to help the other four GIs left behind
collect the Enfield rifles that I had seen being passed out to the Moros on
my last trip up from Dansalan. Someone had told the Japs how many had
been given out so the Japs demanded all of them back. We took a few
drinks before setting out to get the guns — ignoring an officer's objection
to the drinks. But our half-hearted efforts turned up just one gun, although
there were promises of giving over some more the next day.

The following afternoon, I went with Haifley, my housemate at
Bacolod Grande, to pick up the Enfields. We had General Fort's driver take
us in the staff car to carry them back. Before we reached the point where
we were to get the guns, a Moro warrior stepped out in the road waving a
kris. I raised my M-1 rifle so he could see it and told the driver to step on
it. As we came nearer, I fired a few bursts near him. He jumped aside as
we passed, cursing us for surrendering to the Japs. Farther on, we got out
and told the driver to wait for us down the road, where we would meet him
in a couple hours.

After an uneasy wait, a few Moros appeared but brought only badly
worn or broken guns rather than the unused Enfields that had been given
out. They handed them over without a word and left. Others came to say
they had lost their rifles, and some did not show up at all. We sensed hostility from them all and were glad to get back in the car. The driver said he
had been afraid to stop and wait so he just kept moving — Moros would

*Appendix A lists most Americans and associated civilians who were surrendered.

grab anything the Japs might get from the surrender. The handful of dam-aged weapons we brought back was not enough to turn over to the Japs, the officers told us. We asked if anyone else wanted to try for some more, but nobody volunteered. Most of us were glad the Moros wouldn't turn in their rifles, believing they would use them against the Japs, as General Fort had in mind.

19

Prisoner in Dansalan and Camp Keithley

June 2 to July 1, 1942

Most of the Filipinos marched down to Dansalan on May 27, 1942, to surrender with the Americans. But some stayed to load the GI trucks with supplies that were to be delivered to the Japs. The barefoot Filipino soldiers staggered through the mud with heavy sacks of rice, sugar, and salt the day before we were all to leave. They were clothed in rags and dripped with perspiration. Yelling Filipino officers beat them, but the men were already on their last reserves of strength. When a sack broke open and spilled, Moros and Filipino civilians scooped the contents out of the mud. As news spread that supplies were being loaded and trucked to the Japs, Moros in the region swarmed into camp with excuses of wanting to get something that didn't have to go to the Japs. Before we knew it, they were carrying off everything they could lay hands on and were disrupting loading of the trucks.

When the drivers returned from delivering supplies to the Japs at Dansalan, they told us the Japs were a little jumpy about their going back and forth to our camp. So far the prisoners had been treated well. Yet I thought this benevolent behavior would end after the supplies had been delivered and all of us taken in. But if the Japs continued to be relaxed, we might be able to escape.

Most discussion, however, was about not going down to Dansalan at all. A friendly Moro talked with Major Navin for hours about going off into the hills, and another Moro urged Major Schroeder to do the same. I confided my plan to escape soon after surrendering, to Ganasi, who had

142

been helping me with food supplies. When he urged me to escape right away, I answered that I could not disobey orders. Ganasi said he would help me to escape later if he could. Meanwhile, I gave him my compass, a map, knife, and ammunition for safekeeping. I gave another friendly Moro my prized M-1 rifle to hold for me. It raised my spirits to think about escaping after going through with the surrender. Others made similar agreements with other Moros, but none of us told each other. My decision to surrender and escape later eased my mind, and I forgot about breaking away right then.

The day before our scheduled departure on May 30, 1942, the Moros gathered in a cordon around the area where we were loading the trucks. Now and then one or two would rush toward a truck to steal something. Major Schroeder and other officers fired their pistols over the heads of the crowd and cursed them. Finally, the officers stationed guards at the corners of our dwindling area; the guards kept the Moros at bay by firing machine guns over their heads. We manned the guns all night. On signal the next morning the guards grabbed their guns and clambered aboard the loaded trucks as the Moros surged forward behind them. As we roared away, hundreds of Moros rushed into camp, trampling each other in the mud to loot what we had left. Incredibly, we had gotten away without losing a man in the three days of loading. Down the bumpy, one-lane road we came upon more Moros, standing beside the road and staring at us. Farther on, other Moros called us cowards and traitors and yelled curses at us while brandishing krises and guns. I'm certain they would have attacked if we had not been armed.

After getting past the Moros, we fell into glum silence. Almost at hand was the long-feared surrender to those yellow slant-eyes, who had chased us everywhere and killed our buddies. How could anyone believe they would treat us as hostages instead of prisoners, and how could anyone let Americans surrender like this? I couldn't figure it out and yet I rode on, feeling trapped and miserable. Then I came back to the idea of escaping as soon as possible after obeying General Fort's surrender order. I would look up Ganasi to get some things I left with him, find Sgt. Manook, and become a guerrilla.

Our trucks continued downward and finally brought us to a cleared area near Lake Lanao that belonged to a Moro farmer. Some healthy Brahma cattle grazing there looked inviting. We stopped and began to fire at two of them. Our shots crippled one animal, which started to run. The volley of shots that followed aroused the Moro farmer who ran toward us yelling and waving his arms. But we fired at him, purposely missing but driving him back. We proceeded to butcher the animals and carried away large choice pieces. We had done wrong; thoughts of our surrender and the lack of food we expected had turned us from our previously respectful treatment of civilians. As we drove away, I had the feeling that I knew the Moro we had treated so badly. We had not been close enough for us to recognize each other, but I believed him to be the Moro I had given my M-1 rifle.

After loading the meat, we drove on toward our surrender. I felt terrible. It was all I could do to keep from jumping out of the truck. But then I would be a deserter. How foolish to surrender like this. My buddies felt the same way, but we believed if we didn't turn ourselves in as General Fort had agreed, our comrades already in Japanese hands would be shot. So breaking away now would plague us forever. There was no other way than to surrender and escape later.

The familiar route to Dansalan took us past Moro gardens gone to weeds and shacks now deserted, as well as signs of skirmishes and an occasional dead animal. At the edge of Dansalan dozens of destroyed and deserted houses came into view. We kept looking for Japs — we thought they might fire on us so we would have a final battle. But the first Jap we saw was a short, scrawny sentry, who stopped us and motioned where we should go. His Japanese words meant nothing to us, and his scowl made us question the wisdom of our surrender. Inside town we passed more Japs, walking or riding in trucks, who directed us onward without raising their guns.

Dansalan was a wreck. The Japs had bombed it and our demolition troops had made it useless for them. But the little Catholic church and the Moro cottages along the lake were untouched, as were the homes of the missionaries. Finally a Jap stopped us at the printing house, where the earlier group of Americans was standing. Japanese soldiers directed us to a vacant lot across the road while our friends watched in silence. Small signs in English showed where we were to place various items — guns in one stack, bayonets and knives in another, and ammunition in a separate pile. Then we had to lay out our personal belongings. Inspection of our personal things took time because a Japanese interpreter carefully recorded and described each item. He took the knife I had hidden and was about to take my boyhood Sea Scout Manual, but then decided to let me keep it. The Japs carried out the shakedown in a firm but civil manner. After they finished, they sent us across the road where we joined our comrades.

Getting together with them made us feel better and thankful to be alive. Our buddies told us that these Japs didn't know what to do with us or how to treat us. They had been shock troops who took Singapore and fought in Burma but had no experience in holding prisoners of war. Their relaxed attitude continued after we arrived — they didn't bother us but kept us in a specified area around the printing house most of the time.

The earlier prisoners enjoyed the fresh meat of the Brahma cattle. The Japs wondered how we had obtained the meat, and it looked like they might take it away from us. But we ate it hurriedly and gave some away while they were still uncertain. Some of the meat went to the Filipino troops held back of the printing house in deserted Moro shacks. I volunteered to take a choice hindquarter to the missionaries who were billeted across the road — other missionaries were also confined there whom the Japs had picked up elsewhere.

The missionaries were surprised to see me because they thought I had taken to the hills. They greeted me warmly, and informed me that Major Heidger had come over the second morning after the surrender to deliver a baby. Miss Amelia Pitco was there — a big, handsome woman, she had shown me how to prepare tasty dishes for the GIs when I was mess sergeant at Camp Keithley. Now, seeing my bare feet, she gave me a pair of tennis shoes she had saved for herself.

Rev. Downs said that the missionaries were glad to surrender and not be left to the mercy of the Moros. I later talked to Mrs. Lane and her child. The Japs had sent her beautiful flowers from the missionaries' gardens and gave her husband a formal funeral befitting his rank.

I had been in the prison camp only a short time when I was detailed to work in the kitchen with Sgt. Jimmy Palmer, still weak from malaria. Palmer had recently refused to help feed the group from Camp Y when they arrived at General Fort's headquarters en route to surrender. But now his attitude changed, and we got along extremely well. Two old buddies who had helped me before, Coty and Pupario, again worked in the kitchen, and Lt. Robert Pratt, 81st Division Finance Officer, was now our mess officer and tried hard to get food. I didn't like the assignment although we were free of Japanese supervision. The men on outside details told of being constantly under the eyes of the Japs. Yet they managed to get away with something now and then.

The Japanese gave us no food. Nevertheless, we accumulated and hid several sacks of flour, salt, and rice. But they soon discovered our hoard and took all the flour. When we protested, the Japs said they would reimburse us with rice. But instead they took most of our rice, too. I spent a lot of time buying food from Moros at the Dansalan open-air market — the Japs liked the idea of not having to feed us. I used money collected from the men; before the surrender we had been given large amounts of emergency money that the Moros continued to honor. The Moros charged exorbitant prices, which we gladly paid for chicken, duck, eggs, bananas, mangoes, tomatoes, and potatoes. A big problem, though, was to get enough of one item to feed everyone at one time.

The Moro merchants had other things to sell, including American goods, and clothing. I noticed a Moro with a number of shoes, which I began to go through since I didn't have any except the tennis shoes from Miss Pitco. I found a pair that was a perfect fit. I looked closer and realized they were my own, which had been stolen months before. I wished I could get my hands on the thief who had left me barefoot. But there was nothing to do but pay.

At first we had considered the emergency money as "play money," not realizing its usefulness. Oddly enough, it had been printed in the printing house where we were held. In the early days of captivity we had plenty of time on our hands. The result was a lot of gambling. Many lost all they had while others amassed large amounts. Palmer, my fellow mess sergeant, won an enormous sum and flaunted his winnings before the losers. Yet, whenever food or other essentials were needed for the kitchen, Palmer was more than generous in his contributions.

While some gambled, some slipped away to practice sumo wrestling with Bill Knortz — it was the same group who had established Camp Y beyond General Fort's headquarters, where Major Heidger had found us. We used a vacant Moro house, which had several large mattresses in various rooms — the Moro must have had a few wives — which we placed together for a practice mat. We posted a guard, realizing we risked our lives. Major Heidger didn't know about our wrestling, but every time we discussed escape plans, he sensed it. He proceeded to lecture us about our duties as POWs. He warned us not to try to escape, and promised to press desertion charges against any man who did. He made this threat constantly, and the Japs declared that if anyone tried to escape, they would automatically shoot ten of the escapee's nearest friends. All of this held us back from trying anything.

While we were prisoners at the printing press, Jap soldiers would make nightly visits to American officers who were quartered on the top floor. They brought saki and wanted to party with our officers, who could not say no. They joined the Japs in drinking toasts and singing songs — the Japs' favorite was "Auld Lang Syne." This was amusing at first but got old fast, especially when the raucous singing continued into the night while we were trying to sleep below. More galling, we had to stand at attention while the visiting Japs paraded through the building with rifles and fixed bayonets, and clanked up the stairs with hob-nailed boots. Sometimes they would come late at night, drunk, and awaken us. We were quick to obey their order to stand at attention, fearing one of them might stick a bayonet into a laggard.

Nevertheless, worse was to come. These rough-and-ready soldiers moved on, probably to more combat duty. Their replacements were occupation troops — extremely young men and a number of veterans, too old to keep up with the front-line fighting. We soon learned the difference.

At muster the new Japs foisted a new counting system on us. The previous Japs had counted us twice daily, but the replacements forced us to count ourselves by calling out Japanese numbers in sequence as we stood in formation. Anyone slow in learning Japanese numbers or making a mistake got a hard slap on each cheek. I soon realized that the best place to line up was in the middle of the formation because prisoners in the front rank or ends of ranks were convenient targets, and often got slapped when anyone missed the count.

About June 10, 1942, the guards invaded our quarters with fixed bayonets and searched each of us for any item of Japanese origin. They seemed to be looking for things taken from Japanese civilians, who were imprisoned by Filipino authorities after the war started. The soldiers also wanted the contents of Japanese stores that had been confiscated. During the search, the Japs abused and beat us severely, giving rise to urgent talk of escape. We were disgusted with the American officers who had talked us into surrender on grounds that the Japs would treat us well — a far cry from what was happening. The next night the Japs stormed in and woke us up in the middle of the night. The roll call showed everyone to be there — our escape talk had only been talk. But the Japs and our officers, who were standing by, were surprised that no one had vanished. (It looked like our own officers had betrayed us to stop an escape). The Japs were jumpy and picked out some of us at random to beat up. After they left, Major Heidger gave us another lecture and repeated his threat to bring desertion charges against any who escaped.

While guarding against our escape, the Japs tried to impress the Moros with lengthy practice-firing of all guns and elaborate bayonet drill. Yet fear of the Moros restricted Japanese activity to open areas not exposed to surprise attack. There were rumors that Moros had killed several Japs. Two Moros who hung around the camp looked ready to kill Japs at any opportunity, confident they would ride a white horse to paradise if they died fighting their enemy.

On June 14, 1942, the Japs became disturbed enough to march us across the river to Camp Keithley on the makeshift bridge our boys had constructed for them. We were assigned one of the few buildings still standing. Directly across the river stood the Dansalan Hotel, site of the Japanese military headquarters. Now that the river separated them from the Moros in Dansalan, the Jap guards seemed less jittery and their control over us loosened. Many of us constructed comfortable beds with wood and burlap sacking. I used a wicker woven frame for a good bed, which I hid beneath cardboard during the day.

We continued to provide our own food. A Jap guard took us across the river to the Moro market. The Japs still liked the idea of us getting our own food and at the same time providing the Moros with customers. It was also a chance to flaunt us as prisoners. When my guard's back was turned, I would buy choice items the merchant quickly brought out of hiding. Sometimes a buddy would attract the attention of the guard while others hustled back across the bridge with black market purchases. I used Philippine pesos and sometimes dollars for sales and purchases from both Moros and Filipinos. Discovery would have put my life at risk, but I was getting confident and reckless. The Japs moved the market closer to the river, where the guards felt safer. But I kept on dealing without being caught.

Before we had moved across the river to Camp Keithley, the Japs had called for enlisted American and Filipino volunteers to drive trucks, repair roads, and build a bridge across the river to Keithley to replace the bridge we had destroyed to halt the Japanese advance. These prisoners were very useful, and the Japs treated them with consideration and favor. But a couple of our men taught the Japs how to use and repair some of our firearms — most of us resented this and had little use for these men. I felt that way about Clark, who had helped me take the truckload of supplies for Major Heidger up to General Fort's headquarters. Now Clark showed the Japs the way up there.

The American officers had very little to do. They slept, read, talked, and sometimes quarreled — more than once about who would win the war. The officers wanted as much food as the men who had been working all day — sometimes more. But I served equal portions to everyone and seconds to the men who worked. My decision was supported by Lt. Albert Chase of the 81st Division, the mess officer then. Chase also backed me up when I complained of officers getting in my way by making peanut brittle when I needed the kitchen to prepare our regular meals. They would buy the ingredients of rice, candy, peanuts, and brown sugar from the Moros. Furthermore, Lt. Chase got the kitchen organized so that everyone who ate had to help out. Many officers liked this because it gave them something to do. The few who protested soon fell into line.

Work came in bunches. One day we had a great many beans, which took hours to shell. But sometimes we had to wait several days before we could get enough eggs or fruit to go around for one meal. Constant minor jobs consisted of grinding and roasting native coffee, sorting rice, making rice meal by hand, and making milk from coconut meat. Nevertheless, our food situation worsened: Prices got higher and food more scarce.

Then the Moro chief, Ganasi, came to the rescue. He had befriended us just before our surrender. Now he sent a boatload of eggs, bananas, and camotes (sweet potatoes). Other boatloads of food followed. (The Japs did not interfere because of their effort to keep the Moros friendly.) A messenger from Ganasi said his chief was ready to help us escape — if I tried alone, his men would help me past the guards. The M-1 rifle that I had left with a Moro was ready for me. But I was not ready to attempt a break, fearful of the retaliation against my buddies left behind.

Despite the tension, we found time for recreation. In good weather, officers and men played baseball in front of the barracks. The Japs looked on, at first with amusement and then with hate and envy in their eyes because the Americans were having a good time. It was different with sumo wrestling. We found the guards did not object to this familiar sport. They watched with interest as Bill Knortz helped us improve our skills. Soon the guards wanted to participate, and we had to agree when they insisted.

Since I was a fairly good wrestler, some of them wanted to take me on. I tried to make these contests a tie and usually could do so. But when I unintentionally got the best of one Jap, it made him furious. Then others tried to exhaust me by requesting one match after another. I decided to quit, fearing injury if they realized I was stronger than they. The Japanese officers disapproved of their men wrestling with us and finally forbade all wrestling — they believed our keeping fit was part of an escape effort.

The Japs continued to hold General Fort. Fort's orderly now was our small buddy, Dick Beck — he had become delirious after enemy aircraft attacked us aboard the *Mayon* en route to Mindanao. Beck had stayed overly dependent on his buddies, and even as a prisoner, our officers had arranged this easy job for him. Although General Fort mostly kept to himself, he sometimes would come into the kitchen and insist on doing something. He ate what the rest of us had and complimented us on our fare. Fort made his own cigars out of strong native tobacco sold by the Moros. Sometimes he placed a cigar upright in his pipe to smoke it, staring across Lake Lanao toward his hideout in the mountains where he had expected to continue the fight. Even after his cigar had turned to ashes, he remained gazing into the distance. I imagined he was recalling incidents all the way from his boyhood to the recent past — his life had centered around Lake Lanao, where he was born and had risen to peacetime command of the Philippine Constabulary in the region.

After mid-June, the Japs sent large patrols into Moro country beyond the small area in which they had previously been content to operate. Some patrols returned with many badly wounded, whom our doctors treated. But in Dansalan the Japs staged big parades and practiced firing all their guns every evening to discourage a Moro attack on Camp Keithley. The Moros, however, continued to ambush and kill patrolling Japs.

One day while I was cleaning up the kitchen after breakfast, I saw a figure stumble and fall a couple hundred feet across the parade ground. As I hurried out, the man rose and moved forward. He was a walking skeleton, garbed in rags, who carried a crooked stick for a cane. Huge, infected wounds covered his body; each was nearly a foot long and an inch or so deep, and looked as though it had been made by a curved Moro kris. He appeared to be in great pain. Even after Major Heidger treated and dressed the man's wounds, he did not speak. I found him something to eat, and while I was feeding him, he managed his first words. In a low monotone, he told me his name was Kildritch. He was an American civilian who had left his plantation in Pagadian to volunteer his help when the Japs struck at Ganasi in early May 1942.

He gazed off into space as he told his story. We didn't interrupt him, even though we didn't catch everything because of his low voice and long pauses. During the Japanese advance, Kildritch and Commander Teasdale had been cut off from their lines and found themselves in the company of a strange Moro, who offered to show them the way back to their own forces. But the Moro wanted Teasedale's shoes in payment — the commander refused because he couldn't last long in the jungle without them. As twilight enveloped them, the Americans tired. Worse, they sensed the Moro was leading them around in circles. They stopped to rest by a jungle stream. After taking off their shoes to cool their feet in the water, the Americans bent over to splash water on their faces. Kildritch heard a thud behind him and turned around just in time to see Teasedale's decapitated head rolling into the stream. Before Kildritch could get up, the Moro was swinging his wavy kris toward him. Kildritch threw himself forward and raised his hands to protect his head. After that he remembered nothing until he regained consciousness later that night. In the moonlight he could see that he had rolled about 20 feet down an embankment into a ditch beside a road. Teasedale's body lay beside him, minus weapons and shoes. Two other bodies close by were the remains of Martin and Defenbaugh from the 14th Squadron — members of a three-man scouting party that had not returned. (We learned later that the third man, Cook, had joined Lt. Col. Fertig's resistance forces.)

Kildritch was bleeding badly alongside the road and then lost consciousness again. When he opened his eyes, he was looking into the face of another Moro. He was certain his life was ending. But his panic gradually fell away as the Moro told him in English that he was a schoolteacher and wanted to help him. The friendly Moro brought Kildritch to a small Moro settlement but had to move him again when the Japs got close. After initial improvement, his condition worsened. His high fever made him so delirious that the Moros had to hold him down with sandbags. They treated him with native medicines but didn't have the kinds of food he needed. Kildritch stayed with them for two months before deciding to give himself up to the Japs, thinking he would get good medical care by being with American prisoners.

Under Major Heidger's care, Kildritch did improve. He spent much of his time in the kitchen trying to help me. Because he was a civilian, we tried to persuade him to join the missionaries instead of staying with us. But he insisted that he was a soldier at heart and was getting excellent medical treatment from Major Heidger. We felt this was a bad decision, especially now that the Japs were treating us more brutally.

Meanwhile, the local Moros were growing bolder despite ever larger displays of Japanese arms and men. They crowded more thickly to the edge of the Japanese restricted area. The Japs shot off rounds of ammunition to scare them off, but the Moros stood their ground and waved their krises. By the latter part of June 1942, other Moros were inflicting still greater casualties on Japanese patrols. Without doctors of their own, the Japs kept ours busier than ever. Both the casualties and their reliance on our doctors made the Japs lose face, and encouraged them to turn to barbaric treatment of us — a safe place to vent their anger.

Our lives became miserable. Sports were forbidden, and we could not whistle or sing. The Japs barged into our barracks at any time, taking anything they wanted, whether sentimental or practical, such as watches, rings, razors, lockets, and cigarette lighters. They even took our homemade beds and our shoes. When they noticed someone's resentful expression, they gave him a brutal slap in the face or hit him in the pit of the stomach with a closed fist. Worse, they would kick a resentful prisoner in the groin, trying to rupture him, or try to break his shins with their hob-nailed shoes. Our officers did not escape brutal treatment. More than once in the evening when they were playing cards, the guards burst in, claiming they had seen a light that they believed to be a signal to the Moros across the lake. No matter what it was, the guards took out the Japanese frustration about the Moros on the American officers, hitting and kicking them or stomping on them with their heavy shoes. At the same time the Japs tried a separate policy toward the 300 Filipino prisoners. A few of them who claimed to be pro-Japanese were freed, but the Japs threatened to kill those who refused to renounce America. They were tied to trees. Then Japanese soldiers whipped swords at them, barely missing their heads.

Verge Haifley and Captain Wyatt made plans to escape but were betrayed by an unknown stool pigeon. By luck, they were not executed. I kept my plans to join Ganasi to myself. But I was stopped from doing anything because of the Japanese threat to kill ten friends of anyone who escaped. On the other hand, Cpl. Bill Knortz, Pvt. Robert Ball, and seamen James S. Smith and Bill Johnson of the PT boats were talking openly of escaping. Knortz asked Sgt. Herbert Zincke to join them, but he refused. I tried to talk Knortz out of the idea, pointing out it would be better to escape as a unit. Then we would have a fighting chance, and no one would be left to face the consequences. But Knortz turned a deaf ear.

One evening we heard a commotion between our barracks and the Filipinos' quarters. We rushed outside and saw several Japanese soldiers standing around a struggling horse. They were stabbing it again and again with their bayonets. Looking closer, I was horrified to see that it was my horse Calio, which I had left behind when the Japs broke through our lines. This cruelty revolted my comrades and me, but we knew the danger of showing how we felt. Calio finally fell struggling to the ground, and then they spread his hind legs with ropes while others beat him in the groin with clubs until he died. Bill Knortz declared, "If the Japs can torture a dumb animal, just think what could happen to us if we're stupid enough to stick around. I'm fed up and I'm going to get out of this mess no matter what."

The Japs cut up the horse and brought a large portion to our barracks. If we didn't eat it, they would give us no more meat of any kind. Many of us believed we couldn't eat Calio but thought we had better prepare the flesh and put on some kind of a show of eating. We ground the meat and made horse burgers. I shall never forget how the Japs stood there watching to see what would happen. Some were so hungry that they ate heartily while others just went through the motions, slipping their portions to those who could eat. At first I couldn't swallow, remembering how I had enjoyed riding Calio, but then my hunger drove me to eat my share. We learned later that the Japs had tortured Calio because he had thrown a Japanese officer who had abused him. Many Japanese soldiers had been watching, so the officer had lost face. His revenge had been to have Calio tortured to death.

Eating Calio did not help our critical food shortage. Col. Mitchell, the senior POW officer under General Fort, and other officers tried to get the Japs to help us with our food supply. They had done nothing to provide food heretofore, and we had used our own money to buy food from the Moros. Now the money was almost gone, and the Japs had cut off our contact with the Moros. Col. Mitchell finally worked out a temporary deal with the Japs. Each day, when it was convenient for the Japs, a guard would take a few enlisted prisoners to the Moro market across the river. But we could make our purchases only after the Japs had bought what they wanted. Under this arrangement I could not purchase enough food to prevent the men from being hungry most of the time.

However, the Moro merchants and I tried to make the best of the situation. The Moros would display and sell only poor or not very desirable food to the Japs. Then when my turn came and the Jap had moved away, the Moros would bring out the better food. Once, when the guard caught me buying the better food, his blows left me stunned for the rest of the day.

All of the confusion, hate, brutality, and hunger had created a constant tension by late June 1942. A few men helped the Japs in small ways to get a little more to eat. A few of the officers were fighting among themselves, and some enlisted men came to blows. We found that one of our best friends was the stool pigeon who had often betrayed our escape plans.

We were freed from Major Heidger's constant threats of desertion charges for escapees when he was reassigned. Instead of being CO of the enlisted prisoners, Heidger now treated sick Japs full time. The Japs needed him because so many of them had contracted venereal disease and were in bad shape. The local women's success in weakening the Japanese garrison amused us.

Captain A. H. Price, who had fought the Japs so persistently with his mountain guns, took direct charge of the enlisted men in place of Major Heidger. He called us together for an encouraging talk that I'll never forget. He was delighted to have us — the first Americans he had led in the Philippines. His previous assignment had been to train Filipinos. In the days that followed, he made a great hit.

Price persuaded the Japs to let me and a few others purchase a quantity of food at the Moro market. We bought all we could carry, believing it might be a long time before we could get more. On the way back we passed the electric-light plant where Knortz, Smith, Ball, and Johnson were working — the foursome who talked so much about escaping. They saw me struggling under a large bunch of bananas and begged for a few. I told them I was sorry, but the bananas would be distributed equally at meal time. They were peeved, and grumbled as they walked to the barracks with me. I could understand their attitude because all of us were beginning to think, "to hell with the other fellow, it's now survival of the fittest."

20

Mindanao Death March

July 1–7, 1942

A few mornings later Smith and Ball went off to their routine work at the electrical plant. Knortz and Johnson said they were going to wash their clothes in the river. At noon, none of the four had returned so I saved their portions of lunch, thinking they would be a little late. Later that afternoon, two friends and I were allowed to go to the market for food, but there was nothing much to buy. Coming back, we saw a large group of Americans out on the parade ground. I sensed danger, but we were too close to make a break. Approaching, we realized that most of the Americans were standing in a single line at attention. and were surrounded by Japs with machine guns and fixed bayonets. Several Japs were counting the men. At bayonet point, Japanese soldiers pushed the three of us into the line. I knew immediately that Knortz, Ball, Smith, and Johnson had escaped.

The angry Japs counted us over and over again to make sure of the number missing. Finally they trained their machine-guns on us. We thought this was the end — what a fool I had been to surrender. The Japs carefully counted a last time. Then they ordered every second prisoner to step one pace forward — I was one of them. But nothing happened. In the sudden stillness, I could hear Col. Eugene Mitchell, a large, calm man who had commanded the 61st Regt. in the 81st Division, pleading with the senior Japanese officer to give us a fighting chance. The prolonged conversation was going through a Japanese interpreter. I finally gathered from Mitchell's words that the immediate danger had passed. Then I heard something about a death march but could not tell when or where to. Suddenly the Japs ordered us into the barracks.

Next morning, July 2, 1942, I got up early to fix breakfast. I had barely started when a Jap guard burst into the kitchen with drawn bayonet — he was undoubtedly edgy about escapes. Fortunately, a cup of coffee calmed him down, and he let me proceed with my work. Right after breakfast, the Japs ordered us to bring out all our possessions and line up on the parade ground again. As I picked up my belongings, I realized with a start that I had made notes on the pages of a Catholic missal about the various plans of escape we had discussed. I had no way of disposing of it now — if I left it in the barracks, we would all be threatened until I confessed. Full of anxiety, I included it in my pile of belongings. But the Japanese soldier who looked through my stuff leafed through it without interest and dropped it to the ground. He may have been familiar with Catholic missals carried by Filipinos and some Americans, and figured my jottings in English were of a religious nature.

Then the interpreter came along and threatened me if I didn't point out who had been friends of Knortz, Johnson, Ball, and Smith. I explained that they all bunked together in a separate room and also worked together at the electrical plant — not closely with anyone else. I did not know them well. Apparently no one admitted to be a close friend of the escapees or knew of anyone who was. The frustrated Japs took Sgt. John Hughes across the river to their headquarters in the Dansalan hotel.

Meantime the interpreter asked me why we had surrendered. It was hard for him to understand because it was so unlike the Japanese tradition of dying in battle rather than being taken prisoner. He insisted we had put up a good fight around Bacolod Grande. He may have been fishing for the names of the American officers who had engaged them at that time. I told him we had surrendered because of the Japanese advantage in airpower, equipment, and manpower but did not mention our combat leaders.

In the afternoon a pale and shaken Sgt. Hughes and three others who slept near the four escapees returned from being interrogated across the river. I asked Hughes about it in case I was called, but he refused to say a word. Sometime later, we heard volleys of shots outside, but being confined inside, we could see nothing. A little later a guard came and motioned to Hughes and two others to come with him. Afraid they were goners, we were greatly relieved by their return an hour later. This time they talked to us.

The Japs had sent them to gather up the personal effects of Col. Robert H. Vesey, Captain A. H. Price, and Sgt. John L. Chandler, whom the Japs had executed. (Chandler had become CO of the 14th Squadron, but his promotion to Lt. did not take effect through lack of General Fort's signature.) I can only speculate that the Japs had selected these leaders because they had determined them to be the combat leaders who had slowed the Japanese advance along Lake Lanao. Captain Price may also have been a candidate because of his vociferous objection some days before when a Jap soldier rummaged around his room for souvenirs. The hotheaded American had thrown a mess kit at the Jap and driven him out.

The Japs continued questioning some of us the next day, prolonging my dread that they would find out I had been a close acquaintance of Knortz. After the questioning ceased that afternoon, I began to think the Japs had not succeeded in identifying any close friend of the escaped four, making us safe from immediate execution. But there would be more Japanese retaliation. They told us we were to begin the 100-mile march to Cagayan the next morning, on July 4, 1942 — the date a deliberate humiliation. The Japs announced at Dansalan that there would be a Fourth of July parade down the National Road to Iligan — the first segment in the march to Cagayan.

Still free to work in the kitchen on the day before the march began, I made some peanut brittle for the men to carry. At breakfast next day everyone hid a little of it in his clothing. I set aside a can of pineapple juice for myself and then forgot it when the Japs suddenly called for us to line up on the parade ground. I hurried back and grabbed the juice, but a Jap was already there to scrounge any food that was left. He chased me out the door, but, juice in hand, I kept running and joined the other POWs.

On the parade ground the Japs arranged the Americans in a column, four abreast, and then tied us in place with wires through our belts. They ran the wires the length of the column and also crossways to keep each rank of four abreast. The Japs tied the officers in with the enlisted men except for General Fort, Col. Mitchell, and Major Heidger, who rode in trucks. The 300 Filipinos making the march were not tied together — none of them had escaped and they were treated better for the time being.

One Filipino driver whispered to me a warning of the brutality we could expect — he was aware of the Bataan Death March, which we did not know about. He told me, "They will kill you if you lag or stray to the side." I passed the word as well as I could without attracting Japanese attention. I worried that our Death March might be worse because the Japs had lost so much face from the Moro attacks and the escape of four American prisoners.

We headed north, mostly downhill, toward the coastal town of Iligan, retracing our mid–January route to Lake Lanao. The Japs had publicized the march to flaunt us before spectators, but the onlookers mostly stayed hidden in the jungle. The Japs pushed us along at a fairly fast pace, but we kept up pretty well, as did the Filipinos, who weren't tied together but who did have to suffer being barefoot. General Fort rode ahead of the Americans. He sat alone, trying to keep erect on the bed of a lurching truck. He was a slight, spare figure with thinning gray hair, proud in his silver stars. Col. Mitchell rode on another truck with Major Heidger.

I had guarded against the sun with a fatigue hat with grass underneath it and a piece of towel over my shoulders. I wore a fairly new pair of shoes, but a guard noticed them. I showed no resentment when he made me give them up, and then tossed me the softer, well-worn shoes he was wearing. His shoes were a perfect fit for me.

We had not gone far when Kildritch, the planter who had turned himself in to get medical treatment, collapsed on the road and had to be carried by the three prisoners wired with him. They were soon exhausted and called to Col. Mitchell that they couldn't do it much longer. Mitchell dropped back and explained the situation to Lt. Osawa, who was in charge of the march. But Osawa angrily replied, "This march is my responsibility." He ordered Mitchell to get in the truck with him. Soon I noticed an extremely ugly, bearded, older Jap take Kildritch to the rear, supporting the American with his left arm and keeping his rifle under his right arm. Mitchell hoped Kildritch would be put in a second truck. Instead, the Jap led him 75 yards behind the column and took him into some bushes. A shot rang out, and the guard came back into sight. Then Osawa screamed at the guard and pointed his finger behind his head. The ugly Jap returned to the bushes, leaned over, fired another shot and rejoined the column. He walked up beside me and insisted I take the tobacco and peanut brittle he had taken from the dead Kildritch. Hiding my revulsion, I accepted. The Jap grinned.

By mid-morning we were near Momungan when a Moro suddenly came into sight, rounding a bend in the road ahead. Armed with a large bolo, he pulled his cart directly toward us. The Japs nervously prodded us to the side of the road with bayonets to give the Moro a wide berth. But he ignored us and went on.

About midday, we were still being pushed at a steady pace when my friend, Major Navin, fell to the ground just ahead of me. I offered him my pineapple juice and tried to get him on his feet. I asked a nearby medic to help, but he just stared at me. The juice did not help. Navin passed out and fell back on the ground. The Japs shot him right there.

On a bluff overlooking the road, two Americans stood in high grass and helplessly watched as Navin was killed. Lt. Col. Wendell Fertig and Capt. Charley Hedges had been evacuated from Luzon but had not yet decided what to do. Fertig had been content to stay hidden and tend his vegetable garden. Next day, however, Fertig told Hedges, "Charley, you and I are going to make it as rough as we can on those little bastards." In time, Fertig did organize resistance on Mindanao Island.

After Navin had fallen, we came upon a Filipino POW crawling beside the road and pleading with a Japanese guard for his life. The pair had dropped back from the Filipino prisoners ahead, who had slowed down. Soon the guard grew tired of prodding the helpless prisoner along with his bayonet and used it to kill him. By the end of the day, the Japs had slaughtered three or four other Filipinos — one of them was a medical officer with a Red Cross band on his arm.

Lt. Col. Barnes, our older medical officer, had loaded himself down with bedding. By afternoon he was staggering and keeping up only because he was being pulled by Lt. Pratt, a young, good-sized officer who was first man in Barnes's column. Finally, Barnes discarded his extra gear but was so exhausted he still depended on Pratt to pull him along and save him from being shot.

Another lucky survivor was Dick Beck, who had been maneuvered into a safe spot as General Fort's orderly while a prisoner at Camp Keithley. Now Herb Zincke, a sturdy sergeant, managed to be tied next to the small Beck and kept him going all the way to Iligan. Without help Beck would not have made it through the day.

When we reached Iligan, the Japs stopped the march and let us sit down. The Jap who had taken my new shoes that morning had done me a favor. His old shoes had given me no blisters while my new shoes had given the Jap several, which he was now examining. Apparently he would have lost too much face by exchanging with me again during the march. When I lay back and held my feet in the air to help circulation to the rest of my body, I attracted the attention of the ugly guard who had shot Kildritch. He nudged me with his bayonet and asked why I had my feet up. I explained, and he seemed to agree it was a good idea. He seemed to have taken an interest in me — he had given me poor Kildritch's peanut brittle and now gave me a friendly nudge with his bayonet.

After a brief time, the Japs herded us up the stairs of a two-story schoolhouse across the street from a Catholic church. Tired after the 25-mile march and having gone without food since morning, some Americans barely made it to the second floor, even with the help of friends. The Japs confined the 300 Filipinos on the first floor below us. I wondered why God was allowing this brutality. At the same time I was thankful to be alive but was so angry I wanted to kill any Jap within reach.

The guards pushed the Americans into an 18-foot-square room and shut the door. It was so crowded it was difficult to sit down. When we tried to lie down, legs became entangled. Some growled at each other like wild animals while others were too weak or sick to care. The worst and the best of both officers and men came out in the ugly confusion. But the natural leaders established some semblance of order — partly because most could understand the danger of the old building's ancient, wooden floor breaking through and tumbling us on top of the Filipinos. Therefore we stood huddled around the edges of the room. When we moved around, we carefully stayed away from the sagging planks in the center.

Upon entering, I had noticed the only window and was lucky enough to get there first. I had just settled down when the door opened. There stood the old Jap who had taken an unwelcome interest in me. He pointed at me through the crowd and demanded in Japanese to see the "Old Man." Someone yelled, "A friend of yours is here, Vic." There were suppressed chuckles. I worked my way around the room to the Jap, who had brought a few bananas, which I divided with others. Then I returned to the window — the rest of the men had honored my first-possession rights.

I was so thirsty I pulled out a piece of sugar cane I had picked out of the mud on the street in Iligan. I quenched my thirst by chewing it slowly until I dreamed that rain was falling in my open mouth — the best drinking water I had ever tasted. Then I became conscious of real rain. I heard water running down a drainpipe just outside. I reached for it. But when the window creaked, the guard outside aimed his gun at me and yelled. I jumped back and sank below the sill. There I had to listen to the running water while I cursed the Japs under my breath.

Then I was distracted and annoyed to hear Lt. Col. Barnes complaining about the personal effects he had lost on the march — oblivious of his good fortune in being alive. He surely would have been shot if Lt. Pratt — at the head of the column in which Barnes was tied — had not been able to drag him along for mile after mile while the Japs were yelling at him to speed up. Pratt had been the mess officer when I was the cook under the Japs at Camp Keithley. Now, Pratt lay vomiting close to Barnes, who took no notice, though he was a physician. When Pratt had to vomit, we rushed him to the window, but the guards yelled at us to get away. Poor Pratt, therefore, lay there messing up the floor while we tried to comfort him. Barnes and Major Heidger, our 14th Squadron surgeon, said there was nothing they could do for him. Then Pratt fell into a coma.

By 4 A.M. we were all desperate for water — the men were more than irritable. My old friend Captain Katz went downstairs and worked his way through the crowd of Filipinos to the door. There he talked the sleepy guard into letting him go to the hydrant nearby. He drank all the water he could and filled his canteen. When Katz begged the guard to let us all go out, the Jap called his sergeant, who decided to let us all line up since we would be easier to handle if we had water. He posted guards along the line to the hydrant as we satisfied our thirst and filled our canteens. We brought water back to those who could not go for themselves. We all felt better but knew the Death March might continue at any time. And we needed food badly.

Now Pratt, who had been in a coma for a couple hours, came to. Two of us tried to get him to drink water and snap out of it before the Japs forced us to march again. But every time he took a swallow, he became sick. He was rational so we tried to rouse him and promised to help him in every possible way if he made the necessary effort. But he only shook his head and muttered, "It's no use. I can't make it." Then he mumbled, "My finance book will never balance." After another shake of his head, he lay still — dead in my arms with a faraway look in his eyes. The others stared down at him. Seeing him die and knowing him well, I became almost blind with rage and vowed to take it out on the Japs. Pratt was the son of a minister in Madison, Wisconsin, and had just reached manhood. His upbringing had served him well through the hardships we had undergone. In the final days of fighting Pratt, as Finance Officer of the 81st Division, had signed for food in values greater than authorized. The fact that he would personally have to make good the large discrepancy after the war preyed on his mind. I could not talk him out of this obsession earlier or as he was dying.

When we reported Pratt's death to the Japs, they ordered that three of us should bury him nearby. I volunteered and the three of us got him down the stairs. But when we reached the door, I was too angry to go farther. I beckoned to a good friend of Pratt's to take my place. I could not stand still but paced back and forth, thinking of how to avenge Pratt's death. My friends told me to take it easy — nothing could be done now. I was calmer by the time the men came back from the burial. They had dug a shallow grave, atop which they placed a wooden cross with Lt. Pratt's dog tags. Before his body was carried out, one American, showing and feeling no disrespect, had taken his shoes; others took his mess kit and some of his clothes, which they sorely needed.

Just then the hideous Jap who seemed to be my pal came into the building, calling for the "Old Man." When he found me, his face lit up in a way that sent shudders up and down my spine — I feared I was being singled out for punishment. He exclaimed that he had come to keep his promise — what promise? He handed me a sack that contained two boiled eggs, several bananas, and some cheap candy. When I asked if he minded my sharing the food with my buddies, he nodded his head as if he really felt sorry for us. But he stared stupidly at the men who wolfed down every thing he had brought. He also gave me a few cigarettes, which I likewise shared. I thanked him for his kindness and asked if I could repay him, but he shook his head. I wondered if he had bought these gifts or stolen them.

He shook his head again when I told him we needed much more food to stay alive. Then he told us he thought we were not going to march that day and now said with grin we might get some food. Once he had left, I tried to figure out this hideous Jap's actions — he had killed Kildritch willingly but seemed to be fond of me. My buddies said it was a good thing to have a Jap who was interested enough to bring supplies. But when I asked them if they would like to be in my shoes, they shook their heads.

A little later that day a Japanese sergeant and guard asked for volunteers to get some rice at the dock. I decided to go for the fresh air and possibility of food, even though I feared an enemy trick to separate some of us to torture or shoot. Lt. Chase joined me — he had been the mess officer who backed up my allocation of food in the prisoners' mess. Eight others decided to go. We bade the rest goodbye as if we would never see them again and boarded a large GI truck with three guards and a driver. He jolted us past the ruined buildings of Iligan, now a ghost city. But the cool air felt good as we passed Jap soldiers and some civilians. One Filipino risked his life to secretly make a "V" sign. We reached a large dock with gaping holes that was surrounded by wrecked and disabled craft. Finally we came to a portion of the dock still intact where large sacks of rice lay outside a warehouse. We were eager to load them on the truck, but they were heavy and we were very weak. We loaded some sacks with great difficulty and would have liked to stop but were told we couldn't leave until the truck was filled. We had about reached the end of our rope when a staff car pulled to a screeching halt beside us.

An angry Jap officer with a sword in hand got out of the car. The guards snapped to attention, saluted smartly, and yelled to us at the top of their voices. We dropped our bags and also stood at attention and saluted. We held our breath while the Jap officer looked us over as if he would like to cut off our heads. Suddenly he turned to the guard in charge, half drew his sword, and tongue-lashed him for letting us out. He slapped the chief guard in the face, glared at us, and sped away. The intimidated guards hustled us on the truck, not bothering about the sacks we had dropped on the dock. During our wild ride back, we came close to turning over and were almost thrown out by the sudden stop at the schoolhouse. There the guards rushed us inside where we rejoined the others with great relief. All thought the ten of us had had a tight squeeze. I thought that the excited officer might have been in charge when Knortz and his companions had escaped at Camp Keithley and was still angry from losing face.

While we were gone, the Japs had been asking for money to pay for the rice we were bringing from the dock. To cook it, they let some Filipinos out to build fires under large cauldrons. After the rice was dumped in, it took forever to steam. Then it was brought to the schoolhouse where the starving prisoners waited — almost 300 Filipinos on the first floor and 40 or so Americans on the second. The Filipinos on the first floor had the advantage of location so a few of us Americans took a large ammunition can out through the mob of hungry Filipinos, filled it with rice, grabbed a small can of dried fish, and carried the food up to the second floor.

But at first all the Americans, including officers, were so hungry that there was a wild struggle as each tried to get as much as he could. Yet natural leaders somehow restored order so everyone got some rice and a tiny, stinky fish. In the first greedy moments, however, some pushed aside others and made enemies. I felt less than human myself as I squatted down to eat the rice and a stinking minnow with eyes that stared as if pleading to be spared. Nevertheless, the group's general mood improved.

Next day there was no bustle to indicate the dreaded march would continue so we made the most of this waiting period. Some slept and others mended shoes or traded for a better fit. Others traded with the Filipinos on the ground floor for empty containers to carry water. I watched crowds pass under my window, some going to market but more going to the Catholic church across the street. That night I awoke in the darkness to find everyone asleep. I prayed to God that He would keep us from continuing the march. I said the 23rd Psalm, then fell back into sleep.

The next morning we began to stir soon after daylight. Surprisingly, we had rested fairly well despite our cramped space. We were stretching ourselves and rubbing each other's backs when my Japanese friend appeared with a big smile on his ugly face, asking for the "Old Man." My friends hid their amused smirks as the Jap handed me a cigarette, two rice cakes, and a banana. He believed there would be no march that day and that we might get pork and rice. Of most importance, his command — which conducted the Death March — was being relieved. For a few minutes he smoked a cigarette in silence, not saying a word. Then he said he would not see me again, shook my hand, and bowed low before turning quickly and leaving. I never saw him again, and to this day I do not understand his reasons for liking me. My large beard may have drawn him to me because his own beard stood out among the hairless-faced Japanese soldiers. He may have had some Ainu blood — the Ainus were Japanese aborigines who have been almost entirely absorbed by the present Japanese population. It was hard to figure.

I learned later that the four men who had escaped joined the guerrillas under Lt. Col. Fertig. William G. Knortz, the escape leader, had been a good friend of Lt. John Chandler, who was one of the three POWs executed in retaliation for the escape. Knortz took Chandler's death hard and threw himself into reckless operations against the Japs. Knortz died in action September 11, 1943. It was rumored that he had been paddling toward a pier guarded by several Japs. As usual Knortz had slung two bandoliers of ammunition over his shoulder. It was not completely dark and the Japs discovered him before he could begin firing. To avoid their fire, Knortz slipped into the water only to sink and drown under the weight of his ammunition.

21

Malaybalay

July 7 to late October 1942

We were still talking about the old Jap when there was noise at the doorway. Young Jap soldiers with childish faces stepped in abruptly. They were quite different from the Japs who had taken us on the march. They differed also because they spoke fluent English. But their attitude was not good — they strutted around looking for anyone who did not stand at attention or salute to their satisfaction. The POWs who didn't satisfy were subjected to slaps as well as blows from Jap rifle butts and hob-nailed shoes.

They told us they expected the utmost respect, and that we should realize we were POWs. Then they demanded ten pesos from each of us for the rice and pork we were to have that day. Because some of us had no money, the Japs collected more money from those who had already paid. At the same time, they eyed our personal effects and helped themselves to anything that suited their fancy, such as blankets, mosquito nets, rings, watches, and shoes. The shoes taken from Lt. Pratt's body went to a Jap.

Another item that attracted the Japs were some pieces of eight, old coins that Pvt. Doe, had gotten from a Moro. After the Jap who took them had moved away, Doe made some insulting racial remarks that infuriated the English-speaking Japs on the other side of the room. Now all the Japs stomped out, threatening to deal with us later. We knew we were in for a hard time from these new Japs — completion of the Death March or something else. We began hiding our money in cracks of the ceiling and floor as well as in our clothes and shoes. Two men stuck money on their bodies with adhesive tape that they painted with iodine to look like a wound or sore. In an effort to keep their shoes, two men cut holes in good shoes and scuffed them to give a worn-out appearance.

There was no sign yet of retaliation for Doe's insulting language. The new Japs put the Filipino prisoners to work cleaning a pig and heating huge cauldrons of water in which the animal would be cooked with rice. We watched the simmering pork and rice hungrily, although the small pig would provide little meat when distributed among the Filipino and American prisoners. When it was ready, there was the familiar scramble. Each American managed to get a can of rice and broth plus a piece of pork the size of the end of a thumb. After we had eaten and drunk as much water as possible, we quieted down to wait and see what the Japs would do. I tried to relax at the window by watching people going to church; I imagined they were praying for us. Our nervous wait was ended by the sudden appearance of the Jap guards.

We all came smartly to attention and saluted, but they were not appeased. While they yelled and rained blows on us, we noticed Col. Mitchell was there — he had been brought to watch our punishment. We stood at attention, trying to ignore the beating that one or another of our buddies was taking. The Japs struck us so ferociously I believe it showed the resentment of our feeling of racial superiority that Doe had foolishly brought to their attention. Suddenly they stopped shouting and beating us so Col. Mitchell could speak.

The colonel's expression showed a grimness we had never seen before. He pointed out the Japs' displeasure at our attitude during the shake-down — they had been especially offended by the "pieces of eight" episode. For the insulting remarks made at that time, they were going to shoot someone. If we did not identify the culprit, they would pick someone out at random and shoot him. The guards would give us five minutes to decide.

Now they went outside, leaving Col. Mitchell with us. We were a sick crowd, forced to decide who was to be executed. We all knew it had been Doe who had shot off his mouth and reasoned that he should be the one to pay for the blunder. Yet even though he had not been an ideal officer, no one wanted to send him to death. But none of us wanted to be the one to walk out and be murdered, either. Should we turn Doe over or should we sit tight until the Japs picked someone out and then all fight for him, trying to convince them it was someone else? As we stood there sweating it out, Col. Mitchell tried to get us to decide. When we couldn't, the colonel said he would try something that might work if we stuck together.

When the five minutes were up, the Japs came back and demanded the man to be shot — they pointed their guns at us in case there was resistance. Col. Mitchell declared in a firm voice that it had been difficult to find the right man and it would be of no use to shoot the wrong one. We held our breath. The Japs looked displeased but listened as the colonel went on: "If you do not take anyone out to be shot this time, then all the Americans agree to hand over anyone guilty of a similar charge in the future." Mitchell added that if we failed to point out the culprit, he would offer himself to be shot. The Japs did not look at all satisfied but little by little cooled off and finally accepted the proposition. But they assured the colonel that next time somebody would surely be shot.

The Japs did not leave but walked around looking for anything they might have missed in the first shakedown. They also watched for any signs of resentment. But we had learned our lesson. They took all the money they could find — we didn't believe their excuse that it was needed to buy our food. After they left, we wondered out loud how long we would be able to stay alive. These Japs had no personal grudge against us like the Death March soldiers, who had lost face because four Americans had escaped from them. Yet Doe's racial insults had stirred the new Japs to brutality that threatened our survival.

As if to confirm our despair, the guards came back late that evening and beat and knocked us around some more with lots of shouting. We could do nothing but stand at attention and salute, hoping they would get tired or bored. They finally did cease and loudly told us they had news. We expected it to be bad. Actually it was a proposal. If we gave them 700 pesos, they would purchase boat passage for us to Cagayan, the destination of the march. Then the Japs left, again leaving us in a quandary.

We didn't know when they would come back but thought we should make up our minds quickly in case they returned soon and demanded a decision. We thought there must be a catch. Was this an easy way to get money that had escaped their notice during the shakedowns? Or did they figure it was impossible to collect that much so they could taunt us all the more during the march to Cagayan? Gambling to avoid the march, we began to collect the money. Half the men had none, but a few had managed to hide a considerable amount and made it possible to reach the needed total. I contributed my last 10 pesos — I was now broke except for my postal savings bonds, which the Japs had looked at repeatedly without interest. The 700 pesos were collected, but its lack would leave us destitute and no longer able to buy food.

The Japs didn't come back until next morning, loud and strutting as usual. When we handed them the money, they were surprised. They told us we would be put on a boat the following morning. Nevertheless, we scarcely believed them and anxiously waited all day and then slept fitfully that night, fearful the march would continue next day.

The Japs came early in the morning and ordered us to get ready for the boat trip. Yet we were still afraid — we imagined being taken on the road again with the result of quick death for the older men and those weakened by dysentery and malaria. Expecting the worst, we took as much water as possible and very little else. The guards ordered us out of the building, and we were soon trudging by the ruins of Iligan. Our anxiety suddenly eased when the Japs headed us toward the docks instead of along the highway that followed the coast to Cagayan. Ragged Filipinos watched the sad procession with pity. Upon reaching the waterfront, I recognized missionary friends going in the same direction. They nodded and smiled as they passed silently by.

We halted beside a 40-foot launch that showed the name of *Tito Maru* on its stern. The guards ordered us aboard. All of us had to climb down into the hold except General Fort, Col. Mitchell, and Major Heidger, who stayed topside with a dozen guards. We barely had standing space but were happy at the moment to be sailing instead of marching. After some bickering among the Japs, the *Tito Maru* cast off its lines and headed out to sea, leaving some Japs on the dock yelling protests from the pier. The lifting mist exposed us to the blazing sun, which beat down while we tried to get into comfortable positions in the crowded hold. Above, armed guards peered down as though ready to fire or throw hand grenades at the slightest provocation. As the sun rose higher and struck more directly, human stench and engine smoke added to our misery.

Major Heidger pointed out our horrible situation to the senior Jap officer, who then decided to let one man at a time go topside to the latrine. This was relief beyond words. At first, each man took so long it made for long waits below. Then we organized ourselves so each trip was quicker, and everyone could go more than once. Someone found a bag of sugar along the way and passed the word so everyone got some. From reports each brought back, we observed the ship was keeping the coast to its starboard side as we proceeded north. When the sun was overhead, the ship turned and followed the coast eastward. During the afternoon the sun gradually sank on our stern and gave us some relief.

Yet it was still miserably hot in the hold when we docked in Cagayan. As we came up on deck in the twilight, however, a strong wind suddenly chilled us. Our guards marched us off at a fast pace, leaving behind the missionaries who had sailed from Iligan on a different ship. Our fast march out of the wrecked town and miserable day aboard ship had brought some to the point of collapse. We worried that the Japs wanted to get someplace where it would be convenient to shoot stragglers. A deserted grove of coconut trees increased our foreboding, but just beyond we stopped at a yellow schoolhouse. The guards searched each prisoner on the porch before sending him inside with orders to stay there. We said we were hungry so they took two Americans to their quartermaster. The men brought back a small can of fish for each three men and a sardine can of water for each man. We ate in silence, thankful that we had survived the voyage on the *Tito Maru* and ended the day with something to eat. But night brought no rest from the Japs.

We had just finished eating when a Jap officer strode in front of us with drawn sword. He engaged in a prolonged mock combat that ended with the decapitation of his enemy. But they did not leave us alone for long. We had just spread out on the floor to rest when the Japs returned and made us stand at attention for a Jap major to say something. He started by asking to speak to "Major" Fort, not realizing our senior officer was a general. He talked to General Fort in a friendly manner but soon gave up because of the language barrier. Before leaving, however, he made us to understand that he guaranteed our safety and the use of the nearby latrine but declared we would die if disobedient or disruptive — no news to us.

After the officer left, General Fort told us he had guaranteed our good behavior in an agreement with the Jap commander whereby the Japs would take his life if we misbehaved. The general forgave us for past conduct that had caused trouble. Now it was up to us to avoid behavior that would bring on deadly Jap reaction. This short speech made us admire General Fort even more. Grateful for his trust and believing we would be safer, we lay down on the floor and went to sleep.

The next morning we stirred early, some rubbing others to ease stiffness and others exercising. But we were too hungry for much activity and soon were motionless as we hoped for chow. Our cramped quarters heated up as the morning wore on. We began to read the schoolbooks that were strewn around, but that helped little. Finally the Japs showed up in mid-morning and asked for volunteers to cook rice. Lt. Chase, two of my buddies, and I stepped forward. We set up a large pot outside the schoolhouse and lit a fire underneath. But we had only small containers to fill it with water. By the end of two hours we were weak from working in the baking sun, but the large pot of rice had cooked and was ready. Everyone got a large mess kit of rice with rock salt as well as refreshing drinks of water. We felt better despite the heat and lay around in the schoolhouse, sleeping, reading, or staring into space.

During this day of unusual peace and relative comfort, we read a lot to keep from thinking about the future. Each man found something there to suit his personality — it must have been a school library. Pvt. Doe gathered a huge collection on the floor beside him that he wouldn't let anyone else touch. I read a little, talked with friends, and then tried to find out something from the Japanese soldiers, with little success.

The next day, July 9, while I was cooking for the boys I saw the missionaries again — they were cooking close by. When the Japs were not looking, we exchanged news. They were faring better than we — they were getting so much food they left some where I could get it for the men. God bless them! The handouts and communication with the missionaries continued for several quiet days. By then it was known that we were to be sent to the POW camp at Malaybalay, but we didn't know whether we were to march or ride. The Japs claimed they were trying to get transportation. After nearly a week in Cagayan, the Japs told us one evening to get ready to move in the morning.

On July 18, 1942, we woke up early and packed a little rice and dried minnows in our mess kits. Then the arrival of several GI trucks eased our worry about another march. Our relief was complete when we climbed up on the flatbeds of the trucks, which were driven by Filipinos. First we drove through the wrecked town, passing by Filipinos who looked on impassively. The trucks headed inland and picked up speed. The road became rougher and abruptly began to climb. The drivers hurtled around a series of hairpin curves. We bounced up and down, afraid of being thrown down a ravine even if the trucks managed not to tip over and crush us. We continued to climb and passed grave markers for Americans, Filipinos, and Japs, as well as equipment abandoned during recent fighting. In deep ravines lay cars and even a B-17 bomber. Then carcasses of cattle cluttered the road at the outskirts of several deserted villages.

We drew up along some grapefruit trees outside another abandoned village. Nearby a spring bubbled out of the ground. Here we drank from the spring and ate the ripe fruit with our rice and fish. By afternoon we were driving past rolling pastures and breathing cool, fresh air. Around a turn, a grove of pines loomed, and as we got closer my buddy Frank Puppario recognized the emergency hospital at Impalutto, where he had been treated before the surrender. Now there were dozens of Japanese guards about and some prisoners, who rushed toward us to see some fellow Americans.

The trucks slowed to 15 mph, and to our amazement we recognized the boys who ran to greet us as buddies from the 14th Squadron; we thought the Japs had killed them in the fighting near Lake Lanao. To see them alive was wonderful. We yelled our news back and forth. They told us some of the nurses there were among the evacuees from Corregidor who had reached Lake Lanao; they had been left behind when the repaired PBY took off suddenly for Australia following a reported approach of enemy aircraft.

Our buddies at Impalutto threw pineapples to us that we quickly hid, causing the Japs to threaten us with rifles. Although our stay was brief, our spirits remained high long after we had driven off. The Japs kept the trucks moving at a fast pace — we believed they wanted to reach a well-guarded destination before dark. A steady breeze and drizzle chilled us while we jounced along.

Finally we descended into a valley and reached the edge of a good-sized town. Many Japanese and Filipinos stared sullenly at our approach. But unseen by the Japs, two Filipinos made "V" signs as we passed. Our guards relaxed when we reached an intersection where we stopped to await orders. They searched us and said we were going to a large concentration camp. They warned us to behave — they considered us rebellious prisoners. In a short time we reached the edge of the camp, where a guardhouse swarmed with guards. They ordered us to fall in, and in steady rain and growing darkness we marched into the large prison camp of Malaybalay. We were amazed to see a great many shacks with lights and the large number of prisoners — about 600, as we later found out.

It had been an easy day, but those who had gorged themselves with the fresh pineapples thrown to us by our old buddies at Impalutto had awful stomachaches. By next evening, however, they were able to enjoy the feast given us by the senior American officers' mess. We sat at tables with dinnerware and were served by the waiters who usually served the general officers. But the waiters told us not to expect that treatment again. That night Pvt. Cawthorn, a medic of the 19th Bomb Group, and I became so nauseous and weak we could barely move. At first we thought we had eaten too much, but nobody else was suffering. Later we blamed the pieces of sugar cane we had both picked out of the mud in Iligan to quench our thirst after the Death March. We stayed miserably sick. Major Heidger said we had hepatitis, but had nothing to recommend.

After three or four days, an old acquaintance, Cpl. Richard Hough, barged in — not the type to make a sympathy visit. Now, with the loose Japanese control at Malaybalay, Hough saw an opportunity to take control of the junior officers' mess. I was a crucial part of his scheme because of my baking ability. We would gain access to more food and perhaps better living conditions. I was willing but didn't think I would ever get well. Hough left abruptly and soon returned with a large can of pineapple juice — he claimed that was all I needed. I drank a good deal of it that night, as did Sgt. Cawthorn. For whatever reason, we had both recovered after our first week in Malaybalay.

I settled down in my job of baking for the POW junior officers' mess at this lenient prison camp. Cpl. Hough was the top non-com and Lt. Andrew Bukavinski the mess officer. They were easy to get along with and liked my baking. I didn't mind the situation even though I had a makeshift oven that required me to feed in yeast every three hours, day and night. Unlike my bakery at Malabang, I had no Filipino helpers so I had to get up myself during the night to keep the process going.

Bukavinski, the mess officer, was a large, loud-mouthed Pole, who early in the war had won a battlefield commission with the 31st Division in fighting around Davao. I enjoyed sitting in the kitchen with him listening to the radio—the Japs thought they had found all the radios in the formerly American camp. But one day a Jap sergeant unexpectedly came in and grabbed the radio from Bukavinski and shouted at us. Bukavinski sprang to attention and kept his mouth shut. Other times he would say to me, "Vic, why don't we get out of here?" We discussed how we might escape, and he gave me a military map of Mindanao, a compass, and a bolo for safekeeping until we were ready to take off.

At Malaybalay one American prisoner was so much of a bully and troublemaker that even the relaxed Japs noticed. They offered to take care of him for us. At first, the American officers were tempted to accept the offer. After some discussion, however, they decided against the idea because then the Japs would feel more free to pick out any prisoner who displeased them for brutal treatment. The American officers told the Japs that we would take care of the situation ourselves. We built a small enclosure inside the prison compound in which we confined the bully. His attitude became worse, and he even injured a medic who was trying to treat him. But life became easier for the other prisoners.

Our situation was not to remain static. As the first step in dismantling this easygoing camp, the Japs sent all American generals and colonels to Manila on September 6, 1942. Among them was General Fort, who had surrendered the remnants of the 14th Squadron, other Americans, and 300 Filipinos at Dansalan. He took with him his orderly, our buddy Dick Beck, whom we had looked after ever since the *Mayon* had almost sunk in late December 1941. Later the Japs sent General Fort, but not Dick Beck, back to the Lake Lanao region, hoping he would help them pacify the Moros. But he didn't fulfill Japanese expectations and was executed.

In mid-September the Japs asked the prisoners who had technical skills to volunteer for work in Japan. Many claimed to have the "technical skill" of driving a truck or some skill from civilian life that might impress the Japs. But I maintained my lack of any technical skill—not expecting good treatment if sent to Japan. The departure of the "technicals" spared them a gruesome experience.

Now Malaybalay contained the "non-technical Americans" and several hundred Filipino POWs—the Japs had always kept the Filipinos separated from us but treated them in a relaxed way, as they did us. The Japanese benevolence ended suddenly after two Filipinos who had tried to escape were recaptured. The Japs tied the soldiers to posts and mustered all prisoners, American and Filipino, to witness the executions. The Filipino soldiers showed courage and faced their deaths with defiant faces. The firing squad riddled them with bullets, leaving their heads slumped over. The whole thing sickened me. And then the Japs left the bodies hanging for the rest of the day, as though we hadn't already gotten the message.

In late December 1942 the other "non-technicals" and I were on our way to the Davao Penal Colony on the southeastern coast of Mindanao—a former Philippine, self-sustaining prison farm that still contained some Filipino criminals. First the Japs trucked us back north to Cagayan, the way we had come to Malaybalay. There we stayed in the same schoolhouse, and I again volunteered to unload cargo—as usual anxious to look around. One of us spotted a keg of tuba in the hold of the ship we were unloading. As each man went aboard, he stopped and took a good swig. We had not had any liquor for a long time, and it was a strong brew. After a few trips to the hold, the tuba really jolted us. But we managed to keep steady enough to escape notice of the Japanese guards on the dock.

After a day or two in Cagayan, the Japs put us on a coastal vessel that continued our eastward course along the north coast of Mindanao that had begun in July when the Japs packed us in the hold of the *Tito Maru* in Iligan. Now conditions on the ship were more tolerable. We kept generally eastward, in sight of land to starboard until the coastline turned south. Then we followed the east coast of Mindanao southward.

When we neared Davao, Lt. May asked us to let him mingle in the crowd of enlisted men. Like Lt. Bukavinski, May had fought the Japs around Davao in the early days of the war with the 31st Division and won a battlefield commission. Now he feared he would be identified as the American who had shot several Japs. But although the Japs knew they had prisoners from the 31st Division, May was never recognized.

22

Davao Penal Colony — Sawmill

October 30, 1942, to February 1943

After the Japs herded us off the ship at the port of Davao, they asked for 20 volunteers to unload cargo that afternoon. I was ready for any activity after the long, confined voyage. Besides I wanted to delay or skip Japanese inspection of my barracks bag that held the escape items Bukavinski had given me in Malaybalay. But late that evening when I climbed off the truck at the penal colony, the Japs were still ready to inspect our gear, as they did for all incoming POWs. I feared the worst as I carefully spread out the contents of my bag, including the map, compass, and bolo. The stunned and excited inspection guard shouted for the sergeant and an officer to show what he had found. The interpreter and a soldier with a threatening bayonet also gathered around. The sergeant demanded, "Why do you have this stuff?" I tried to look calm and then said the smartest words of my life: "I've had these things all the time. Your soldiers didn't pay any attention to them and didn't take them away, sir." My attempt to draw attention to Japanese carelessness elsewhere instead of my own wrongdoing worked. They seized the gear, glared at me, and continued the inspection.

As we drove among the camp's dilapidated buildings, I remarked to my companions that it looked like a tough place. The guard understood and growled, "It is tough, and you're here because you killed Japanese." Many of the Japs understood English, but I quickly resorted to pig Latin — it was always a mystery to them. Next day the senior Japanese officer, Major Maeda, greeted us. "You're not here for lazy but to work," he said in broken English. "We'll see that you do." He was stout and middle-aged, and wore a jacket covered with World War I ribbons.

Entrance to Davao Penal Colony, looking out. *(Photo by Glenn Nordin, courtesy Carl Nordin.)*

Our shipload of prisoners entered Davao on or near October 30, 1942, and brought the number of prisoners at the penal colony to about 1,000. On November 6, another 1,000 prisoners arrived. These men had survived the Bataan Death March. They had been shipped from the Cabanatuan prison camp on Luzon Island. We thought we had been through a lot until we saw these men. A six-foot skeleton, named Cowan, wanted to buy a can of sardines from me. He offered five pesos, but I told him he could have it — it was my last can, but I felt good about helping a buddy. The next day, however, old Cowan sold my can of sardines for 30 pesos. In the next few days the Davao prisoners learned something from the boys from Bataan about dealing and surviving that we didn't know before — some of them managed to secure the only soft jobs in the camp organization.

Cpl. Kenneth Day, a deep-voiced, lanky soldier from the 5th Air Base Group, remembered that the Bataan men "had turned totally bitter in their bare-knuckle struggle for existence. The will to live had taken the place of the Golden Rule." In contrast, the morale of the prisoners from Malaybalay had been preserved by the decent life there. In an effort to cheer up the Bataan men, a singing group that had been organized at Malaybalay serenaded them one evening. Day described the response:

POW non-coms' barracks, Davao Penal Colony. Protestant church services were sometimes held outside. *(Photo by Glenn Nordin, courtesy Carl Nordin.)*

> As we sang "Honey," "If I Had My Way," "Old Man Noah," and "The Ranger's Song," they came out of their barracks to listen. These men, starved physically and spiritually, stood like scrawny statues, drinking in the music. We sang as we never had before, inspired by the tears running down their faces.

Cpl. Day also recalled that the new arrivals had brought hordes of lice to camp so "we were picking the little bastards out of the seams of our clothing and crushing them between our fingernails." Bedbugs subsequently reduced the lice population, but they were just as bad and equally hard to eliminate.

The bugs bothered me so I volunteered to work at the sawmill a few miles from the main camp. The Japs had stationed 50 of us there to cut down and ship mahogany to Japan. Prisoners sliced large slabs off the logs to rid them of bark. My partner Ramey and I had the job of lifting the discarded slabs onto a handcar — the slabs were so large it took both of us to lift one. Then the handcar was pushed on rails to a spot where the slabs were dumped into the ocean.

Ramey and I were together most of the time. At night we slept under the same mosquito netting in a lumber shed. He had traded off his netting, but mine was big enough for both of us. One night I had just fallen asleep when I gradually became aware that Ramey was dickering with one of the local guards, who wanted Ramey's blanket but wanted it cheap because it was full of holes. Tired of the chatter, I said, "What the hell," and let Ramey trade off my blanket instead of his — it was dirty anyway. Thus we came to share a tattered blanket as well as the mosquito netting. Nevertheless, Ramey was usually adept at trading.

Since there was seldom enough to eat in the chow line, we traded U.S. cigarettes for extra food for ourselves and some weak prisoners — our Red Cross packages provided us with the cigarettes. The Japs forbade this barter and would ferociously punish anyone they caught doing it. To make the trading safer, the Filipino who provided us with food would hide it for us to pick up, and I would pay him by quickly slipping into his hand a Filipino cigarette pack filled with American cigarettes. So food continued to be exchanged, and I actually gained weight.

In early 1943 Ramey got the crazy idea of trading for eggs to celebrate Easter. He had our Filipino trader put six eggs in the usual hiding place. The next thing I knew, Ramey rushed by me with the eggs and pushed them under the blanket of a POW who was down with a severe case of malaria. Unfortunately, a Jap guard caught up with Ramey and dragged him away. I retrieved the eggs and threw five of them in the latrine. I ate the sixth with distaste — the first raw egg I'd ever eaten. Soon the thoroughly frightened Filipino came around. Fearing that Ramey would give in to Jap torture, the Filipino was considering immediate flight to save himself and his family. I assured him he would be safe.

Hours later poor Ramey struggled back in awful shape. I lay down beside him to give him comfort and learn what had happened. But he was obsessed with the thought of eating the eggs, and I had the sad job of telling him what I had done with them. Then I found, as I expected, that my partner had betrayed neither the Filipino nor me.

At the lumber camp I learned to play chess from Pease, a big Swede, and Brown, a small, red-haired Irishman — another of the partnerships frequently formed by prisoners. Pease and Brown carved chess pieces from the reddish mahogany and black ebony — one color for each player. I soon learned the basic moves, but was slow to become proficient, partly because a small, dainty, young Jap hated to see me play. He would interrupt me by pulling my long beard and calling me an old man. After a month, when I won my first game — not against Pease or Brown — it was a big thrill. Thereafter, I won my share and made my own set. A number of us learned to play, but not all were good losers — some would not speak to their opponents for a couple days. But the games relieved our boredom.

Our daily routine started when a siren blew for wake-up and breakfast. The POW cooks had already boiled rice and tea. Everyone hurried to get in the chow line to make sure of a full serving. But at midnight on

December 31, 1942, someone sounded the siren to salute the New Year. It jolted Blackie Grossman out of a sound sleep and soon he was standing, bleary-eyed, at the head of the chow line. Our laughs thoroughly awakened Blackie, and soon he was laughing himself.

Blackie, a short, blue-eyed, swarthy New Yorker, had the knack of keeping our spirits up. One afternoon the Japs kept us working after dark, making it difficult for them to round us up and get us back to the lumber sheds. But the Japs heard a cackling in the darkness and stopped to search the bushes for a chicken dinner. They asked us to help out. Just as they were about to give up, the cackling came again nearby, so we all searched some more. By this time we realized that the chicken was Blackie. We whispered to him, "Stop it or we'll all be in bad trouble." Blackie's cackling had delayed the roundup only 10 or 15 minutes but had given us a big chuckle.

I tried to play my own joke on the Japs. One guard asked me how he could get the POWs to work harder. I advised him to say, "Take it easy! Take it easy!" When he tried it, he got only blank stares from the prisoners. Discovering my trick, the guard smacked me across the face a few times, but that was all. He probably didn't want to make too much of it, hoping the other guards wouldn't find out how he'd been duped.

I almost got in another scrape one morning before work when no guard was about. I wanted to get a view of the surrounding area so I climbed on top of a lumber shed. There, in the early morning sun, I dozed off. I woke up to the chatter of a young officer and six home guards. They had not noticed me, but I couldn't get down without attracting their attention. I didn't know what to do because of the risk of being late to work. As I waited, hoping they would move, I decided these Japs didn't look aggressive. I jumped down right in front of them and walked briskly toward my work group. They were too shocked to make a move. The regular guards never questioned me about this incident. In a few days, however, I got into another dangerous situation.

A small, 100-pound guard learned that I was a sumo wrestler — Bill Knortz had secretly taught me and others while we were being held at Dansalan. I couldn't refuse the guard's challenge — it was an order. I tried to let the guard win after I put up some realistic resistance. But when he was about to subject me to a dangerous leg-sweep, I had to save myself. I picked up the little Jap and held him yelling and struggling over my head. Another guard rushed up, ready to use his bayonet, and ordered me to drop my opponent. I let loose of him over a mud puddle and hurried away to my work detail. I wasn't punished — apparently my opponent would have lost face if he retaliated. But a few days later I was sent back to the main camp of the Davao Penal Colony.

23

Davao Penal Colony — Rice Paddies

February 1943 to mid–February 1944

I worried that I had been transferred to the main camp because I was considered a troublemaker at the sawmill. Now I hoped to lose myself among 2,000 prisoners. But my good physical condition might make that difficult. However, the Japs just assigned me to the daily work detail at the Mactan rice paddies along with most of the other 700 healthy POWs. The rest of the prisoners were excused from heavy work for legitimate medical reasons or the pretext of them. Some of these fellows had light duties close to the compound.

The rice paddies took up about two-thirds of the 2500 acres of the Davao Penal Colony. Other parts of the farm produced a variety of tropical fruits and vegetables. But we were always hungry because much of the food production was shipped to Japanese garrisons elsewhere in the Philippines.

Every morning 650 of us headed for the rice paddies aboard a narrow-gauge "Toonerville Trolley." A small diesel engine pulled us through the jungle on 20 flatcars, each crowded with 30 prisoners and one or two guards. As we chugged along at 15 miles per hour, I wistfully watched monkeys cavort in the trees and throw bananas at each other. A 20-minute ride brought us to Mactan and the hassle of everyone trying to get off at the same time and then finding or being assigned his work detail. Going back at the end of the day, hungry and tired, was even worse. Fifty

The "Toonerville Trolley" track to the rice paddies, Davao Penal Colony, as it appeared in 1955. *(Photo by Glenn Nordin, courtesy Carl Nordin.)*

volunteers, however, stayed out there all the time to drive and take care of the carabaos, which did the heavy plowing in the paddies.

I had been going to Mactan for a week when the rest of the sawmill detail came back — the Japs had shut down their timber operation. My partner Ramey came back, seemingly recovered from his beating by the Jap guards, but in a few days he came down with cerebral malaria. He wandered around in the stifling heat, shivering under a raincoat, and didn't know me when he died a few weeks later.

About when the sawmill detail returned, there was a serious escape effort. From the end of the work-day until muster and work assignments the next morning, the Japs kept the prisoners securely inside a 100-by-200-yard compound, enclosed by a barbed-wire fence. The compound was surrounded by swamp and nearly impenetrable jungle, and sentries paced the perimeter all night. During the day, however, different prisoner details worked at various places under different kinds of supervision.

Captain Marion Lawton recalled that one group, working on the coffee plantation, pointed out to the Japs that it was behind in pruning the coffee trees. The ten Americans in the group and two Filipino convicts who supervised the pruning offered to work on Sundays, their day off, to catch up. By the third Sunday, April 4, 1943, the Japs had relaxed enough to let the prisoners work by themselves. On that day, the two Filipinos guided the Americans through the jungle and in a few days all reached the main guerrilla organization on Mindanao, led by Lt. Col. Fertig. Then most of the escapees were taken to Australia by submarine.

The two Filipinos who had escaped were among the two dozen hard-core Filipino criminals the Japs had inherited when they took over Davao. They used the convicts to teach the Americans how to operate the sawmill and produce rice, fruit, and vegetables, as well as to tend the coffee plantation. The Americans were shocked to learn that some of their instructors were convicted murderers. After the escape, the Japs stopped all American contact with the Filipino convicts.

The escape left the rest of the prisoners terrified because of repeated Japanese threats to execute prisoners in retaliation, as had been done at Camp Keithley and other places. Although there were no executions, the Japs confined everyone to the barracks next day, and rations were cut severely for a time. The guards became meaner and more suspicious. But the worst development was the loss of Lt. Yuki, a Roman Catholic who supervised all the work details. Yuki's rules were lenient, making for a pretty good camp. He was shipped out.

The Japs also stopped all American contact with a popular Japanese guard we called Ufi. He spoke fluent English and regularly guarded a large Scandinavian named Winter, who chopped the wood needed by the camp to maintain a supply of boiled water for safe drinking and cooking. The huge prisoner and small guard often chopped wood together to provide the daily supply.

Soon after my return to the main camp, I found a new friend, a Pole from Philadelphia named Raskovitz. Like Ramey, Raskovitz was an extrovert and an adept trader. Since I was quiet and conservative, we made a good pair. I talked him into volunteering for the group stationed at the rice paddies rather than enduring the hassle of going back and forth from the main camp every day with the bulk of the healthy prisoners. I pointed out the likelihood of more freedom there, but I had the additional reason of wanting to work the carabao bulls. It was a job shunned by most prisoners because they had never worked with animals. The Japs were glad to have us join the permanent group at Mactan.

Raskovitz and I used the few days before the move to acquire all the cans of corned beef we could, even giving up American cigarettes in our trading. Raskovitz gave up the cigarettes willingly, even though he was a great smoker. We took along 14 cans of corned beef. At first our partnership worked well because the can of corned beef we split daily was a welcome supplement to the thin fare the Japs provided. Sometimes I was able to sneak some mangoes and other fruit from small islands of native growth in the rice paddies, where I could forage without being seen by the guards. In a week or so, however, Raskovitz and I parted company, mainly because he traded away some of our corned beef for the cigarettes he craved.

At Mactan we slept in rough shelters close to the bulls' corral. The first day I went out with a carabao, it wouldn't work for me. Since I hadn't cultivated any rice that day, the Japs gave me a painful beating. Sleeping near me, though, was a Filipino criminal who still was being used with Americans at the rice paddies. He explained to me how to manage the carabaos and how to talk to them — they understood Spanish or Tagalog, the Philippine dialect. Next day I did better and thereafter had no trouble with the animals.

I liked to start early to get as much work done as possible in the cool part of the morning. The guards gave us a certain amount to do for the day so with hard work I could finish by mid-afternoon and wash off in the river. To speed up the work I took two carabaos out each morning so I could leave one resting but restrained in the deep mud, while I worked the other behind a plow until he became tired. We had one-handed plows with steel blades to cut deeply in the mud to prepare for planting the rice. The plowman grasped the plow with one hand and guided the carabao with the other.

To reach the paddies in the morning, I had to lead my carabaos a half-mile on the top of a dike. The narrow top forced me to proceed single file with one carabao in front and one following me. They were difficult and scary to catch in the morning, but once I had run a rope through the rings in their noses, they were docile and worked intelligently. Thus the lead carabao walked along the dike at a reasonable pace, and the carabao behind me knew enough to maintain the same pace. A guard followed behind.

After I had learned how to lead my carabaos, the guard must have become bored. He jabbed the rear of the carabao bull behind me with his bayonet to see what would happen. It jerked me and the carabao ahead of me to a halt. I told the guard to stop, but he laughed and did it again in a few moments. The next time he jabbed harder. As I turned around, the carabao behind me turned his head and snagged a horn in my rib. I tumbled off the dike into the muddy ditch with a broken rib. The Jap laughed harder than ever, but I was beside myself with rage. I got up and threatened in suddenly proficient Japanese to kill him if he did it again. My outburst scared him. He might have shot me but didn't — perhaps they were short of plowmen. Instead, this short, mean-looking guard stayed back a distance but kept his gun pointed at me the rest of the way to the paddies. Even when I started plowing, he stood on the dike pointing his gun at me while I worked. I was so uneasy I tried to keep the carabao between me and him when I could. However, next day I managed to be put with another guard — each oversaw three or four plowmen.

I kept my cool in another rice paddy incident. I came upon a guard beating and prodding a prisoner who could barely stand up. I insisted that the guard beat me instead because the POW was too sick to work. The guard stopped and gave me an angry look but didn't bother to beat me.

Cpl. Kenneth Day also worked carabaos at the rice paddies. He and a companion found that by working together on adjoining paddies they could complete their daily quota faster than by working in separate paddies. (Each prisoner was required to plow one paddy daily, a bit more than half an acre). Besides not having to turn the animals as often, Day thought the carabaos liked each other's company, or maybe the competition.

One day the two plowmen got six others to join them to test the idea on a large scale. They lined the eight animals abreast along the first dike, planning to plow in a straight line across dike after dike until they reached the end of the row of paddies. Then they would all turn and come back, thus avoiding the tight turns required inside a paddy. The guards watched the preparations but did not interfere. The eight plowmen all barked their command, and the carabaos started together rather smoothly. But soon one animal got a little ahead of the others. Then the animal next to him couldn't stand that and speeded up. The others reacted in the same way. Before they reached the next dike, the whole thing had turned into a race. The men had never seen carabaos — plodders by nature — move fast before. But now the prisoners could barely hold on to the plow handles and guide ropes. Soon the animals broke loose from Cpl. Day and his seven companions, and dragged the plows across the dikes, tearing holes in them, while the guards yelled bloody murder. The plowmen fell down in the mud, laughing at the grand sight of the loose carabaos galloping off in every direction. It took the rest of the morning to catch them and most of the afternoon to repair dikes and plows.

As mentioned, Cpl. Day loved to sing with the prisoner choral group. He was so intelligent I wondered why he wasn't an officer. When I played chess with him, he would lie relaxed in the shade beside the chessboard with a towel over his face. Thus blindfolded, all he needed was for me to inform him of my moves and tell me where to move his pieces. He never needed many moves to beat me.

About this time the Japs needed more of the trained carabaos to work the paddies. A solution was to train one of the carabao cows that wasn't giving much milk to be a work animal. My handling of the animals made the Japs think I could do the job. I took it as a challenge and spent all one morning with the cow and training sled without making much progress. I couldn't even get a little milk from her when we were out of the guards' sight. In the middle of the day I broke for us to rest and tied her loosely enough for her to get some water at a low spot. An hour later I was still resting at the POW shelter when a friendly Japanese interpreter we called "Pittsburgh" rushed in and reported, "Your cow is drowned. Be careful!" The cow had become entangled in the rope and fallen into the mud and water where it had not been able to get up.

I worried the rest of the day about what the Japanese guards would do. As night fell, we heard loud, angry voices from the guards' quarters. I asked Raskovitz to sneak over to the guards' shelter with me — we no longer shared our cans of corned beef, but he would be a good partner in this risky business. We found the guards all inside still shouting at each other, trying to divide the meat from the carabao cow. Then we noticed that the animal's large head was lying on the ground outside. Each of us grabbed a horn, and we lugged it as quickly and quietly as we could back to the prisoners' shelter. We cooked it, and four or five of us feasted that night before we buried the remains.

While plowing in the rice paddies, I always looked for frogs. When I saw one jump, I shifted the reins to my plow hand and snatched it up with the other. I was too quick for the guard on the dike to notice me. On a good day I strung 15 or 20 frogs in a wire loop under my clothes. Since there was no body search when my daily task was finished, usually long before the sun went down, I would feast on frog soup. I boiled the skinned frogs in my mess kit with pepper and salt water by closing it and then exposing it to the still-intense sun. While cooking, I kept a sharp lookout for guards who might come into the prison compound. But I was never caught.

One day I noticed a guard had set aside a foot-long mudfish behind a little dam in the rice paddy. When my plowing brought me there, I grabbed the fish and hid it in my clothing — the guard had moved some distance away. Later he came back to pick it up but searched and searched in vain for the feast he had planned for so carefully.

A scheme for picking breadfruit required two prisoners, and could be successful if the nearest guard was too far away to recognize the men. One prisoner climbed a tree and threw down a few six-inch breadfruits to his partner, who ran off with them. The man in the tree scrambled down, jumped to the ground, and headed in a different direction.

The Japs thought I would be valuable as supervisor of the 50-man crew that harvested the rice. I didn't like bossing fellow Americans on behalf of the Japs but felt I had little choice. Besides, some of this rice fed fellow prisoners, just as criminal prisoners had worked these paddies to feed themselves under Philippine administration before the war. Once our guard offered to shelter me from a downpour under his big umbrella. But I stayed out in the rain, realizing how taking favors from the Japs would look to fellow prisoners.

One of my crew was Blackie Grossman, whose cackling like a chicken had fooled the Japs and amused Americans on the sawmill detail. At Mactan, wild chickens lived on the islands wild growth among the rice paddies and occasionally scurried by the workers. One morning a prisoner grabbed a chicken while working and managed to kill it and hide it in his clothing without being seen by the guard. That night the prisoner plucked, cooked, and ate the chicken in the compound. Unfortunately, he left telltale feathers that our guard noticed later. I feared that next time it would be my neck as crew leader so I warned the crew in strong terms to leave the chickens alone.

The next day another chicken scampered by and disappeared. The guard caught this out of the corner of his eye but couldn't tell what had happened to the chicken, though he suspected it had been caught. At the end of the day, he lined us up two abreast, rather than the normal four abreast, to search each prisoner as we entered the compound. After Blackie had passed the checkpoint and gone on a few paces, he let out one of his cackles. That confirmed the guard's suspicion that someone had caught the chicken. But now he had to start the search all over. I sweated it out, fearing they would discover Blackie's trick and take it out on me as well as Blackie. I cursed Blackie under my breath. Finally, the watchtower guard became impatient at the delay and demanded an end to the search. We all filed in, leaving our guard angry and still unaware that there was no chicken. I relaxed but later confronted Blackie and told him I would punish him myself if he did it again.

I got another promotion I didn't like when Gallegos, boss of all the carabao drivers, became so weak I had to take his job. His condition and that of some others in the rice paddies resulted from cuts made by brushing against the sharp-edged cogon grass there. Scratching turned the cuts into welts that would not heal. Neither the Japanese nor American doctors understood what was happening. I was also afflicted by the cogon grass — although less severely than Gallegos — so I was a poor choice to replace him.

I was especially reluctant to take the job because my chess friends, Pease and Brown, had recently escaped into the jungle. With the increased Japanese edginess, I feared what would happen to me if some of my carabao drivers were to escape. I had seen the executions of our three leaders at Camp Keithley after four prisoners had slipped away. But I had no option but to take my new "position." My health did not improve. After only a month I was constantly nauseous and could barely walk.

In January 1944 an American doctor sent me back to the main camp. There I was assigned to a half-day detail, weeding radishes on the prison farm. I worked in a gang of twelve prisoners under a guard who walked behind and made us keep a steady pace across the field. Nevertheless, I was able to pull up a radish now and then and take a bite before shoving the plant back in the ground. Then I weeded like hell to get away before the plant began to wilt. I got caught a few times and suffered hard blows. However, the work on the radish field helped restore my health. Other hungry prisoners snatched radishes, but some prisoners were quite ingenious in getting even more to eat.

One POW, who drove an old tractor on the farm, stayed fat among the scrawny prisoners. No one knew why until the tractor broke down. Then the Japs discovered a little basket inside the radiator in which this guy cooked corn and potatoes while he was driving. Food had spilled out of the basket and clogged the hoses. Another prisoner who satisfied his hunger for a time was a big, rugged, blue-eyed Scandinavian named Fitzjohn. He wore civilian-style shoes that he had made of wood and leather. One night as he came through the gate, someone accidentally hit the heel of his shoe. Rice poured out of the hollow heel. The Japs took the shoes and whacked his ears unmercifully. Then they forced him to spend two weeks in a cage that was so small he could neither sit nor stand.

In my weakened condition, fellow prisoners helped me out. An old 14th Squadron friend, Doc Haddock, who worked in the POW mess, gave me a can of parched and pounded fish bones. Every day I took a spoonful of the salty stuff. Once on the way to the radish field, a Jap ordered me to move a 200-pound bag of sweet potatoes — a task well beyond my strength at that time. But the POW officer in charge of farming, Lt. Roy Y. Gentry, saw my plight and moved the bag for me. I eventually regained enough strength to play chess again, although the mental exertion brought on headaches.

I became strong enough to be assigned to repair of roads near the prison farm. We hauled rocks in wheelbarrows and dumped them into potholes. One day a hired guard started humming "Onward Christian Soldiers" — he was Formosan or of some other non–Japanese extraction. When I told him I was a Christian, he asked me to share his lunch. First, however, we bowed our heads in silent prayer. One day I was eating a snack by myself when this guard accosted me with, "You are no Christian. You don't even pray before you eat."

At the main camp I joined the Boy Scout troop, which Col. Emeral

This substantial house at the Davao Penal Colony very likely was the residence of the camp's senior Japanese officer, Major Maeda. *(Photo by Glenn Nordin, courtesy of Carl Nordin.)*

Cane had formed — he had called out the 200th Anti-Aircraft band to march and play music immediately after the first shattering attack on Clark Field. A few men, myself included, were Eagle Scouts, and there were many other Scouts as well, including West Pointers and Annapolis graduates. Belonging to the Scouts kept up our morale, and our educational meetings relieved the boredom. We'd pick a man who had traveled some place out of the ordinary, such as Alaska, and have him describe his experiences. Scouts stood guard at each end of the room so the Japs couldn't surprise us. The speaker didn't have to be outstanding for me to enjoy talks on interesting subjects.

One day, feeling much better, I volunteered to ride out to the rice paddies for a day's work. As we boarded the Toonerville Trolley for our afternoon return, a tropical storm broke. Sheets of rain drenched us on the open flatcars. Halfway back the tiny engine chugged to a stop, unable to make the grade because of the slippery tracks. The guards ordered us to get out and push. In the gathering darkness, one prisoner began to sing "God Bless America." Gradually, others joined in, and the 600 of us belted out the song while we pushed the train toward the main camp. Major Maeda, the camp commander, turned on all the lights in his house and peered into the darkness, wondering if he had an uprising on his hands. He watched us go by and file into the compound. It was totally dark — unlike the normal return that was timed to get us inside while it was still light. The next morning Maeda issued extra rations and loosened camp routine for a time. But this easygoing interlude at the prison farm did not survive the spring of 1944, when advancing American forces threatened the Japanese hold on Mindanao.

24

Lasang Airstrip
Mid-February to August 20, 1944

By early 1944, the Japs had begun to worry about the defense of Mindanao, the first large island of the Philippines in the path of General MacArthur's drive to retake them. The drive began on March 2, 1944, when Americans landed in the Admiralty Islands, which lay 1800 miles southeast of Mindanao. In the following months, American forces captured a series of thinly held island locations that had airfields. The airfields were then used to base aircraft for the next advance. On September 15, the capture of Morotai in the Moluccas brought MacArthur's forces to within 300 miles of Mindanao. The advance since March 2 had covered 1400 miles and isolated 140,000 Japanese troops.

In mid-February, the Japanese commander at the Davao Penal Colony informed Lt. Col. Kenneth S. Olson, the senior American officer, that 650 healthy prisoners were needed to expand the Lasang airstrip, ten miles to the southeast and five miles northeast of the city of Davao. To furnish 650 prisoners, Olson had to take some of the Americans who had been on light duty at Davao, as well as the 500 more-healthy prisoners who had been working full-time at the Mactan rice paddies.

I was in the lineup of the light-duty prisoners to be considered for Lasang. When Lt. Yosumura, the Japanese doctor, walked along the line of prisoners, he passed me by because I managed to look more unfit than I was. But another Jap noticed how sickly one of the POWs already selected looked. Then he noticed me, now not so slumped over. One jerk of his thumb sent me to Lasang in place of the sickly prisoner. Later, in May and June of 1944, the 1,200 remaining, less-fit prisoners at the prison farm were moved back to Cabanatuan on Luzon, where many of them had been held after the Bataan Death March.

The night before the more-fit prisoners left for Lasang, Lt. May wrote a petition that protested working on the airstrip as contrary to international law, which forbids use of prisoners of war in support of military effort. In the dark we crept over, one by one, to sign — so quietly that the Japs didn't know what was going on. Lt. May left the paper with senior POW officers, hoping it would survive as postwar evidence of Japanese wrongdoing. But nothing was ever seen of it. A similar protest was presented to Japanese officers by Navy Comdr. W. R. Portz. It was read and rejected.

Before our departure next morning on March 1, 1944, the Japs issued each of the 471 enlisted men and 179 officers two Red Cross food packages and a pair of shoes. At 11 A.M. we climbed on trucks and headed south for Lasang. Beside me stood a short, scrawny Air Corps man from New Jersey, who told me his name was Kid Marlow. He didn't seem downhearted and was full of comments about what was going on. We reached Lasang in about an hour. Since our last names began with "M," Marlow and I were assigned to the same sleeping shed, where we managed to get adjoining sleeping boards.

Our shed was one of four that the POW construction crew had built a half-mile from the strip. They were thatched with the long leaves of nipa palm trees. Another shelter housed the kitchen and camp staff. Two latrines to the rear were later moved between the sheds because the odor had reached the nearby Jap officers' quarters. The changed location was much too near the wells and prisoner sheds for good sanitation, but the Japs rejected all requests to move the latrines a second time. They kept a large oil barrel full of drinking water outside, which was kept sanitary by a fire underneath that was stirred up occasionally to bring the water to a boil.

The Japs promised the American mess officer 650 grams of rice and 500 grams of vegetables per man per day, as well as sugar, salt, cooking oil, and frequent meat and fish. But we received only 550 grams of rice daily during the first two months; the total shortage reached 400 kilograms per month.

The vegetable issues came in as promised, but there was no make-up for spoilage, which often amounted to more than half the issue. The vegetables were camotes (sweet potatoes), squash, and a water weed called "kangkong." There was no variety from day to day — camotes might be available for five or six days, followed by a number of days of another vegetable.

Meat and fish were rare items. When the Japs butchered a carabao, they kept the four quarters, entrails, and neck for the 200 guards and left the head and ribs for the 650 prisoners.

Our first task was to clear everything up to the ten-foot fence topped by barbed wire that bounded the compound at a distance of 100 feet from the sheds. In the process we destroyed a number of healthy orange trees, which made me worry about the food supply. Next, we were to cut off the shoulders of the mile-long runway to provide adequate drainage. For the first few days, we refused to do any real work, while keeping up a semblance of activity. Japanese civilian engineers assigned separate tasks for each work group of 50 prisoners to do for the day. But we leaned on shovels and talked — the hired guards put little pressure on us although the engineers kept us out until 6 P.M. Yet they couldn't get any group to complete its task. Lt. Hosida, the camp commander, threatened us daily through his interpreter, Mr. Nisamura. Hosida even hired a few civilians from Davao to shame our performance.

At roll call on the evening of the third day, Hosida scolded us through Nisamura: "I cannot understand why you will not work. You are surrendered POWs and must do as we ask or suffer dire consequences. You are receiving much more food than civilians in Japan, who only receive 400 grams of rice per day.* Your assigned work is not hard. You did much more work at the Mactan rice paddies and now should do as much on the airfield." In conclusion Hosida asked pleadingly, "Will you do the work on the airfield?" He repeated the question three times.

There was a pause, and then an officer stepped up, saluted, and said, "Mr. Nisamura, I am sorry I cannot work on the airstrip. As an officer in the U.S. Army, I can do nothing to benefit your war effort against my country." Nisamura replied, "You don't know what you are saying. You cannot speak for the group." But Lt. Col. Rufus Rogers, the senior American officer, immediately declared, "This officer expresses the feeling of the whole group of Americans here. We did not come to Lasang of our own free will but on Japanese orders. If you force us to work, we will probably have to do as you say. But actually the men are against working on the airfield and wish to return to the Davao Penal Colony." Those words ended the talking that night.

But the prisoners were getting tired of staying out on work details until 6 P.M. every day and then having little time to wash their clothes, shave, and talk before stretching out for the night on their sleeping boards. This

---

*The shortage of rice for POWs at Lasang reflects the reduced official daily rice ration for the Japanese soldier from 850 grams in 1942 to 400 grams in late 1944, reported by Gavan Daws in Prisoners of the Japanese, 1944. Daws points out that in the same period American submarines increasingly interrupted Japanese shipping — sinking one ship every three days in 1942, one ship every day in 1943, and sinking more ships in 1944 than the combined total sunk in 1941, 1942, and 1943.

feeling came into the open early in the afternoon of the fifth day, when it began to rain. That, and the chilly wind coming off the sea, made one group decide it was foolish to stay out longer than necessary. They finished their assigned contract as soon as they could and came in.

After this breakdown of organized resistance, the prisoners considered other approaches. Captain McGowen, chosen by the enlisted men as a leader, believed that we should deal with the Japs on the contract basis. We should agree to do little enough so we could finish work at a decent time and make life at least bearable. On the other hand, Captain Wald would use the contract system only if the Japs agreed to the size of the tasks proposed by the Americans. In time, the Japs removed Wald as a sub-detail leader and threatened him with severe punishment if he caused trouble in his work detail. There was so much controversy among the prisoners about work that Lt. Col. Rogers issued orders that prisoners do as little as possible but complete contracts if reasonable, and come in early to get rest and have time for personal needs. Rogers also tried to settle things down by rearranging the officers and men — the Japs had originally mixed them together within work details. Now, he put the officers and non-commissioned offices together and segregated the privates in their own details under competent leadership.

But dissension about how much to work continued. At times the Japs had the guards use clubs to get the men to work harder, or to punish individuals who did little or no work; some of those who didn't do their share were a burden to others. Lt. Hosida and his second-in-command, Lt. Hosimoto, made general threats every night at roll call.

The Japs rewarded groups that finished their tasks faster by letting the men swim in a nearby creek. A few Americans hated to see slow or sloppy work as a matter of principle so would try to get the rest of us to do a better job. But I didn't pay any attention when an American sergeant urged me to work harder.

The basic Japanese requirement for a prisoner was to dig out two-thirds of a cubic meter of dirt a day to form drainage ditches along the airstrip. Most work groups finished their contracts by 11 A.M. and had the rest of the day off. But the coral detail did not benefit from the contract system. Its men were hauled two miles every day to the Tabunco coral pits to load large chunks of coral that were trucked back to the airstrip.

I volunteered for the coral detail because I wanted to move around. On the way to Tabunco the first day, we passed many civilians who looked as though they wanted to cheer us up. One of them shouted, "Victory Joe!" The Japs stopped the trucks, and while we watched in horror, they almost beat our cheerleader to death — I doubt if he survived. At the pits we wrestled with huge chunks of coral that required two men to lift them on the trucks. The glare of the sun on the coral almost blinded me.

As weeks went by, the sun burned us black all over since we wore nothing but G-strings. My feet were covered with calluses, but I still got cuts from sharp pieces of coral. I weighed about 100 pounds — my prewar weight was 170. I was still missing the four top front teeth that a nervous soldier had knocked out while jumping off a truck at Ganasi. My beard had been bleached white by the sun. I hadn't shaved it off, having long before traded off my razor blades. Occasionally the guards took us down to the river where we'd use sand to scrape the dirt off each other. But the best time to wash was during a good rain when we stood under the eaves of our huts and let the warm water fall over us.

About April 7, 1944, on the way to Tabunco, we noticed three wounded guards on a passing truck that belonged to the main Davao prison camp. We suspected an escape attempt there and learned later that about that time four or five Americans had fled into the jungle after bashing their guards with shovels. The Japs sent out patrols, but the Americans reached Lt. Col. Fertig's headquarters, where some or all of them joined his guerrilla forces. One escapee was my friend, Lt. Andrew Bukavinski — we had often discussed escape plans at Malaybalay.

The day after we saw the wounded guards, Lt. Hosida ordered all prisoners to turn in their shoes, thus depriving us of the new Red Cross shoes we had worn only a little more than a month. This effort to discourage escape was roughest on the coral pit workers, whose feet would be easily cut. Lt. Col. Rogers urgently requested sandals, at least for the coral workers, but none were issued.

Soon after coming to Lasang, Kid Marlow and I started to share our Red Cross food packages and any other food that either of us obtained by trading. Once Marlow showed up with an open can of beans. I asked, "Where did you find it? Japs or another GI could come after you. Don't ever do it again." I hid the beans in a box and shoved it out of sight, and Marlow drifted away. I acted none too soon because Pork Maderis, a burly, aggressive chow hound, came looking for his can of beans. He even sniffed but smelled nothing. When I nonchalantly assured him I knew nothing, he went looking elsewhere.

I got involved with another greedy chow hound through my old friend, Vergil Haifley, with whom I had shared the Moro house by Lake Lanao in Bacolod Grande. Verge asked me, "Vic, would you teach me some judo? There's a guy I want to put in his place." I answered, "Verge, that bully is too strong for you — one blow will finish the fight." But Haifley insisted, so I began to show him some moves. Just then Marco Caputo, a muscular chow hound, stronger and more feared than Vergil's enemy, interrupted our training.

Caputo snarled, "I'll show who's strongest around here!" With that he grabbed me in a bear hug that forced the air out of my lungs. Fearing serious injury, my mind raced to find a way to save myself. Suddenly I relaxed and then in one motion lifted my arms above my head and slid downward, helped by the perspiration on our bodies. With one hand I lifted Caputo's leg off the ground and with the other shoved upward against his chin. He hopped around on one foot, trying to shake himself loose. But one wild hop into a hole unbalanced him, and then I threw him to the ground. Even though we were close to the Japanese officers' quarters, the fight had been so brief the Japs had not noticed it. I fled, fearing we might have been seen. In that case "Little Caesar" Hosimoto would have forced Caputo and me to fight to the finish, or close to it. My small friend Haifley later challenged his own enemy but was felled with one blow, as I had feared.

Near the end of April the Jap officers and NCOs talked to us almost every day about a prisoner exchange that was to take place in September or October. As a first step, they would soon transfer us to Manila. The Japs removed our officers from the airstrip and assigned them to camp maintenance and grass cutting around the outer edges of the compound. Rations of meat and rice increased after Major Tagasaki became the new CO of the Davao Penal Colony.

But the small increase in meat and rice didn't last. After May 1 we steadily lost weight, and our health and vigor declined because the Red Cross food packages and vitamins were used up — the Japs had dispensed them just before we left for Lasang. The lack of vitamins brought some of us down with beri-beri and pellagra, and affected the eyesight of many. The Japs began to treat us more harshly. They knew they were losing the war and no longer worried about exposure of conditions at Lasang since the prisoner exchange apparently had fallen through.

In early July 1944, Tagasaki moved his headquarters to Lasang after the main-camp prisoners had been shipped back to Cabanatuan. Upon his arrival, Tagasaki announced that all prisoners would go on work details, including Lt. Col. Rogers, the senior prisoner, as well as chaplains, doctors, and medics. After a short stay, Major Tagasaki left for Manila, leaving us again in the hands of Lieutenants Hosida and Hosimoto.

Despite our weakened condition, the Japs feared us more since there was now no prospect of prisoner exchange. To keep us intimidated, the guards would suddenly shout "Banzai" and rush toward us with drawn bayonets, stopping just short of thrusting their bayonets home. To increase our terror, they picked times when we had no tools that we might have used to defend ourselves.

One afternoon when an officer work group did not finish its contract, Hosida ordered the guards to line up rails from an abandoned track. He forced the whole detail of 50 officers to kneel with their shin bones against the sharp edge of the rail. The guard then made the officers rise slightly so their weight rested entirely on the rail. While keeping the officers in this painful position, Hosida ordered the rest of us to finish the officer's contract. We completed it in 25 minutes. Then Hosida made everyone run over a mile on the gravel back to the compound. Hosida and Hosimoto grinned as we winced whenever our bare feet struck a piece of coral. On another occasion, officers who had completed their regular task were ordered by Hosida to wash the clothes of the enlisted prisoners — apparently to stir up bad feelings between enlisted and officer POWs.

Hosida was slender and had an aristocratic bearing, but his second-in-command, Lt. Hosimoto, was a stocky and muscular judo expert. He took care to observe our work and look for laggard performances. If a prisoner fell short or looked at him the wrong way, Hosimoto went after him. It was not difficult for him to throw his victim to the ground, who by now had lost weight and was weakened by reduced rations. Once his victim was down, "Little Caesar" viciously kicked him. The typical, bloodied victim was able to get up and stumble back to the compound.

But Hosimoto picked on one prisoner who was not so easy to overcome. He was Lt. Bolen, a Navy officer who was of average weight and height, and who, at 42, was considerably older than the rest of us. Little Caesar noticed Bolen chewing on a piece of sugar cane after his work detail had finished for the day. When Hosimoto seized it Bolen grabbed it back, and we thought Little Caesar would have another easy victim. Yet each time Hosimoto tried to upset him, the Navy officer shifted his feet and stayed upright. The muscular little Jap became more and more exasperated. Finally, he brought down the flat of his sword on his victim's ear. The ear bled a lot but was not severed. Apparently satisfied, Little Caesar walked away.

The Japs began to patrol during the night just outside and even inside our sleeping sheds, worried that prisoners would try to escape since there would be no exchange. I slept on a plank, suspended three feet above the ground next to my partner, Kid Marlow. I woke up one night, needing to urinate but afraid to go to the latrine; a few nights before, a prisoner heading for the latrine had run into a lurking guard, who bloodied him with a bayonet jab in the rib.

To avoid that risk, I stayed put and relieved myself in my canteen.

Then I emptied it outside through a small hole in the shed's wall. Immediately an excited shout of "Buckaroo" scared me out of my wits. A Jap guard rushed inside, stood next to me, and called the other guards over. Their flashlights showed him splattered from the waist down with my warm urine. Meantime I had gotten under my blanket, hoping they would think I had been asleep all the time. But Marlow had been aroused from a deep sleep and sat up. The guards turned on him as the guilty one and began to beat him. I stopped them by admitting that I had done it. I spent the next day pounding coral rock with a sledgehammer while the guard who had suffered stood over me with a bayonet. It was a rough day for me, but the hot sun apparently got to the guard because that was the end of my punishment. The story of the incident spread. That evening, Lt. Col. Rufus Rogers, the senior American officer, took me aside and whispered, "Vic, you exactly expressed the sentiment of all of us last night."

The Japs did their best to break down an enlisted man named John McCloskey, who worked in the mess crew. They found wire snippers in the bottom of a basket of sweet potato vines he was carrying. His confinement in a tiny barred enclosure prevented him from stretching out. But after 20 days on rice and water, McCloskey still looked reasonably fit. Then Hosimoto surprised us by letting McCloskey out. Hosimoto may have admired McCloskey's stamina because of his own obsession with physical fitness. What Hosimoto and the other Japs did not know was that Major Heidger and other American doctors had slipped vitamin pills to McCloskey every night. Hosimoto was puzzled by McCloskey, and absolutely baffled by American victories over Japanese forces. He was heard to mutter about the failure of Japanese gods and the success of the Christian God.

Our acts of defiance continued. Despite the extreme danger, a slight prisoner named Abernathy had developed a trading relationship with a guard the Japs had probably recruited in Formosa. One night Abernathy crept up to the fence through the darkness to wait for the Formosan — he owed him some money. But when Abernathy tossed the can of money over the fence, he heard only angry shouts instead of the Formosan's familiar voice. Abernathy fled back to his bunk and lay there with pounding heart. He bunked near me, and after calming down he told what had happened. Next morning Hosimoto ordered Lt. Col. Rogers to produce the culprit. But by the following day, Rogers had not delivered the offender. Hosimoto now informed Rogers that he would pick out one or more prisoners at random for execution if he did not have the guilty person the next day. On the third morning Lt. Col. Rogers stood before Abernathy and stated that all evidence pointed to him as the one sought by the Japs and told him what the Japs would do if no one came forward. Abernathy saluted and replied,

"I'll come with you, colonel." Abernathy was confined in the same small enclosure that McCloskey had occupied.

The Formosan to whom Abernathy had tried to toss the can of money feared the worst when the Japs seized the American. But Abernathy refused to betray him. The Formosan in turn was able to slip extra food to the confined American. Another American, Sgt. Denver Rose, also worried about the situation because he had had dealings with the Formosan. Rose had the soft job of tending the diesel engines that generated electricity for the camp.

Starting around August 1, 1944, searchlights played in the sky nightly, and there were frequent air raid alerts. On August 4 the Japs stopped work on the airstrip and we realized they were getting ready to take us away. That night I was still half awake about 1 A.M. when I heard an approaching aircraft that didn't sound Japanese. I went to the door to listen and realized the low-flying plane was American. I yelled to everyone to stay put because the guards would be there soon. Then the plane swooped lower and dropped three small bombs before flying off. Excited guards rushed into the compound and stationed themselves at all the barracks' entrances. We had little sleep for the rest of the night — the tense guards standing there kept us on edge and fearful.

Next morning the guards would not let us out of our sleeping quarters — they probably didn't want us to see how much damage the bombs had done to the airstrip. Although they gave us back our shoes, we didn't leave that day.

The following day, the Japs took back our shoes, so we figured we weren't leaving soon after all. Then they cut our rice ration to 300 grams — half the 650 grams promised upon our arrival at Lasang. Our vegetable ration dropped to 300 grams, as compared to the promised 500 grams. Now they let us out into the barren compound. There was a ten-foot strip of green just inside the boundary fence; the guards had orders to shoot anyone on that strip. In the days that followed I would dart into the danger zone to grab some water weed for Marlow and me; he stayed by our bunks to protect our small store of food.

Once I stopped short when I noticed a Japanese soldier in a neat uniform standing outside the fence. He gave me a snappy salute. When I returned the salute, he strode away. I never saw him again — he was apparently a visitor who showed his respect for a fellow soldier. In contrast, the guards and other Japs seemed amused by our desperate scrounging for food. They went so far as to feed fat monkeys and parrots just outside the fence while we hungrily looked on. I took new notice of my pet cat.

After the drastic cut in rations, some of the boys around Marlow and me remarked, "Vic, if your cat knew what you were thinking, it wouldn't stay around." I resisted for a few days but finally realized the cat could mean life or death for Marlow and me. I throttled and skinned it, then cooked it in my mess kit over the glowing coals under the big water barrel. Unbelievably, Marlow and I were so hungry that the meat and broth tasted pretty good. The senior POW officer in our barracks got wind of our stew and enjoyed the small portion we offered him. Another officer, a captain, was so crazed with hunger that he lost all of his humanity in begging for a share. We gave him some, but he was furious when he found out what it was.

Ten days after the airstrip had been bombed, the Japs told us to be ready to leave the next day and that we would get our shoes on the boat. That night we had stewed carabao and rice — we called it the "Last Supper." The following morning, August 20, 1944, we arose at 3:30 A.M., had breakfast, and were ready to go at six. At 6:30 we were herded into several large groups. A rope around each group tied all the outside men together, preventing the inside men from getting out. Thus tethered and barefoot, we had to walk carefully to avoid tangling ourselves up. We headed toward the water at Tabunco on the road I had ridden so many times to the coral pits. A truck carrying a mounted machine gun led the column. Guards with automatic rifles rode in the lead truck, and another armed truck with guards brought up the rear. The Japs probably feared an attack by guerrilla forces.

Lt. Col. Wendell Fertig, the guerrilla leader who had observed our Death March on July 4, 1942, by this time had organized the largest resistance group on Mindanao. But Fertig had refused months earlier to carry out a plan proposed by General MacArthur's headquarters to release by force all prisoners at the Davao Penal Colony. Fertig said his own men were short of food and could not possibly feed the 2,000 POWs who were to be released, especially since many were sick and wounded. Fertig also feared brutal retaliation against any village where the prisoners might be aided or found.

25

Torpedoed

August 20 to September 7, 1944

After the guards had herded the tied-up groups of prisoners over the two miles to the pier at Tabunco, we got our shoes back. A good-sized freighter stood just off shore. Small craft took us out to her, and then we had to climb swaying landing nets to reach the deck. We were so starved we barely had the strength to pull ourselves up. As we boarded, the guards put 400 of us into one hold and 350 into another — 650 men from the Lasang detail and 100 from another work group. We were all aboard by noon, August 20, 1944. We were just jammed in — we had hardly enough room to sit down, let alone stretch out. The Japs crowded us even more by loading baggage into our holds.

There was no organization. We were on our own. Guys were hollering for "Joe" or "Bill" — everyone was trying to find his buddy with the result that we just climbed over each other. But there were a few natural leaders who tried to calm us down: Father LaFleur, some West Pointers, and a guy who was a self-appointed bouncer. An officer's rank didn't mean anything. We finally quieted down out of sheer exhaustion. Then the Japs told us our rations would be 300 grams of rice and 300 grams of vegetable per day — the same starvation rations announced on August 7.

The heat in the holds was terrible and made worse because the Japs piled sacks of vegetables over the hatches, leaving only side hatch covers free to let in air. The guards lowered four latrine boxes into the hold that held 350 prisoners and followed a similar procedure for the other hold. About 2 P.M. they called for prisoner mess cooks to prepare the food. That evening each of us received one handful of rice and an inch of watery soup in the bottom of his canteen can. This serving did not come close to the very small ration promised. From then on the soup was made from camote peelings or squash, and was so rancid that it was scarcely edible.

That afternoon the freighter moved to the harbor for Davao City. Some prisoners saw a high-flying, four-engine aircraft through the hatch, and then we heard a bomb swish into the water at some distance. A machine-gun clattered on the deck, and the side hatch covers banged closed. We sweated it out for three hours with no fresh air and no circulation. Some got sick, and some passed out from lack of oxygen. When the hatch doors opened again, there wasn't a sound because we were all too weak to say anything. Lt. Col. Rogers vigorously protested and then begged the Japs to give us more air.

The next day, August 21, we moved south along the coast and entered Sarangan Bay. That night the Japs allowed the prisoners to rig an American parachute on the ship's boom to divert air into the prisoners' holds. But the parachute was taken down the next morning when we sailed out into the Celebes Sea. At 10 A.M. guns on the ship fired, and the guards closed the hatches again for several hours. The ship stopped, apparently having found cover along the coast. But when night fell, we were underway again. Until August 24 we generally followed the same pattern of being underway at night and staying hidden during daylight.

Once a day the Japs would lower a five-gallon can of water into the hold. We organized ourselves into groups of ten. Each group could fill one canteen. From the canteen, each person got eight GI spoonfuls of water. Some fought over who got the last spoonful or licked the last drop from the canteen. At that time the Japs dispensed our daily dab of rice. But I saved mine until we returned to the hold after our daily salt-water hose-down on deck — needed to relieve the stench. When on deck, I soaked my shirt in salt water to take below. There I squeezed the salt water on my rice for seasoning and a little water. Some boys almost died trying to drink salt water. During this time most of us became dehydrated. At first, when we were able to sweat, steam from our bodies would form on the steel plates of the hold so I would wipe up some moisture with my T-shirt to cool myself. After they gave us our tiny water ration, we'd perspire a little bit immediately, but that was all. We urinated only once in a great while, and with excruciating pain.

I teamed up with Captain Richardson, a handsome officer next to me, to share our rations of water and rice. We used his canteen to store about half our water ration to drink later. Also crowded close to me was Abernathy, who had been severely punished at Lasang — in order to save the entire camp from massive reprisals, he had admitted trading with a guard. Now I praised him for confessing and tried to cheer him up, but he felt he would not survive, and seemed resigned to his fate. Another companion near me was Father Joseph LaFleur, an Army chaplain who had volunteered to come with us on the prison ship. He once gave his water ration away. Many were desperate for water, but there were also some phony "desperates" who yelled for water. I knew they weren't in any worse shape than anyone else. I had heard they drank blood on other ships. On ours they drank urine. It almost caused a murder. When one guy passed out, his buddy drank his water and then pissed into the empty canteen, thinking his pal wouldn't know the difference. But when the pal came to and took a couple swallows, he realized what had happened and almost killed his buddy before being restrained.

Another guy went crazy and kept yelling, "Get thee behind me, Satan!" The men around the poor fellow feared the Japs would fire down into us, as they had threatened if we didn't keep quiet. The man's companions tied him up, and every time he began, "Get thee —" you could hear a whack, a blow from a canteen that cut him short. Next morning, I crawled over to take a look at him; he was unconscious and still tied. I don't know what happened to him.

On the evening of August 22, the holds remained shut for ten straight hours. As hour followed hour, everyone else lay down flat to avoid the least exertion. But I propped my head up slightly, hoping to get a little extra air. Some men who thought they were dying asked Father LaFleur to give them last rites, and he did so. The doctors — Lt. Col. Colvert, Major Heidger, and Major Tremaine — could do nothing in this crisis. But everyone survived.

In the late afternoon of August 24, we slowed and heard sounds from other ships. Soon we dropped anchor. But where were we? We found out after the Japs demanded some volunteers to bring the latrine boxes out of the hold and dump them over the side — the Japs had neglected doing it for so long that they didn't want to face the foul smell themselves. We chose some Navy men to go on deck, believing they might recognize the harbor. It turned out to be Zamboanga, a good-sized city at the extreme southwest corner of Mindanao. We were 250 miles due west of Davao, but the freighter had sailed much farther to get around the large bulge on the south coast of the island. We were still on our once-a-day water ration, and men blacked out frequently. Others were tormented with heat rash.

Ten days passed before a ship tied up next to us. Then on September 4, after our daily salt-water hosing on deck, the guards motioned us with guns across the gangplank to the ship alongside — it was called the *Shinyo Maru*. Immediately it was into the holds again — 250 prisoners into the forward hold and 500 into the large central hold. There I settled next to an iron pipe that extended from the bottom of the ship to the main deck. At 11 A.M. the next day we got underway.

About 4 P.M. we heard a protracted commotion above us. Some prisoners saw an elderly man with a towel around him, ordering the guards to take more covers off the hatches. We believed it was the captain of the ship, who wished to give us more air in the hold. As a result, practically all the hatch covers were left off for the rest of the afternoon and all night.

But the next morning brought another air raid so the guards closed the hatches again. This time conditions became even worse because the guards put tarpaulin over the hatch covers. Luckily, however, this alert lasted only a short time, and we got some more air again. But other alerts followed during the day and into the night while the ship would move a short distance, stop, and then move on again. Sometime before dawn the ship began a steady run.

The next day, September 7, Lt. Hosimoto had the hatch covers rearranged so that there were small spaces left between them — they looked like wide bars running across the ceiling of the holds. Then the guards lashed down the covers with ropes so they couldn't be lifted from the inside. After we left Zamboanga, we no longer had any idea of where we were because prisoners no longer took the latrine boxes out on the deck. Instead, the guards lifted the boxes out of the hold by rope. Nevertheless, by mid-afternoon of September 7 we hoped the worst was over — we had plowed along without any alerts on the run that had begun before dawn.

The sudden sounds of a bugle and rifle firing on deck shattered our brief mood of relief. I could see the bugler through the slats of the hatch cover. Others heard a loud explosion, quickly followed by another, but I may have become unconscious because the next thing I knew I was under water. I wasn't scared but I felt this was it — I'd given up. Then I was conscious of being shoved against the big pipe where I had located myself when I came aboard. Above, frozen to the pipe, was a fellow I knew. I tried to shake him loose, but he wouldn't budge. I had to leave him — I was running out of air. I finally popped to the surface and breathed again. In the semi-darkness of the hold, a few men were floundering among floating barracks bags and gasping for air. But many were still under water. I could hear the ship's whistle blowing constantly, like the cry of a wounded animal. I repeatedly shoved timbers and debris away as the rising water lifted me upward. Now there were bodies all around. Still floating, I reached the deck, but then I caught my leg under a girder. I was trapped there, floating but unable to move. Then the ship lurched sideways. I heard the crunch of solid bone breaking and knew it was my leg. Now it hung loose, and I was free in the water.

26

In the Water

September 7–8, 1944

The ship's hull began to split apart. I was caught in a cascade of water that poured through the crack and into the ocean. I was carried close to some Japs in a lifeboat who were shooting at floundering prisoners. One Jap aimed right at me, but I turned and ducked under just in time. But when I came up for air, the guy next to me was sinking away — hit by the Jap's shot. Before the Jap could fire again, I ducked under and swam away. He didn't see where I came up. Then what I had read long ago in Lowell Thomas's *Raiders in the Deep* flashed through my mind: the importance of getting far enough away from a sinking ship to avoid being sucked under with it. I swam directly away from the *Shinyo Maru*, which was now listing badly.

After coming out of the darkness of the hold into the water and mid-afternoon sunshine, I was in a different world. I noticed a large wooden hatch cover floating close by. It was about 12 by 15 feet, but there were 15 men draped across it or holding to the edges. Some of them were yelling, and others had blood coming out of their ears and mouths. A few tried to act as though nothing had happened.

I knew the hatch cover was too small for so many men, but I worked my way over to it with my broken leg just dragging. Someone helped me aboard. Now the prison ship was sinking lower. As it disappeared into the ocean, it pulled our raft toward it but we stayed afloat. The ship's whistle kept blowing until the end. The lifeboat of Japs who had fired at me had made no attempt to get away and were pulled down with the sinking ship — they just kept firing until the ocean swallowed them. All that was left were a lot of big geysers and bubbles. (The prison ship had stayed afloat after being torpedoed not more than 15 minutes and probably only six or seven, according to 1st Lt. John J. Morrett, a survivor who wrote an official report on the American prisoners aboard). Suddenly it became very quiet except for Americans talking on our raft.

Captain Cleveland, whom I knew only by sight, moved across the raft to look at my leg. It had been numb but began to hurt a little. It was bleeding, and bones were sticking out of my skin — a dangerous compound fracture. Cleveland made a sort of tourniquet out of his belt and fashioned a splint from a board, which he tied around the leg with my G-string.

Nearby was a freighter that had run aground during the attack on the seven-ship convoy of which the *Shinyo Maru* had been part. It and two other vessels had been sunk. Now, from the deck of the grounded ship, Japs were firing at the Americans who struggled for shore about two miles away. With me on the raft was Mike Pulice, a buddy of mine from the 200th Coast Artillery. He also had a broken leg. We agreed that the Japs on the grounded ship would eventually get around to firing on our raft because there were so many of us. With our bad legs, we couldn't get away and would be sitting ducks.

We had just about decided to swim off on our own when a stunned Jap floated close to the raft in his life jacket. After some argument, the men on the raft decided to kill him with his own bayonet. Meantime I kept asking him for some of his water, but he shook his head again and again. Not interested in stabbing him, I reached underwater and grabbed his canteen. Then I did a wrong thing: I gulped down all the cold weak tea in the canteen instead of saving some of it.

I spotted a spar floating nearby that was large enough for Mike and me. We grabbed it and pushed off from the raft, kicking with our two good legs. I knew we had done the right thing when I looked back at the wounded and spiritless men lying on the raft and hanging to its sides. We headed away from the grounded vessel and the shore.

We hadn't gone far when we came upon Lt. Col. Colvert, a doctor and an acquaintance of Mike. He was old to be in uniform but was swimming easily. Finding him seemed like a blessing from heaven — while floating around with two bad legs, we had run into a doctor! He told us he was doing all right. Then we asked if he would stay with us and fix up our legs when we got ashore. We must have looked too healthy because he answered, "I'm sorry, but my job is on the hatch cover over there where there are many more wounded men to help." He pointed toward the men we had left. About ten minutes later a shell from the grounded freighter exploded behind us. I looked for the hatch cover, but it was gone — a direct hit had wiped it out along with the men it carried.

As the sun went down, Mike and I were still together. He was floating on half a life preserver while I clung to an empty saki box. Then Japs on another ship spotted us and opened up with rifles. I spun my box toward them and ducked my head beneath the water. The bullets sounded like nails as they hit the water, and were louder still when I came up for a gulp of air. I tried to submerge my whole body, but that damned wood splint was so buoyant it stopped me from getting either leg completely submerged. A bullet nicked me in the ankle of my bad leg. When the Japs gave up firing, Mike and his life preserver were nowhere to be seen. By now the sky had grown dark.

I figured I had little chance of escaping with my broken leg, but I was going to try. It was hard to stay on top of my saki box because it was too small and the thing kept bobbing up and down. I saw a big timber float by and I started after it, but no matter how hard I kicked, the current pushed it out of my reach. Finally I realized the current was carrying the timber in a large semicircle so I swam to intercept. When I finally climbed on I was thoroughly exhausted but happy. The sounds of gunshots and barking dogs came from a long way off in the dark. Across the bay I saw a light on top of a mountain; I used it as a bearing with the stars. When I checked a little later, I realized the current was taking me out to sea. Because I didn't have the strength to head directly toward shore, I merely pushed the timber at an angle to the direction of the current.

In time I reached quieter water and was catching my breath when I heard the *chug, chug, chug* of a motor launch coming out of the darkness toward me. I slid off my timber and stayed low behind it. I began to pray. The faces of the riflemen in the bow stood out in the moonlight that shone off and on through the passing clouds. It looked like the launch was coming right at me. When they were almost on top of me, the Japs yelled — possibly a warning not to ram my timber — and veered off. I don't know how they missed seeing me. I felt lucky as all get out except that I had lost my timber.

Suddenly downhearted and lonely, I prayed and floundered in the water. But soon a long board, two feet wide, floated toward me. As it came closer, I saw that it was two boards nailed together with nails sticking out the top. I grabbed it anyway. I climbed aboard with difficulty, tearing my chest on the nails. In a while I couldn't stand the pain of lying on the nails so I slid back into the water, scraping myself some more. Then the movement of the water grated my helpless leg back and forth on the rough wood underneath while I hung on the side. When I couldn't stand it any longer, I climbed back on. I changed back and forth all night — standing one torture as long as I could before suffering the other. Throughout this ordeal I was terribly thirsty.

Just before dawn it began to rain. A floating palm frond brushed against me, which I stuck in my mouth, hoping to catch some water. I held it up, looking like a big bird, and swallowed a little rain. The pain in my leg had become so bad that I prayed for a shark to come along and bite it off. As the sky grew lighter, I made out a small boat a long way away. I yelled and shouted but no one heard. Now the current brought me closer — it was a local boat. I yelled again, but it suddenly took off and left me. The sun came up, and then the sky became overcast.

When the sun broke through the haze in mid-morning, I could see toward shore, where the vivid green of shallow water contrasted sharply with the deep blue water where I floated. Oil had collected on my beard the day before as I passed through three miles of slick. There was so much of it that my beard acted as a buoy and kept my head above water. But the oil had washed off my body, which was held to the surface by the leg splint; I could not escape what was by now a blazing sun. I was getting badly sun-burned, especially in the rear. When I could think, all I wanted was to get ashore, drink some coconut milk, and hide. Then I'd lose my train of thought and want something else.

Meanwhile, the tide had been carrying me closer to land, and I was floating in the green shallows. I could see a small shack and something moving that looked like a dog. I was maneuvering myself toward the break-ers when a Japanese observation plane with two pontoons began to fly in circles near me. I put all the effort I could to get into the whitewater where the breakers formed. Suddenly, an outrigger canoe with two men was rac-ing toward me. They came alongside, pulled me aboard, gave me a banana and raw egg, and handed me a T-shirt full of holes to cover my damaged skin. The Japanese plane swung back and gave us a burst of machine gun fire. My paddlers yelled like hell and paddled to the crest of a large wave that carried us flying into shore.

27

In the Hands of the Guerrillas

September 8–29, 1944

I was afraid the Filipinos might leave me on the beach as the plane banked for another run. But my rescuers picked up the outrigger canoe with me in it and carried it under a large palm tree. There a Japanese flag flew. I didn't know what to think as the Filipinos jabbered with each other. What did the flag mean? But because I knew some Spanish and Filipino dialect and they knew some English, I got their conversation. They told me I was still on Mindanao, on Sindangan Bay, only three hundred miles across the island from where I had boarded the first freighter. This news surprised me because I thought I might be in Indochina.

The Filipinos treated my leg with some white powder they told me was sulfathiazole, which they claimed had come in by submarine. This obvious lie added to my distrust at seeing the Japanese flag flying there.* When I asked to see one of their new, short-barreled rifles, they refused but showed me the "43" on their ammunition. Then I knew they were telling the truth because the ammunition we'd had on Bataan was 1941 or earlier.

After the plane had been gone for a time, the Filipinos moved me into a shack. Soon an old woman brought in a coconut shell of water. I was dying of thirst, but she gave me only spoonfuls while holding me in her arms. Next she fed me cornmeal and chicken gruel. The family that lived

---

*Flying the Japanese flag did not necessarily mean Filipino support for the Japs; it often was a tactic to escape persecution or even a cover for guerrilla activity. See S. A. Mills, Stranded in the Philippines, p. 91, for the thoughts of a guerrilla leader on this matter.

in the shack kept peeking in the window at me as though I were a freak — and with my big dirty beard and emaciated body, maybe I was. I felt a little better, but it would be several days before I got over being startled by any sudden noise, however slight — probably the result of the torpedo exploding so close to me.

Later that day a couple of Filipinos came into the shack with a wild story. They thought they'd seen a ghost in a nearby cornfield, but it turned out to be a naked American wandering around. When they brought him in, I recognized a fellow prisoner of the 30th Squadron from Utah. He wore only a straw hat and carried a clay jug of water. Seeing me, he said, "Hey, Mapes, who am I?" Up to that moment I had known his name like my own, but now I couldn't think of it. He didn't say anything about my bad condition, which he didn't even notice. His only thought was who he was. When he headed for the door, I asked him where he was going. He replied, "I'm just going to keep going until I remember my name." I asked the Filipinos to watch him and help him if they could. I worried that the enemy plane would fly back and see him. But he soon came back with a big smile on his face and announced, "Hey, I know who I am, I'm Bill Lorton." Then I remembered, too, and we both laughed.

That evening the Filipinos told me I had to be put in a gunnysack and taken away from there. They tied me in and fastened the sack to a pole. Two of them lifted the pole to their shoulders, and we started off in the darkness. Bill Lorton was no longer around, and I wondered what my rescuers had done with him. We hadn't gone far when a commanding voice brought us to a halt. An armed Filipino stepped out of the shadows and demanded, "What are you carrying in that sack?" My Filipinos answered, "Oh, that's just some carabao meat we're delivering." Then my heart sank when I heard, "Fine. I'll just come along to protect it."

In a short time I was dumped on the ground and then lifted into a canoe. Paddlers and our unwelcome guard got into another canoe, and both canoes shoved off. As we sped along, I whispered to the Filipinos to slip away from the other canoe. But when we dropped back, the self-appointed guard motioned with his gun for us to stay close. We paddled for several hours before the two canoes came ashore and the sack of carabao meat — me — was roughly dropped to the ground.

I peeked out to see one of my Filipinos motioning to the guard to come away with him briefly, as though to show him something. They didn't come back right away. After a time, only my Filipino returned, hefting the guard's gun. Then I was untied so I could stretch out. I looked around and was amazed to see Mike Pulice lying on the ground not ten feet away. He caught my eye and shouted, "Vic, what happened? How did you get here?" But I refused to show that I even knew Mike. In spite of the guard's disappearance, I still suspected these Filipinos because Bill Lorton had vanished. It took Mike a long time to convince me that the Filipinos were friends.

We later learned that we were in the hands of Lt. Col. Fertig's guerrilla organization. He was overcome with remorse at the sinking of the *Shinyo Maru* because he had not tried to free the American prisoners earlier. Now his men and local Filipinos were gathering up the survivors. The *Shinyo Maru* had been torpedoed by the U.S. submarine *Paddle* (SS-263) in Sindangan Bay on the northwest coast of Mindanao. Besides the *Shinyo Maru*, the *Paddle* had disabled and probably sunk three other ships of the seven-ship Japanese convoy.

In a half-hour or so, Mike and I were turned over to four bearers, who looked even smaller than the average, slight Filipino. They put us on stretchers and headed inland. After an hour's climb in the dark over rough ground, they set us down in a cornfield — apparently too tired to go farther. They promised that others would come to pick us up. They disappeared and we lay there, gazing at the bright stars and hearing the protests of howler monkeys close by. We thought our luck had finally run out by the time another crew appeared. These bearers may have been succeeded by still another crew before we reached the top of a small mountain and were deposited in a makeshift hospital. Several other badly wounded survivors from the *Shinyo Maru* were already there.

They laid Mike and me side by side at a spot from which we could look out over several miles of jungle to the ocean. While we waited for the guerrilla doctor, a boy named Clarence entertained us with a one-stringed coconut instrument. The local Filipinos tending the hospital fed us green bananas, eggs, and carabao milk — one lactating woman even donated her own milk, hoping it might help my leg. When I had to go to the john, I used half a coconut shell, which the Filipinos would dump in the jungle. My beard was so full of sand and oil I couldn't lift my head. A guerrilla soldier started to shave the dam thing off with a dull, mess-kit knife, but it hurt so much he had to stop when only half-finished. He completed the job the next day. I looked awful because now the lower half of my face was all white instead of tanned like the rest of me.

Meanwhile, Fertig's guerrilla command had ordered Dr. Santiago Calo to leave his station at a regimental infirmary and proceed to the vicinity of Sindangan, where the survivors from the *Shinyo Maru* had come ashore. Calo covered the 55 miles by horseback in eight hours, even though he had to hide for some time in thick undergrowth to escape machine gunning by two enemy aircraft. Calo reported to the local guerrilla leader, Captain

Fangon, who sent the 40-year-old doctor to the mountaintop where Mike and I had joined the other serious cases.

Dr. Calo thought I looked much older than my 27 years because of malnutrition and four missing front teeth. When the doctor looked at the bones sticking out of my leg below the knee, he said he might have to amputate to save my life. But I pleaded with him to save my leg. He said later that my determination caused him to postpone the operation for a few days.

I had a constant high temperature because of infection — penicillin was not available, but the doctor gave me sulfathiazole. He tried to clean the maggots from my gangrenous tissue and exposed bone marrow with Dakin's solution. Every slight movement was torture. For dressing the wound, the doctor used banana leaves that had been passed over flames for partial sterilization. Day after day I lay in constant pain. Each night was an eternity. I would grip Mike's hand when the pain became too great. When he groaned, I did the same for him.

But after a few days the gangrenous process stopped, and the foul smell disappeared. Yet I could still feel maggots crawling over the wound. We had been there almost three weeks when Dr. Calo came into the shack one morning, whistling while he wiped off a rusty saw. Mike and I turned to each other with looks that asked the question, "Which of us is going to lose a leg?" We were terrified because he didn't have any anesthetic — he didn't have anything except this old saw. The whistling continued as the doctor sat down and began sawing some bamboo splints. He explained that we would need the splints for our transport to the beach, where a submarine was to meet us.

At 5 A.M. next morning on September 27, 1944, we heard a commotion outside. It was our transport, which consisted of two wooden sleds, two carabaos, and their drivers. As the drivers tied us to the sleds, Lt. Col. John McGee came by to see that all the patients were on their way. He had been a prisoner at Davao who had escaped from an earlier prison ship at Zamboanga. Now he had charge of the *Shinyo Maru* survivors. He cheered us up but wrote later that he doubted I would make it.

We knew why we had been tied so tightly as soon as our jolting trip began. It was much rougher going down than coming up. When we passed through a coconut grove, the coconuts bobbed up and down in crazy rhythm. My leg almost drove me crazy. At a brief stop, Dr. Calo gave me a cigar, telling me it would help.

I had just lit up when we heard Japanese planes approaching. The Japs had been bombing the nearby town of Sindangan daily. They had come earlier than usual that morning so we were caught on fairly open ground. The drivers unhooked the carabaos, hid us under some small bamboo, and hurried to the edge of the jungle. From there they and the doctor watched two enemy planes strafe and bomb a deserted village — according to the doctor, they wrecked one house and killed one chicken. I was puffing on my cigar and didn't notice a thing. The cigar had put me to sleep — it must have had some opium in it. That was the first real rest I'd had in weeks. The drivers returned quickly, and the awful bouncing started again. But the agony didn't last. Soon we were transferred to litters, on which four bolo men (volunteer guerrilla supporters) gave us a more gentle ride. It was still early in the morning when we reached the beach, where a few fishing boats from a nearby village had been drawn up. No one was about yet.

A damp wind chilled us as we waited — we didn't know for what. Then two other badly wounded survivors from the *Shinyo Maru* were deposited beside us. Before long, a husky fisherman approached the bolo men and pointed out a large outrigger canoe. The bolo men loaded Mike, the two other badly wounded survivors, and me on the large fishing boat. All of us stretched out and were covered with tarpaulin. Villagers helped the bolo men push the fisherman and his craft through the breakers for a day of offshore fishing. He put up sails and used an oar to set an eastward course along the coast. Full daylight brought enemy planes which flew lazily over us, but the pilots saw nothing that interested them. Underneath the tarpaulin I gratefully soaked up the trapped warmth of the sun, as I was still cold from my wait on the beach.

After the aircraft disappeared, our fisherman spooned some hot rice for us from the barbecue pit he tended at the stern. We moved steadily along the coast until late afternoon, when we headed for shore. The breakers took us into shallow water, where the fisherman jumped out to push us in. But the current almost pulled the boat out of his hands. With a tremendous effort he kept us from being swept out to sea. He finally shoved us up on the beach. Then we heard a bunch of Americans chattering and were overjoyed to realize that the other survivors from the *Shinyo Maru* had gathered among nearby palms.

They had been enlivened by three weeks of rest and food provided by the guerrillas and local Filipinos. There seemed to be a lot of us there, but it turned out that only 83 of the 750 POWs had made it to shore. Every one of the survivors had had close calls but none closer than that of Sgt. Denver Rose, who had operated the electric generator at Lasang. I soon heard his story — it had already become common knowledge among the healthier prisoners.

As I listened to how Rose had escaped, I forgot my painful leg. Like others, Rose was fired on by the Japs while swimming away from the sinking *Shinyo Maru*. Hours later, about 6 P.M., he was only 100 yards from shore when a Japanese patrol boat scooped him up. Rose was taken to an anchored oil tanker where the Japs had gathered about 30 other POWs who had been picked out of the water. The Japs tied the Americans together and tied the hands of each behind his back. The POWs were herded to the rear of the ship, where the Japs prepared to machine gun the whole bunch. Then they changed their minds. Instead, they cut loose the lead American from the rest and took him to the aft end of the ship. There a Jap sailor shot him with a rifle. Two others followed in a like manner while Lt. Hosimoto, second-in-command of the Lasang prison camp, stood by, getting a big kick out of the way his plan was working.

Meanwhile, Rose, the next in line, had been rubbing the rope that bound his hands against a rusty steel cable. Just as the Japs released him from the other prisoners, Rose was able to break the rope and free his hands. He fled forward on the main deck. The Japs were so stunned that he was able to duck briefly out of sight in front of the forward deckhouse. He couldn't jump overboard because he could easily be shot in the water. In the fastest decision of his life, Rose slipped over the side of the ship at the bow. His foot caught the edge of the hawse pipe — the large opening through which the anchor chain held the ship at anchor. There was enough space there for Rose to be invisible to anyone looking over the side. The Japs scurried around for a long time — it seemed even longer to Rose — but they finally gave up. Rose climbed down the anchor chain after dark and swam to shore.

I was glad to see Bill Lorton among the survivors. I had worried when I saw no more of him after the guerrillas took me to safety in a gunnysack. I was surprised to see that Chick Gardner had made it. He was the scrawny kid with big ears who could hear enemy aircraft before anyone else. Only Gardner, Ike Haegins, and I had survived of the 16 members of the 14th Bomb Squadron aboard the *Shinyo Maru*.

Among the 667[*] who did not get ashore were Captain Harry Katz and Lt. Albert Chase, officers of General Fort's 81st Division. I knew and liked them both. Katz had helped set up my bakery at Malabang and had obtained water for everyone the night after the Death March. Chase and I had volunteered for cargo-unloading prisoner details together.

Dr. Calo was there with the bulk of the *Shinyo Maru* survivors — he

---

[*]*The slaughter of the POWs trying to escape from the* Shinyo Maru *was consistent with instructions given by a higher command to a POW camp on Formosa prior to August 1, 1944, which are quoted in Appendix B.*

had left Mike and me that morning and proceeded by land to the beach rendezvous. We had moved northeast and were now just north of Lanboyan Point, near the village of Siari.

Calo was worried that my dangling leg would prevent my getting through the narrow entrances into the submarine. The only solution was to set the leg. Dr. Calo had only Novocain for local anesthesia, but I was allergic to it. Nevertheless, he had six men take hold of me and pull. My yell could be heard for miles, but my leg was straighter than before. Yet the pain was so great that Calo spent a sleepless night with me.

We didn't know how many of us the submarine could take so Lt. Col. John McGee, in charge of the survivors, had everyone draw from a hat that contained 100 numbered slips. My friend Cletus Overton drew "72" so he thought he had little chance of getting aboard. McGee ruled that I should be "1" because of my condition. McGee himself, not having been a survivor from the *Shinyo Maru*, did not plan to go with us unless there was space for all. He wanted to go on active duty elsewhere rather than stay with the guerrillas.

An hour before dusk that day, McGee accompanied guerrilla Captain Thomas down to a large canoe at the water's edge, where two Filipinos waited. Thomas settled himself in the canoe, holding a large American flag tied to the end of a pole. The two Filipinos pushed off the canoe, climbed in themselves, and paddled Thomas away from shore. McGee stood watching as the canoe disappeared behind Lanboyan Point. He waited as dusk turned into darkness and then still another hour before Thomas returned without finding the submarine. Thomas then dismissed the group of civilians who had assembled boats to take out the survivors and bring in supplies. He told them to be ready for a possible rendezvous the next evening.

Although the submarine's skipper informed the guerrillas by radio that he would try again, Captain Thomas had no better luck the following evening of September 28. That night the guerrillas took Mike, me, and the two other stretcher cases into a nearby village to spend the night. They put us in an old shack that smelled of dried fish and left us in the care of a large woman with a rifle. In the middle of the night a Japanese launch pulled ashore and the woman slipped out. It turned out the Japs were just looking for food as the woman and another guard observed them in the dark. Even after the Japs had gone, I lay in the dark, thinking it was a bunch of hogwash to hope we would ever escape.

Next morning, September 29, it appeared my foreboding would be borne out soon—five small Japanese cargo ships came into sight. After weeks in the area, it appeared that the Japs had discovered us and were

USS Narwhal, photographed off the Mare Island Navy yard, April 1943. The *Narwhal* carried me to safety in 1944. (U.S. Naval Historical Center.)

coming to recapture or kill us. We could only pray during the long hours it took the ships to pass along the coast.

Late that afternoon the sea became so rough that McGee doubted the men could be safely taken out to the submarine even if it appeared, but Captain Thomas insisted upon trying again. McGee had to help push Thomas and his crew out from shore, and the Filipinos had to paddle strenuously to get past Lanboyan Point. But this time McGee did not have so long to wait. Just as night was falling, he thought he saw a movement past the point, but he could not be sure in the faint light. Then the clear silhouette of the forward 6-inch gun and the outline of a huge submarine slowly emerged from behind the point. The submarine moved deliberately into the cove and paused close enough to the shore to be in full view of us. By that time the heavy seas of less than an hour before had calmed, and the water in the cove was smooth.

On the beach, I raised my head and was amazed at the submarine's immense size — it looked like a battleship. In a few minutes a bright yellow rubber boat headed toward us. Why didn't they pick a darker color? I was getting last-minute instructions from Dr. Calo when the largest guy I'd ever seen stepped ashore and nonchalantly walked toward us. Except for blue dungarees he was naked and as white as a lily after months of submarine duty. He told me he was glad to see me. "Man," I said, "you ain't half as glad as I am!" He pondered and said, "Wait a minute. I've got something to do." He walked away, making me think he had to relieve himself. Instead, he went to the water's edge and wiggled his toes in the wet sand. But soon he and other sailors fitted me in a little rubber dinghy, and the giant paddled me away from shore. Halfway to the sub, some outrigger canoes whizzed toward us, but my paddler just kept up his leisurely stroke. I asked him if we could get one of those outriggers to give us a tow. He threw a rope to the lead canoe. That's how I got to the sub before anyone else.

When we came alongside, the sub looked bigger than a football field — and it was. The *Narwhal* (167) was one of two 371-foot subs — the largest U.S. class. After I had been carefully placed on the deck, the giant paddler left me in charge of a skinny sailor, who squatted down beside me. He was so shaky he lit a cigarette, apparently forgetting the enemy. I protested, and he quickly snuffed it out. Meantime, the outrigger canoes were delivering the other survivors and pausing alongside to be loaded with arms, ammunition, and medical supplies for the guerrillas. When this procedure was well underway, the skipper, Commander J. C. Titus, turned his attention to me.

Titus asked his executive officer, "Should we try to get him in through a torpedo tube?" But the exec suggested lowering me through the conning tower. Titus agreed, so the exec had the sailors devise a hoist to lower me into the sub. It was such a narrow fit that they wrapped a blanket tightly around me to keep my arms and legs from swinging out. Even so, my bad leg was bumped repeatedly on the way down, causing me a lot of pain. Once aboard, I was carried along the main passageway and placed on the deck of the forward torpedo room.

Back on shore, the young Navy officer in charge of the beach party asked Captain Thomas how many POWs there were. A Navy signalman flashed the submarine to find how many could be taken. A reply came flashing back. My friend Cletus Overton — number 72 — held his breath until the Navy officer reported that everyone could be taken. Overton felt born again because he would have been among the last among the prisoners to get aboard if space were limited. Lt. Col. John McGee likewise was relieved. He was anxious to leave and go on active duty elsewhere because his rank was too high to fit into the guerrilla command headed by Lt. Col. Fertig. McGee had been put in charge of the survivors and given himself the lowest priority in getting aboard the *Narwhal*.

28

In the Hands of the Navy
September 29 to October 25, 1944

The sailors quickly brought aboard 80* survivors and Lt. Col. McGee before the *Narwhal* headed into the Sulu Sea. Some of the crew came around to take food orders. A big sailor asked me what I wanted — they had everything but a cow, he said. But I couldn't think of a thing. Finally, I asked for a peanut butter sandwich and tomato soup.

The plentiful food on the sub made the sailors look "great big and robust" to Cletus Overton, who recalled, "When comparing our condition with theirs, we realized how bad ours was. When you only have other POWs to look at, you forget what healthy looks like."

The next morning an old buddy of mine, Jim Green, told me to begin eating, but I replied that I hurt too much and was too sick. I had eaten little of the food the sailors had brought me the night before and now I didn't feel like eating at all. "Well," Green said, "you're going to eat a pancake," and he fed me bite by bite. But I couldn't hold it down.

Later that day the *Narwhal* sounded its general alarm —*ugah, ugah, ugah*— causing the crew to scramble to their emergency stations. The sub spewed and hissed as we began to dive. The angle of descent got steeper and steeper and became almost vertical. The sailors with me in the forward torpedo room were rolled out of their cots, and I was thrown against a bulkhead. Now the sailors were on their hands and knees — some crossing themselves. I thought, "Uh, oh, this apparently isn't normal, even for these

---

**Appendix C lists the 83 survivors who reached shore from the* Shinyo Maru. *Only 80, however, boarded the* Narwhal *because Pvt. Pratchard died of pneumonia on September 17 and two remained with the guerrilla forces.*

guys." But we finally leveled off. A sailor explained that the outside diving plates had stuck so the skipper had used an emergency measure that finally stopped the dive at 170 feet. The skipper, Commander Titus, later reported that it was the fastest dive the *Narwhal* had ever made.

After this scare, we cruised smoothly toward Dutch New Guinea. The Narwhal's pharmacist mate built me a traction splint, but that's all he could do. The young Filipino doctor sent by the guerrillas was so seasick he couldn't help anybody — the sailors even had to help him walk. Meantime, gangrene was eating up my leg — just poisoning me. My swollen leg smelled so bad that the sailors in the torpedo room hated my being there and hated even to pass near me. Few of my friends wanted to come close either, so I was alone much of the time. I just lay there listening to the then-popular song that went, "Get out of here and get me some money too..." The sailors played it over and over. I had a hell of a fever and was sick enough to know I could die soon. But I held on.

The six days the *Narwhal* needed to reach New Guinea seemed like forever. On October 5, 1944, however, all of the POWs disembarked at the submarine base at Biak, New Guinea (which had been captured only that summer by the Americans). The bumping was again awful as they squeezed me out of the conning tower. On deck I was startled to see the base all lit up in the darkness — we were now out of the war zone. Once I was ashore, some of the guys came over and shook hands with me. Their looks told me they thought I wouldn't last long. Cletus Overton recalled, "I just didn't think Vic would live... his leg was as big as a basketball. It had turned black and it smelled like a rotten horse."

Alone again, I also felt my time had come. It was probably a matter of an hour or two. But in a short time sailors from the Navy field hospital picked up Mike and me and took us aboard a shuttle boat just before it pulled away from the dock. In a half-hour we tied up at the small island of Mios Wendi, and soon we were lying on sturdy cots inside a Quonset hut that was the Navy hospital.

The head doctor, a Navy commander, took me in hand. First he put on ice packs to bring down my 105-degree fever. Next I received a direct blood transfusion from a healthy sailor who lay down beside me. I weighed less than 100 pounds, but I was too sick to eat — I couldn't stand the smell of rich American food. The commander told me I had to eat. I told him I couldn't, but he insisted, "Eat it and throw it up. But eat." I did this for three or four days, eating and vomiting time after time. But then damned if my appetite didn't catch on. However, what really saved me was penicillin, which I'd never heard of. The staff worked on my leg day and night. The doctor said it was lucky that the guerrilla doctor had not been able to clean all the maggots from my leg — the remaining larvae had fed on the decaying flesh and exuded substances that had been helpful.

As I lay there feeling a little better, I heard high-pitched voices singing another new song across the nearby lagoon, more softly than the song the sailors had played during my agony on the submarine. The nurses got me over to the door, from where I could see a couple of canoes gliding by, paddled by teen-aged boys who sang again and again, "Pistol packing mama, lay that pistol down." The words faded into the distance, but the crazy song fit in with my growing sense of well being. After three weeks, the commander decided I was ready to be shipped to Australia, but he couldn't guarantee I'd keep my leg.

Mike Pulice had stayed at the hospital with me, but Overton and the other survivors had flown directly to Australia after the *Narwhal* had delivered us to Biak. En route they looked down on an armada of ships steaming northward. There were so many the boys couldn't agree on even a rough estimate of their number.

A couple weeks after the boys reached Brisbane, Australia, they read in the newspaper that the Sixth Army had invaded the central Philippine island of Leyte on October 20, 1944. In striking at Leyte first, American forces had bypassed enemy garrisons on Mindanao by landing 250 miles closer to Japan — a continuation of General MacArthur's strategy of isolating large Japanese garrisons in his approach to the Philippines.

Epilogue

Mike Pulice and I arrived at the Navy hospital near Biak, New Guinea, on October 5, 1944. By late October the chief Navy doctor concluded we had improved enough to be transferred to the 42nd General Hospital in Brisbane. Early one morning sailors picked us up on stretchers and took us on the short voyage back to Biak, where the sub had landed us. A truck fitted as an ambulance picked us up for the short trip to the airstrip, where a light plane was waiting. Two other passengers had taken seats before the sailors carefully took Mike and me aboard and propped us up so we could enjoy the view. Now the plane was full except for the relaxed pilot who climbed aboard and took off. He was oblivious to an unidentified plane flying in the distance, but it worried us.

We flew steadily southward over an empty ocean until dusk. Then we saw hundreds of lights flickering on — they marked a city along the east coast of Australia. The pilot told us it was Townsville. It had a population of less than 50,000, but it looked much bigger to us. The peaceful view of a place so lit up after years of blackouts made me exclaim to Mike, "What a beautiful sight!" The pilot heard us admiring the scene and circled back around the city to give us a better look. Then we flew southward for another two hours before landing at Brisbane's airport, all lit up and bustling at that hour.

Australian soldiers put Mike and me on stretchers and carefully placed us on the ground. But a large Australian woman in uniform was not satisfied — she single-handedly picked up each of our stretchers and set us down a little to the side. She declared, "I'm afraid you'd get stepped on." Before long they transported us to the large 42nd General Hospital in Brisbane, which now had many American patients and doctors. The doctor who examined us found that Mike and I had hookworms. The de-worming process involved taking a huge pill and then fasting until one defecated. Mike was able to complete the process in good time and was waiting impatiently for the nurse to bring him some food. But my system had not delivered. We hurriedly switched some of his stool to my bedpan so I could also qualify for some food. I was still under 100 pounds, but thereafter I ate six meals a day.

We stayed at the Brisbane hospital for about two weeks before we boarded a hospital ship for the U.S. It had been a handsome Lurline cruise ship that had been converted and equipped to carry wounded servicemen. There were 4,000 of us, but the galley served a sumptuous Thanksgiving dinner for everyone aboard.

On the morning of December 10, 1944 —five years to the day after I had left prewar U.S.— word came down to our ward that the very top of the Golden Gate bridge had appeared on the horizon. As we steamed onward around the Earth's curve, more and more of the bridge came into view. The returning servicemen crowded to the side of the main deck that gave the best view of the towering structure. But the large ship tipped so dangerously that the captain sounded the ship's alarm and ordered everyone to get back to his quarters. I was on deck, and the tipping ship had banged the ankle of my bad leg against the bottom of the railing, giving me a painful bruise. The ship, however, righted itself as we passed under the bridge and into San Francisco Bay.

After we docked, soldiers took us off and transported Mike and me to the Presidio, the Army base in San Francisco. We did not get medical treatment of any significance there, but a young flier who had lost both legs in combat made us feel welcome. He had been fitted with artificial legs and now looked handsome in his uniform. He cheerfully brought us up to date abut the current war situation and told us many of the things that had happened in the more than two years we were held by the Japs. As to our future, he advised us to insist upon being sent to Walter Reed Hospital in Washington, D.C., rather than the regional military hospital in Atlanta. It was our right to choose, and at Walter Reed, the flier said, we would get the best treatment.

In a few days we were on a military flight headed eastward, but bad weather forced us to land in Oklahoma City. While we waited for things to clear, an officer at the air base did his best to persuade us to go to the military hospital in Atlanta, which would be closer to my home in Florida. But I stuck to Walter Reed, and Mike followed my lead.

We landed at the National Airport in Washington, D.C., in December 1944. A heavy snow blanketed the ground. A full colonel was there to meet us and ease our transfer to Walter Reed. But he didn't seem pleased with his assignment to meet two enlisted men with bad legs on a snowy night. He bade us farewell with, "Get in touch if you need me." The expression on his face, however, told us he hoped we wouldn't call on him.

At the hospital, we were carried into a ward full of patients. As we were getting settled, they burst out laughing. I thought they found us amusing until I noticed they had earphones; I learned later they were listening to Jack Benny on the radio. In a day or two my mother and father came up from Florida to see me. But they were permitted to see me only one at a time. When I inquired, a WAC captain explained with great tact that my parents weren't allowed to see me together because they had divorced. The possibility of this separation had never entered my mind and it upset me for a long time.

From my arrival, nurses gave me penicillin every three hours, day and night — a pill had not yet been devised that would give prolonged effects to avoid awakening patients through the night. I was in the amputation ward where nurses gave a lot of morphine for pain. Some fellows became addicted, but I usually endured the pain.

A lot of injured men from the Battle of the Bulge in Europe came into the ward in late December 1944 and January 1945. Some of them complained about the food, and one of them threw his salad on the floor. Some seemed impatient to lose legs and arms and be fitted with artificial members so they could get out of the hospital. As for me, the doctors explained it might take two years to fix my leg, and then there would be no guarantee. I told them, "That's fine. I'll try it." I liked the food and care at Walter Reed — so different from my two years as a prisoner of the Japs.

After two years, my insistence on treatment for my leg rather than amputation had paid off. Yet I still carried the parasite that came from my work in the rice paddies. It had entered my body through numerous cuts from cogon grass. Called schistosomiasis japonica, it had infected many of us working at Mactan; snails in the rice paddies carried the parasite and passed it on to us. The doctors at Walter Reed wanted to see what they could do.

They gave me intravenous injections of tartar emetic every other day while I was confined to bed. In a week or so, they had completed the treatment. But the final dose seemed large. When the discarded dispenser was carted away, I slipped out of bed and retrieved the empty dispenser from the waste container. It showed that 22 cc's had been injected, even though the instructions with the drug warned that a single dose should never exceed ten cc's. Shocked and feeling the effects of the huge dose, I crawled back into bed. The next day, however, I felt better.

In a few days, the doctors in charge of my treatment were showing me off to a group of visiting physicians. A Brazilian doctor lingered after the others left and asked me how large the doses of tartar emetic had been.

When I told him about the final dose, he exclaimed, "They gave you enough of that stuff to kill a horse!"

In late 1947 I was able to go on an 18-day Christmas leave, but when I came back, I found I had been discharged from the Army as well as the hospital. In the spring of 1948, I was still considering what to do when I decided to go out to Andrews Air Base to watch the annual air show. But I stopped at Bolling Airfield instead.

There I ran into Captain Shafer, whom I'd known when we were enlisted men in Hawaii. When I told him I wanted back in the service, he took me to Captain Heintzelman, who authorized a physical exam for me. At the infirmary, they examined me, probably thinking it was for *release* from service because of my weak leg. I took the results back to Heintzelman, who took my application before a board of officers. They authorized my reenlistment. Through the grapevine, I learned that one board member, Lt. D. I. McPherson, had strongly influenced the others. McPherson had been a fellow prisoner on the *Shinyo Maru*.

Back in service, I was accepted for Operation Bootstrap, which sent enlisted men to college. Upon reporting for one class at Carlisle Barracks, I thought the alert officer instructor looked vaguely familiar. I finally recognized Lt. Francis E. Le Clear, whom I remembered as a prisoner at the Lasang airstrip. There he had looked so emaciated and weak that I could not believe that he now stood before me fit and healthy. As we shook hands, I thought how strong his will to live had been to have survived the sinking of the *Shinyo Maru* after he was already so weak from work at Lasang. From courses at Carlisle and the University of Maryland, I earned 140 credits. But two years after leaving Walter Reed, my leg collapsed and I had to return.

At the hospital Captain Gustafson, a young, heavy-set doctor, told me he could try to fix my leg with bone and skin transplants but warned I would have to stay in bed a long time and there was no guarantee of success. He used a clear, plastic cast with holes in it. The leg could be inspected without removing the cast, and it could be taken off at night. The doctor's care resulted in a sturdy leg by the end of a year. When the smiling doctor, now promoted to major, visited me the last time, I said, "There's just one complaint I have, doctor. Some of the hair is growing the wrong way on my scar." Gustafson ordered me to get out of there.

By late 1951 I was back at Bolling Airfield with a much better leg. Soon after my return, I applied for an open slot for Master Sergeant. I didn't realize the high quality of the competition, which included former officers. When I was selected, the director of personnel at Bolling congratulated me but was surprised. He said, "You must know someone, Vic." I also thought so and believed it was General Emmett O'Donnell, who was stationed at

Victor and Lou Mapes, happy together, 1995.

the Pentagon. In late December 1941, however, O'Donnell had been in charge of the Air Corps men on the steamer *Mayon* during our passage to Mindanao. After Japanese aircraft attacked the *Mayon*, the then Major O'Donnell had thanked me for bringing seven men ashore who otherwise would have been lost, as described in Chapter V.

Less than a year after my second release from Walter Reed, I was assigned duty in Japan. For a time, the Air Force did not send anyone to Japan who had been in the Pacific war, but I may have become a candidate because of my success in the Operation Bootstrap program. I soon found myself on the northern Japanese island of Hokkaido at the Fourth Fighter Command airfield, where F-86 fighters were stationed to counter Soviet military strength in the Far East.

My main responsibility was education. My supervisor was Col. Chester Ladd, a West Pointer and pilot who had flown in the Korean War. We substantially expanded the Operation Bootstrap for the men at the base and worked together on a variety of other duties. One day we stood at the mouth of a large, dry limestone cave that we were considering as an emergency command post in case of a Soviet attack. We had just agreed it would be suitable when a huge slab of limestone crashed down at our feet. We only had to look at each other to eliminate the cave from consideration.

I was assigned a 17-man Japanese work detail hired by the Air Force to support base operations. One day I noticed a new man painting a classroom door — he looked very familiar. I shouted, "Hey, I know you!" It was a former Japanese soldier who had been at the Mactan rice paddies. Now he was scared to death, but I finally coaxed him to come back and finish his painting, assuring him I held no grudge. Actually this small, bowlegged Jap had patrolled on the dike with a gun but had not mistreated us. I told the other members of the details, some of whom were also ex-servicemen, that I had been a POW but would treat them fairly. Many of the detail took pride in their work. But in the nearby town were unfriendly Japs, whom I avoided.

I stayed at the fighter air base in Japan for 18 months. In 1954 I was transferred to the Strategic Air Command (SAC) station near Plattsburgh, New York, on Lake Champlain. After a year I managed to find an opening at Bolling Air Field. I served there until my retirement in 1959 with 22 years' service. The Air Force granted me ten-percent disability, but the Veterans Administration increased it to 50 percent. I have used a cane for years.

I have lived in the Washington, D.C., area since retirement and have kept in touch with a number of old buddies by visits, reunions, and correspondence.

Military History of
Victor L. Mapes

Victor L. Mapes enlisted in the U.S. Army Air Corps on November 1, 1939, at the age of 22. The recruiting sergeant in Ft. Wayne, Indiana, promised an assignment to Hawaii, and on December 10 Mapes was bound for Honolulu aboard the troop ship *Chateau Thierry*. After basic training at Hickam Field, Mapes attended the Cooks and Bakers School.

In the spring of 1941 Mapes joined the reactivated 14th Bombardment Squadron. On September 16, 1941, the squadron sailed for the Philippines, reaching Clark Field on October 1. Half of the 14th Squadron's B-17 bombers were destroyed by the Japanese attack on December 8, 1941. On December 10 the loss of a crewman when Colin Kelly's B-17 was shot down indirectly led to Mapes's promotion to squadron cook.

On December 29 surviving members of the 14th boarded the inter-island steamer *Mayon*, which headed south, bound for Mindanao. Next morning, after the Mayon had anchored for the day, air attacks drove most of the airmen off the ship — Mapes among them. A number drowned, but Mapes saved seven Americans and one Filipino with a canoe he commandeered on shore. Meantime the Filipino crew had saved the ship, which landed the survivors on Mindanao on January 1, 1942.

Until late May 1942, the 14th Squadron supported the dwindling American air activity on Mindanao. On May 27, 1942, the remnants of the 14th Squadron and Philippine 81st Division surrendered to the Japanese at Dansalan. As a prisoner, Mapes continued to cook for the 50 American prisoners.

On July 4, 1942, the 40 American and 300 Filipino prisoners at Dansalan were taken on a Death March after the escape of four Americans.

On the march three POWs could not keep up and were killed. Thereafter the remaining prisoners were moved by ship and then truck to the large prison camp at Malaybalay. Mapes stayed there from July 7 to late October 1942.

On October 30, 1942, Mapes entered the Davao Penal Colony and stayed until February 1944. It was a former Philippine prison farm, and the American prisoners cultivated rice and vegetables as the Filipino criminals had done.

On March 1, 1944, Mapes and other healthy prisoners began to work on the Lasang air strip. Treatment of prisoners worsened as the Japanese realized they were losing the war. On August 20, 1944, the Japanese packed the Lasang prisoners in the hold of an old freighter, which reached Zamboanga on August 24. On September 4 the 750 prisoners were shifted to the *Shinyo Maru*. It put to sea next morning and was torpedoed and sunk by the U.S. submarine *Paddle* on September 7.

Mapes broke a leg while getting off the ship. Despite Japanese efforts to shoot all prisoners in the water, Mapes was still afloat the next morning. He was rescued by a Filipino, who took him ashore. Now flat on his back with a bone protruding from his leg, Mapes was cared for by the Mindanao resistance organization for 21 days.

On September 29, the U.S. submarine *Narwhal* picked up Mapes and the other survivors from the *Shinyo Maru*— 83 had reached shore out of the 750 prisoners aboard. The *Narwhal* delivered Mapes to Biak, Dutch Guiana, on October 5, 1944. A doctor at the Biak Naval Hospital saved Mapes's life with penicillin and an immediate blood transfusion from a healthy sailor.

In mid–December 1944 Mapes entered Walter Reed Hospital and stayed until the end of 1947. In the spring of 1948 he was assigned to Bolling Air Field, where he was promoted to Master Sergeant in 1952. Soon after he was sent to a U.S. fighter base on the main Japanese island of Hokkaido. He served there for 18 months as head of the Bootstrap Program, which enabled enlisted men to earn college credits. In 1954 Mapes was assigned to the Strategic Air Command in Plattsburgh, New York. He was there a year before returning to Bolling, where he retired in 1959.

Military History of Scott A. Mills

Scott A. Mills joined the Navy on July 1, 1943, when he entered the Navy V-12 Program at Newberry College, Newberry, South Carolina. After eight months at Newberry and four months at the Midshipman's School in Plattsburg, New York, Ensign Mills was assigned to the LCI *1080*, which was being built in Bay City, Michigan. It was 150 feet long and 30 feet wide. With a draft of six feet, it could beach itself and deliver 200 troops to an enemy shore. The ship was manned by a crew of 25 and four officers — Ensign Mills was the Communications Officer.

The *1080*'s route to the Pacific theater of war lay through the Great Lakes to Chicago, down the Illinois and Mississippi rivers to New Orleans, through the Panama Canal, and north to San Francisco. After a stop in Hawaii, the *1080* sailed for Guadalcanal to join the amphibious fleet assembling to invade Okinawa.

On March 4, 1944, the Commander and the staff of Landing Ship Tank (LST) Flotilla 6 moved aboard — the LCI *1080* had been converted from a troop carrier to a flotilla flagship in San Francisco and was now the LC(FF) *1080*. After several days of rehearsing the invasion with its flotilla of LSTs, the LC(FF) *1080* sailed for Okinawa on March 11.

In the bright early morning of April 1, 1945, the LC(FF) *1080* worked its way close to the southwest coast of Okinawa while the column of 90 LSTs of Flotilla 6 dispersed to their assigned landing zones. The invasion fleet of hundreds of warships and amphibious craft stretched away from the coast to the horizon in all directions. The only challenge came from three Kamikaze aircraft that were shot down by intense anti-aircraft fire from large ships near the LC(FF) *1080*. The *1080* maneuvered close to its LSTs, which were discharging tanks and soldiers on the landing beach. Now the Flotilla Commander shouted to the LST captains through a bullhorn, urging them to hurry with the unloading — as though encouragement were needed.

The American landings were unopposed that day, partly because of the preinvasion demonstration on the other side of the island. The first day, however, was not typical. Every night thereafter, enough Kamikaze pilots flew down from the main Japanese island of Kyushu to keep the *1080* and other anchored ships at General Quarters, usually throughout the night. The Kamikaze aircraft that did not reach the main anchorage sank many of the American radar picket ships that were stationed closer to Japan to provide early warning of the Kamikazes. On land the enemy soldiers contested every inch of their fortified cave positions at the southern end of the island. After the *1080*'s stern anchor cable broke on April 10, it was still able to avoid collision with the numerous nearby ships. A few hours later, however, the *1080* retired southward for a quiet anchorage and relaxation on Saipan.

On May 26, the *1080* returned to Okinawa, but the situation had changed little on land or sea — it was not until June 21 that organized resistance ended. The capture of Okinawa cost America dearly: 7,500 killed and 37,500 wounded on land; while at sea 5,000 were killed, 5,000 wounded, and 36 ships sunk. Seventy thousand Japanese died on Okinawa, and at least 80,000 Okinawans, most of them civilians.

On August 11 — after another retirement to Saipan — the *1080* sailed for Leyte, a Philippine island where a fleet was gathering to invade Japan. En route, the news of the atomic bombing of Japan electrified the ship during midwatch on two different nights. When the Japanese surrendered on August 14, 1945, the *1080* was anchored with the invasion fleet off the coast of Leyte. The assembled ships greeted the news with thousands of lights and flares after years of wartime blackout. The celebration marked the end of the sinking feeling that came when one thought about invading Japan — a mammoth task compared to the capture of Okinawa.

On September 29, 1945, the *1080* led 40 LSTs into Tokyo Bay. They carried troops for the occupation of Japan. Ashore in Japan on ship's business and recreation, Ensign Mills encountered no indication of hostility, even aboard a trolley crammed with rush-hour passengers. All reports likewise showed that Emperor Hirohito's call for peace was strictly and universally obeyed.

After returning to the U.S. in early 1946, the *1080* was consigned to mothballing and decommissioning in Astoria, Oregon. Mills, now Lt.(jg), became commanding officer on May 3, 1946, and supervised final preparations for the *1080*'s entrance into the mothball fleet of the Columbia River Group. The *1080* was decommissioned on June 7, 1946. Lt. (jg) Mills was discharged on July 26, 1946, after three years of service.

Appendix A:
Dansalan Surrender List

This list has been carefully compiled by Frederick M. Fullerton, who was among those surrendered.

ARMY AIR CORPS
FROM 14TH, 19TH, AND 30TH BOMB SQUADRONS

Major Luther Heidger, Medical, 14th — Died on the *Shinyo Maru*
Lt. (Pvt.) John Doe, 14th
Robert Ball, Fifth Air Base — Joined guerrillas, survived
Richard P. Beck, 14th — Survived
Edmund Casey, 14th
Cawthorne, 19th Medic
John L. Chandler, 14th — Executed
John F. Clark, 30th — Survived
Jerry L. Coty — 14th
Vergil E. Haifley, 14th
William A. Knortz, 14th — Joined guerrillas, killed in action
Koontz, 19th Medic
McLaughlin, Medic
Victor L. Mapes, 14th — Survived *Shinyo Maru*
James A. Palmer, 14th
Peterson, 30th
James Price, 19th
Thomas Renick, Jr., 14th
Harley E. Shadoan, 14th
Shipley, 19th Medic
Herbert L. Zincke, 14th — Transferred to Japan, survived

Navy

Lt. Commander Strong
David Goodman, PT Boat Squadron 34
William H. Johnson — Joined guerrillas, survived
James S. Smith — Joined guerrillas, survived

Civilians

(Major) Louis Schroeder — Sent to Santo Tomas Civilian POW Camp
(Captain) F. H. Pipe — Sent to Santo Tomas Civilian POW Camp
Kildritch — Shot on Death March

81st Division

Headquarters

Gen. Guy O. Fort, CO — Executed
Capt. A. H. Price, Field Artillery — Executed
Capt. Charles Wyatt, Engineer
Lt. Col. Barnes, Medical
Lt. Landis Doner, Quartermaster — Sent to Santo Tomas Civilian POW Camp
Lt. Robert Pratt, Finance Officer — Died following Death March
Frederick M. Fullerton, Jr., TDY from 75th Ord — Survived

73rd Regiment

Col. Robert Hale Vesey, CO — Executed
Capt. S. M. Byars, Exec. Officer
Lt. Albert Chase — Died after *Shinyo Maru* torpedoed
Lt. Stephen Laro
Lt. John Stephens — Died after *Shinyo Maru* torpedoed

61st Regiment

Col. Eugene H. Mitchell, CO — Survived
Major Richard Hill, Exec. Officer
Capt. Harry Katz — Died after *Shinyo Maru* torpedoed
Lt. Donald Hanning — Sent to Santo Tomas Civilian POW Camp

84th Regiment

Maj. Jay J. Navin, CO — Shot during Death March

Engineer Combat Unit

Lt. John D. Stuckenberg — Died on the *Arisan Maru*

Appendix B:
Survivors from
the *Shinyo Maru*

One of the survivors, Captain John J. Morrett, reported the following list of survivors to the Southwest Pacific Command, U.S. Army, on September 18, 1944.

OFFICERS

MAJ William C. Chenoweth
MAJ Harry O. Fischer

1st LT William Cain
1st LT Richard L. Cook
1st LT Frederick J. Gallager
1st LT James A. Gardner
1st LT John P. Gillespie
1st LT Ralph R. Johnson, Jr.
1st LT John J. Morrett

2nd LT Gene P. Dale
2nd LT Harvey Denson
2nd LT Francis E. LeClear
2nd LT Roy D. Russell
2nd LT Harry J. Skinner

CAPT Robert B. Blakeslee

1st LT T. S. Pflueger
1st LT John C. Playter
1st LT Burt Schwartz
1st LT Felix Sharp, Jr.
1st LT Morris L. Shoss
1st LT Charles A. Seinhauser
1st LT James D. Donlon

2nd LT Murray M. Sneddon
2nd LT Paul S. Snowden
2nd LT F. S. Tresniewski
2nd LT James K. Vann

ENLISTED MEN

PVT W. N. Alexander
CPL J. R. Bennett
T/4 W. F. Biddle
PVT Jesse Bier
CPL Ray Billick
S/SGT Hayes H. Bolitho
CPL John W. Booth
T/4 P. L. Browning
T/65 Marco A. Caputo
S 2/C Charles V. Claborn
SGT O. E. Clem
S/SGT J. P. Coe
CPL V. D. Cutter
PVT Jack M. Donahoe
T/4 William Frederick
CPL Walter B. Gardner
T/SGT Don F. Gillen
SGT Peter J. Golino
PVT Donald J. Grantz
S/SGT J. R. Green
PVT I. B. Haegins
PVT Willard E. Hall
S/SGT W. L. Haskell
T/5 Francis Hoctor
T/4 W. S. Horabin
PVT R. J. Hughes
PVT L. P. Ingley
T/SGT Charles C. Johnstone
PVT J. H. Jones

S/SGT R. J. Kirker
PVT L. G. Knudson
PVT Glen E. Kuskie
S/SGT J. C. Lamkin
T/4 C. E. Latham
T/4 Bill J. Lorton
CPL John Machowski
S/SGT Victor L. Mapes
T/SGT Cecil McClure
T/3 J. F. McComas
T/3 D. I. McPherson
SGT L. S. Moore
SGT E. A. Motsinger
T/5 D. J. Olinger
PVT Cletus O. Overton
T/4 Buster Parker
SGT R. H. Person
PVT James H. Pratchard*
CPL Michael Pulice
T/3 Otis E. Radcliff
SGT George R. Robinett
T/3 Denver R. Rose
S/SGT O. A. Schoenborne
T/4 Marcus N. Simpkins
T/4 John Stymelski
T/5 Lawrence Tipton
Chief A. D. Waters
T/3 H.W. Wilson

Reached shore from Shinyo Maru *but died of pneumonia on September 17, 1944.*

Appendix C:
Japanese Military
Directive

The mass slaughter of POWs trying to escape after the *Shinyo Maru* was torpedoed was consistent with the following instructions, which a higher command transmitted to the Japanese POW Camp HQ in Taihoka, Formosa. This directive appeared in that camp's journal of August 1, 1944:

Under the present situation if there were a mere explosion or fire a shelter for the time being could be held in nearby buildings such as the school a warehouse or the like. However, at such time as the situation became urgent and it be extremely important, the POW's will be concentrated and confined in their present location and under heavy guard the preparation for the final disposition will be made.

The time and method of this disposition are as follows:

(1) The Time

Although the basic aim is to act under superior orders, individual disposition may be made in the following circumstances:

(a) When an uprising of large numbers cannot be suppressed without the use of firearms.

(b) When escapes from the camp may turn into a hostile fighting force.

(2) The Methods

    (a) Whether they are destroyed individually or in groups, or however it is done, with mass bombing, poisonous smoke, poisons, drowning, decapitation, or what, dispose of them as the situation dictates.

    (b) In any case it is the aim not to allow the escape of a single one, to annihilate them all, and not to leave any traces.

Bibliography

Bird, Tom. *American POWs of World War II*. Westport, Conn.: Praeger, 1992.

Brackman, Arnold C. *The Other Nuremberg — The Untold Story of the Tokyo War Crimes Trials*. New York: William Morrow, 1987.

Braley, William C. *The Hard Way Home*. (A Coast Artillery Association Book.) Washington, D.C.: Infantry Journal Press, 1947.

Coleman, John S., Jr., *Bataan and Beyond*. College Station, Tex: Texas A & M University Press, 1978.

Daws, Gavan. *Prisoners of the Japanese*. New York: William Morrow, 1994.

Keats, John. *They Fought Alone*. Philadelphia: J.B. Lippincott, 1963.

Kerr, E. Bartlett. *Surrender and Survival — The Experience of American POWs in the Pacific 1941–1945*. New York: William Morrow, 1985.

Knox, Donald. *Death March — The Survivors of Bataan*. New York: Harcourt Brace Jovanovich, 1981.

MacKay, James. *Betrayal in High Places*. Auckland, N.Z.: Tasman Books, 1996.

Manchester, William. *American Caesar, Douglas MacArthur, 1880–1964*. Boston: Little, Brown, 1978.

McClendon, Dennis, and Wallace F. Richards. *The Legend of Colin Kelly*. Missoula, Mont.: Pictorial Histories, 1994.

McGee, John H. *Rice and Salt — A History of the Defense and Occupation of Mindanao During World War II*. San Antonio: Naylor, 1962.

Mills, Scott A. *Stranded in the Philippines*. Quezon City, Philippines: New Day Publishers, 1994.

Morrett, John J. "Report of Prisoner of War Group Aboard Prison Ship, Torpedoed Off Liloy, Sandangan, Zamboanga, Mindanao, P.I." Memorandum dated September 18, 1944, to Southwest Pacific Command, U.S. Army. Washington, D.C.: National Archives.

Piccigallo, Philip R. *The Japanese on Trial*. Austin: University of Texas Press, 1979.

Quirino, Carlos. *Chick Parsons — America's Master Spy in the Philippines*. Quezon City, Philippines: New Day Publishers, 1984.

Smurthwaite, David. *The Pacific War Atlas, 1941–1945*. New York: Facts on File, 1995.

Spector, Ronald H. *Eagle Against the Sun*. New York: The Free Press, 1985.
United States Navy. *History of USS Narwhal (SS 167)*. Washington, D.C.: Office of
    naval Records and History, Ships' History Section, Navy Department, com-
    piled August 1951.
Weiss, Edward W. *Under the Rising Sun*. Erie, Pa.: Edward W. Weiss, 1992.
Wills, Donald H. *The Sea Was My Last Chance*. Jefferson, N.C.: McFarland, 1992.
Zincke, Herbert L. "Guest of the Emperor." Unpublished manuscript held by Her-
    bert L. Zincke, in Silver Spring, Md.

Index

www.ingramcontent.com/pod-product-compliance
Lightning Source LLC
Chambersburg PA
CBHW021139090426
42740CB00008B/853